JOHN WILLIAM WARD

An American Idealist

JOHN WILLIAM WARD

An American Idealist

Kim Townsend

Amherst, Massachusetts

2014

To

Mary, Haig, Roger, Walker

and

Karen

CONTENTS

Preface

ON SATURDAY EVENING, August 3, 1985, after having had dinner with his old friend Martin Duberman, John William Ward, known to everyone as Bill, went back to the Harvard Club of New York, where he was staying. The Club is an imposing Neo-Georgian building, altered since, but originally the work of the famous architectural firm McKim, Mead, and White. At the heart of it, through a small lobby and a grill room beyond, directly before you, more imposing still, is Harvard Hall, its ceiling forty feet—more than three stories—high, "the finest clubroom in the Western Hemisphere, if not the world," the Club's website claims. Around the walls are large portraits of distinguished alumni who were members of the Club: presidents of the Club, presidents of Harvard, presidents of the United States. We can imagine Ward looking at them before taking the elevator up to his room on the top floor of the building.

He was himself a distinguished alumnus of Harvard. He had aspired to distinction all his life and he had achieved it—as he would never forget—by overcoming odds that few if any of the men whose portraits he was looking at had had to face: he was Irish, not Irish like John F. Kennedy (whose portrait hangs in an adjacent room). "All four of my grandparents were illiterate immigrants in the latter nineteenth century. I am proud of them," he once wrote a student who had changed his name in honor of his African ancestry. "I am proud of that Irish heritage, and no less an American for that pride. Just as you are, and should be, proud of being a black whose people were forced into bondage from Africa, people whose sweat and blood make your life today possible. May both of us hope that generations from now men and women may look back at us with pride." Bearing down on another occasion, he said his grandparents were "illiterate peasants who came to this nation and with muscle and sweat gave their grandchildren a start, and their children's children an advantage beyond even their own wild dreams." They had dreamt the American Dream and it had been fulfilled. He himself was proof that that was so.

Having graduated from the Boston Latin School (where he was captain of the football team), he entered Harvard in the fall of 1941. Intending to become a doctor like his father, he began majoring in Biochemistry, but the following fall he left to join the Marines. When he returned four years later he majored in History and Literature and graduated, with honors, in 1947. In 1949 he married Barbara Carnes, with whom he would have three sons.

After Harvard he went on to the University of Minnesota, where in 1953 he earned his Ph.D. in the field of American Studies, the field in which he first distinguished himself. Indeed, he was a textbook example of what he taught and wrote about as a professor of American Studies—an individual, a self-made man, a citizen who believed in every man's chance to succeed and at the same time every man's responsibility to work for the common good—all, in the aggregate, distinctly American. His dissertation, *Andrew Jackson: Symbol of an Age*, was published in 1955; in the next several years it was widely read in college classrooms; the paperback alone sold over a quarter of a million copies. Beginning in 1952, he taught at Princeton as a member of the English and then of the History departments and chaired the university's Special Program in American Civilization. In 1964 he went to Amherst College as a professor in the History and American Studies departments. The list of honors he received along the way includes two Fulbright Lectureships in England, two Guggenheim Fellowships, a Fellowship at the Center for Advanced Study in the Behavioral Sciences at Stanford, and a Phi Beta Kappa Distinguished Lectureship. Admired as a teacher, scholar, and citizen at Amherst, in 1970 he was elected by his colleagues as one of four members who would serve on the committee that was formed to search for a new president of the college—and he emerged the winning candidate. He was president of Amherst College from 1971 to 1979.

He was president when America was going through radical changes. The nationwide protests against the war in Vietnam and the demands for racial and gender justice that became the civil rights and women's liberation movements shook the foundations on which America had been established. The confrontations and the conflicts that resulted were clearly and dramatically evident on college and university campuses. It was there that the generations were most obviously pitted against each other. "Never trust a man over thirty" was a rallying cry that was taken seriously. The young wanted an America that would not draft them to fight in a senseless war halfway around the globe; they wanted a social and political order that was more truly democratic than the one they seemed destined to inherit. They wanted the education they were offered, or that was required of them, reformed with their ideals in mind, and wanted, moreover, a voice in the determination of how that should be done and a voice in the selection of the teachers who would do the offering and the requiring. One college president summed up the students' goal precisely and memorably: "They want not to be prepared to play a role in society," he said. "They want to change society so they may play a role in it." That man was Ward.

Like all his peers, he wanted to see to it that the institution over which he presided continued to run smoothly no matter how rough the passage through which the country was going; and at the same time, inasmuch as it was an educational institution, he encouraged the expression, and discussion, of views no matter how radically divergent they were. He saw himself as an educator, a seminar leader, he sometimes said, even after he stopped teaching—not just an administrator. What was more, though, what set him apart from other college and university presidents, was how much he understood and shared many of the views of those who wanted American society to change, especially the views of the younger generation, the students. He wanted American society to be more inclusive, egalitarian—in a word, more democratic; he wanted an Amherst education to inspire students to work toward that goal and insofar as it was possible, to have Amherst itself be such a place.

In the spring of 1978, a summary description of him in an article in the *Amherst Bulletin* provided the obvious title for his story up through this stage of its completion: "President Ward's biography is an American success story." The occasion was his appointment by Governor Michael Dukakis to chair a seven-member special commission to investigate allegations of corruption in the awarding of state and county building contracts in the Commonwealth of Massachusetts, or, as it was officially called, the Special Commission Concerning State and County Buildings, or, better still, unofficially, the Ward Commission. The story became more impressive, his success more evident during the more than two and a half years of the Commission's existence. You could see the results: the Commission's findings saved taxpayers billions of dollars; politics in Massachusetts became more democratic, less corrupt; laws were passed that made representatives serve the people who had elected them. Upon leaving Amherst, Ward said repeatedly that his years as president were the most rewarding and exciting of his life; after one year chairing the Commission he said *it* was "the single most intense and interesting experience." And it was. It was "the most intense and interesting," and for reasons we will come to appreciate, the most fulfilling experience of his life.

His work with the Commission was pro bono. After it was completed, he wanted to continue to serve the people of Massachusetts, as president of the Greater Boston Chamber of Commerce, for example, but neither that nor any other job materialized. Needing work, he became a social science consultant for the American Express Company in New York, and then, in 1982, the president of the American Council of Learned Societies, a confederation of forty-three societies that was, by his own description, "the premier organization in the world of scholarship and learning."

The *Bulletin*'s summation went on to say, "with idealistic overtones": "President Ward's biography is an American success story with idealistic overtones." The addition got him right. As a teacher, especially in seminars, as a college president, as a crime-fighter and a consultant (essentially leading seminars), and as an apologist for liberal arts education and defender of the humanities not only in America but behind the Iron Curtain and in China, he was nothing if not idealistic. He gave expression to his idealism in convocation and college assembly and commencement addresses, in the essays that he wrote, essays on his favorite subjects and on figures he admired, and in countless speeches. He wanted the best for everyone, wanted everyone to be their best, as individuals and citizens, the two, he would always argue, being ideally one. He was an idealist, but not alone, not just *an* individual, a single, stirring voice. He was a man who was emblematic of his time. He embodied, in word and deed, the hope that was so strong between the mid-'60s and the mid-'70s that America could be a truly democratic society. Considering what has happened to those hopes since—the enormous gap between rich and poor, the polarization of the citizenry and its political leaders that seems to wipe out the possibility of a commonwealth or a common good—we must admire him the more.

His story, though, is not one of a steady rise to the top. Quite the contrary. His success at every level was followed by failure. But idealist that he was, every time he fell back, every time the stone rolled back, he righted himself and tried to push it not just back up but to new heights. After his academic reputation slipped when he failed to complete the book on individualism that he hoped would take off from where his Jackson book ended, he quite openly aspired to be president of Amherst. The success (and notoriety) of his early years as president was followed by relatively uninspired and uninspiring administrative work, and finally an ugly battle with his faculty that led to his resignation. He then went on to play the rougher game of politics on Beacon Hill, one in which the stakes were considerably higher than at Amherst, and he won.

But after the setback that followed upon the extraordinary achievements of the Commission associated with his name—after he failed to find a job *because* the Commission had been so successful—there was no ascent, not even a recovery. Having, as he said, "to hustle to pay the family bills," he took the shuttle down from Boston fairly regularly to do consulting for the American Express Company and eventually moved to New York with his wife. To others his subsequently becoming the president of the American Council of Learned Societies might have appeared to be another rise to another more distinguished position, but it was not to him. He had known what it was to bring about significant change for the good more immediately and more directly than was possible in the academy. Now he was not even an educator—just an administrator and an apologist for education. In the summer of 1985 he told a man whom he had known since his days at Princeton that his life was now "useless." He felt that way about himself because the job did not meet his expectations, but also because his personal life had become seemingly empty too: in June he and Barbara had filed for a divorce in the Bridgeport, Connecticut, Superior Court.

If we continue to follow Ward as he walked through Harvard Hall and looked at those portraits, we may go further and imagine not just his looking up at them but his thinking that their subjects were looking down on him. He had always been subject to depression, to what some called his "black, Irish moods." William Styron is more specific and thus more helpful when, in *Darkness Visible*, his fine memoir about *his* depression, he says, "Of the many dreadful manifestations of the disease, both physical and psychological, a sense of self-hatred—or, put less categorically, a failure of self-esteem—is one of the most universally experienced symptoms." It is one we know Ward suffered from.

But Martin Duberman, with whom he had just had dinner, did not see what was coming, nor did a former Amherst student who had met with him that afternoon at the Council, nor did the two old friends, Richard Schlatter and Arthur Trottenberg, with whom he had lunch that day, even though they had invited Ward to have lunch with them because Schlatter's daughter Heidi had warned her father about what she had recently perceived to be Ward's fragile state of mind. "There was nothing to indicate the depth of despair," Trottenberg later said.

After leaving Harvard Hall, Ward went up his room, which in those days would have been more like a dorm room, reminding alumni who stayed overnight of their undergraduate days, than a hotel room. He had always been something of a drinker; he had been drinking more and more since the move to New York. He drank heavily that night. Sometime in the small hours of the morning he called his wife and asked for a reconciliation. She said no. And he killed himself.

Suicide is not easy. According to Thomas Joiner, author of *Myths About Suicide*, "the accepted rate [is] one death for every twenty attempts." But Ward was determined; he knew what he was doing. He did not slit his wrists, no tendons were in the way. As the medical records have it, he died from "incised wounds of major vessels." His body was not discovered until early in the afternoon of the following day. Schlatter came and identified it. According to the *Boston Globe*, his wife declined to comment on the note that he left her.

John William Ward: An American Idealist is his story.

ONE

Becoming "Bill" Ward

"Perhaps I have shown it in much of my life, but I am always uneasy with the presentation of self."
(Ward in a letter, September 4, 1973)

JOHN WILLIAM WARD was Irish and he grew up Catholic. He went to St. Gregory's Elementary School in Dorchester, Massachusetts, across Dorchester Avenue from St. Gregory's Church. In nearby Brighton the family lived across the street from St. Columbkille, the looming cathedral in the heart of town that dates back to the 1870s. He was Catholic until the end of his freshman year at Harvard. Over a century before, colleges, Amherst College prominent among them, were founded to shield young believers from Harvard's free-thinking, Unitarian influence. His mother opposed his going there. In 1941, setting out for Cambridge, Ward assured her that he would do his best to preserve the faith in which he had been brought up. His best was a lot: he promised her that he would go to Mass every day for a year, and he fulfilled that promise. If his faith endured, well and good, but it did not, presumably causing a break with his family and a radical disruption of his sense of himself and of his place in the world.

What did survive was his signature, the way he signed off, ended speeches, letters, and conversations throughout his later years. "Keep the faith," he would say. He could no longer say faith in what. It was just whatever was your ideal, whatever you believed in, whatever you were committed to, assuming you believed in something, or were committed to something you felt was worth continuing to strive for. Otherwise it was no more than *Hang in there, Hang tough.*

Ward's Irishness was useful to him and to others. He was, in the words of one friend, "an Irishman who could pass for Anglo, a street person and a learned man." He was arresting, an unusual and attractive combination, one not often found in the academy in the '60s and '70s, at least not in the academies he taught in and administered. Trottenberg, who had known him since their Harvard days together, described him as "a naturally ebullient Irishman who somehow got to know everyone in sight," who "just filled a room when he walked in." On the other hand, when the atmosphere clouded up, when, for example, his anger got the best of him—which, as he was the first to admit, it did on many occasions—his "Irish temper" was to blame. When he was depressed, and especially when people tried to come to terms with his suicide, it was helpful to recall what were considered to be his "black, Irish moods." You could get a lot of mileage out of his Irishness.

But by the same token, you could run into roadblocks. What about Ward's depression, or his anger? His Irishness explained them. No need to go any further, to wonder, say, about the possible relation between the two, about how his low self-esteem might prompt him to strike out at others—and even at himself. After his death one paper reported that, "Critics said he could be arrogant." "Ultimate Smug... suave and condescending," a former president of the American Studies Association has said. Pinning "Irish" on arrogance does not work so easily as pinning Irish on ebullience or temper or dark moods, but perhaps imagining defensiveness or resentment can be of help, not Irish defensiveness or resentment, but rather Ward's defensiveness and resentment about being Irish—more precisely, Ward's defensiveness and resentment in response to the way he thought others viewed his Irishness. An especially telling account of his years as Amherst's president had it that, "Forthrightness, Ward's unwillingness to back away from a fight, was viewed by his former colleagues as both his chief virtue and his major fault." One professor's gloss was, "I don't think there's any question that most of us attributed his assertiveness to his Irish background. But of course that sort of thing is seldom discussed openly in this environment"—not openly discussed but registered all the same, registered not only by others but by Ward himself. Under the circumstances, "in this environment," a man coming from where he came from might well be defensive and appear arrogant.

And where did he come from? His understanding of where he was situated on the social scale would only have made matters worse. Ward would insist that his family was not wealthy. "I don't have money; I don't know people who have money; I don't move in a world where there is money," he once asserted in an interview. He meant he did not come from big money, from inherited wealth; and he was speaking from his experiences of Princeton and Amherst, institutions and towns that rested comfortably at a higher and ethnically a more "respectable" level than the ones around Boston on which his family settled. His earliest years were spent in the Lower Mills section of Dorchester, certainly not one of the more prosperous suburbs of Boston, but the Wards did have a one-family house the likes of which lined Ellison Avenue, and his father *was* a doctor—not your friendly family physician, though, but rather a doctor hired by an insurance company to assist in its dealings with claims. The Wards' move to Brighton was definitely a step up. Their house on the corner of Market and Mapleton Streets is quite large, as large or larger than the houses across and down Mapleton. It is centrally located and solidly middle-class. The Wards had a good home in Brighton. Much would be made of Ward's Irishness throughout his life, much too of his successful ascent to prominence—to success. The farther down the social scale a boy's beginnings are situated, the more impressive the story of his rise; the more ragged he is in the American success story the more impressive is he when he makes something of himself and reaps his rich rewards. But the Wards were not poor. Ward himself never wore rags. The family was not "shanty " but "lace curtain Irish," of the sort, as the stereotype has it, that tries to do everything right in order to achieve bourgeois respectability, all the while hiding from themselves the fact that nothing they do will do the trick. Ward *felt* that he and his family were poor. As for belonging, he was never quite sure.

We live by the stories that we tell ourselves about our lives. In turn, much of what others know about us depends in some large measure on these creations of ourselves. In an effort to understand who Ward was, we are unusually dependent on them. He liked telling stories, he was known for them, some of them he told over and over again. There are the few about his father, who was obviously not a model citizen. His son told of his admiration for James Michael Curley, the mayor of Boston who famously served part of one term behind bars, specifically of Curley's willingness to steal a Cadillac if it enabled him to put food on someone's table. He told too of the ritual his father would perform at tax-time: he would lay out the IRS forms on the dining-room table, go right to the bottom line, to "Amount Owed," ask the family, "How much should we give the government this year?" and then, bearing the answer in mind, work backwards to document it. The most striking story is one he often told about his father's one comment when he told him that he had been elected president of Amherst: "Get a haircut," his father said. But here again, there is a limit to what these stories tell us. The stories were diverting, not just entertaining but also the means by which he threw you off track. If he could come up with a good story about one or another experience or passage in his life, you were led to believe that that was all there was to say about the experience or passage. You were not about to go on and ask, for example, "How did you feel about your father's response to your being named president of Amherst College?"

His speeches and his writings tell us a lot about his ideas and beliefs, but we have relatively few personal letters to or from him, and no journals, no diary. A letter from his secretary at Amherst says that upon his departure he "systematically went through his files and destroy[ed] many papers which he thought not necessary to retain." What the system was, she didn't say.

Who was close to him? Who knew him? He was widely and well liked, he was famously good company, but as Christopher Isherwood once said, "Of course, fun-to-be-with people are almost by definition not those one knows well." When Julian Moynahan, who was a colleague of Ward's at Princeton, was approached as "someone who was close to Bill," he immediately responded by saying, "No one was close to Bill Ward." Richard Schlatter's daughter, who knew him then and thereafter, until the end of his life, has called him "an alien." Barry O'Connell, a young Amherst colleague, admired him enormously, but referred to him as "a stranger." Leo Marx, whom he often described as his best friend, said Ward "believed so much in the autonomy of the self that it was very hard to find out what he was feeling." All the stories, and yet what you might hear behind them was silence; what you came to know was a man determined not to let you in, a man determined to be strong—to be self-sufficient, self-reliant.

From Emerson's "self-reliant" man, jump ahead a century. Ward was, and cultivated, the image of a man—a "real man"—of the kind that came of age in the first half of the twentieth century. Medium height, sturdily built, blue eyes, short, straight, dark hair, his voice had a twang that made it clear that he was not to the manor born. His laugh (you wouldn't say laughter) was restrained. He was not the kind of man who would ever throw his head back in sheer delight, or break up uncontrollably. He liked strong drink and strong (i.e., unfiltered) cigarettes—Lucky Strikes—and he had espresso in the morning. American coffee, he said, was just like hot water. When he rested his sunglasses on his head, he looked to some as if he might have just come off a movie set. In 1979, a *Boston Globe* columnist came up with another image: "Walking across the Common recently, his appearance did not belie his Irish background. Of medium build and height, with a shock of grey-flecked hair topping a furrowed lived-in face, the professor could have passed for a world-weary plainclothes cop." He loved the image.

He was the more manly, necessarily tougher, for growing up where he grew up. He knew the territory. As a youth (and thereafter) he played poker and frequented a local pool hall; he was a good athlete. He knew not just the social and economic territory but the political territory as well. In a "Talk of the Town" piece on him in the *New Yorker*, he spoke about "that special odor of corruption that flows over Boston." He had gotten strong whiffs of it early on from his father. When Governor Dukakis made him chairman of the Special Commission Concerning State and County Buildings he underscored the appropriateness of his choice by pointing out that the culture of Boston was "intensely political and part of that is its Irishness," which Ward, in turn, confirmed with a personal example. Ward had caddied for the police commissioner of Boston, Joseph F. Timilty. Not long after he got his driver's license he was stopped by Timilty. Timility leaned out the window of his limousine and said to Ward that he didn't think he was old enough to drive. When Ward proved that he was, Timilty wrote, signed and handed Ward a note that read, "Bill Ward is a very close personal friend." "Do you know what that means?" Timilty asked. Forty years later, in telling the story, Ward shook his head and said, "Even a kid in high school knew how to fix things."

WARD PLAYED his cards close to his chest. Dealt the requirements of a man of his generation he was very hard to get to know—the harder in his case because of his resentment over his Irish background and his insecurity about his social status, and the anger they produced.

But deep down in him too was a sense, a sense that developed into a belief to which he remained faithful all his life, that discrimination based on differences of religion or race or ethnicity or class were baseless and unjust, and that they had no place in a democracy. It is more than likely that the seeds of that belief were planted in the fall of 1935, when he started the seventh grade at Boston Latin—i.e., when he entered a world in which such discriminations did not matter. Fostering that belief was, and still is, one of the school's strongest claims to fame. There are, of course, the flashier ones. Boston Latin is the first public school and the oldest existing school in America. It was founded in 1635, a year before Harvard was founded so that, as Latin School students liked to say, their school's first graduates would have a place where they could go to continue their education. No school can boast of such alumni: Five of the fifty-six men who signed the Declaration of Independence went to the Latin School; among its famous alumni are Cotton Mather, Emerson, Charles William Eliot (the most well-known of the five Harvard presidents who graduated from Boston Latin), George Santayana, Joe Kennedy, Bernard Berenson, and Leonard Bernstein. Ben Franklin is the school's most famous dropout (Louis Farrakhan is another), yet also the endower of the Franklin Medals, awarded each year to the students at the top of their graduating class. The school is famous too for its demanding curriculum, what with five years of Latin required of students entering in 7th grade and four of those entering in 9th (the points of entry) when Ward was there. Those requirements have since been reduced by a year, but the tradition of the "declamation" (pupils in the 7th through 10th grades must give an oration in their English classes three times a year) has remained unchanged.

Competition for admission is limited to residents of Boston, it is strong, and—most important to any educator whose ideals are genuinely democratic—students are admitted solely on the basis of their academic achievement and potential and they are all held to the same rigid academic standards. In the words of Theodore White, another alumnus: "The Latin School was a cruel school....It accepted students without discrimination, and it flunked them—Irish, Italian, Jewish, Protestant, black— with equal lack of discrimination." Nat Hentoff, a Jew from Roxbury who was in Ward's class, surely speaks for thousands of students for whom the school was welcome "neutral ground": "Under the purple-and-white flag of Boston Latin School, we were all united—the Irish, the Italians, the Jews, the Greeks, the Scots, the Armenians, the relatively few Yankees who were still there (the others no longer applied because all the rest of us were there), and the far fewer blacks," he wrote in *Boston Boy*. On that neutral, level ground, he went on, the masters paid little or no attention to their students' sensibilities or their souls: "They gave us something a good deal more important—respect. Whatever our backgrounds, we were in the school because we had shown we could do the work. The masters, therefore, expected at least that much of us, and that was why we came to expect even more from ourselves." The school's motto is *Sumus Primi* (We Are First), *primi* in existence and, arguably, *primi* among public schools in the rigor of its standards, right up there with New England's elite private schools.

The democratic ideal that governed the school's selection of its students and the kind of education their masters tried to give them once they were there would strongly influence Ward's life as a scholar, a teacher, a college president, and a citizen. Working from a perusal of the 1941 *Liber Actorum*, his senior yearbook, he once said, "It so happens that I gained my growth early in life." The growth he had in mind was not the kind that was reflected most prominently in academic achievements. For him, getting a good education was not synonymous with doing well in school. He was himself, he said (using a cliche he hated), "to put it bluntly, a dumb jock in high school, not a very good student. That puts it mildly. I actually flunked a year of high school." He is being too hard on himself, underestimating, undercutting himself, perhaps to make his ascent to the richness of his later life the more impressive. He did flunk a year, but then, so did many Boston Latin students. On a very rare occasion a student might complete two years in one, but failing a grade was not unusual. Only a third of the students finished in due course, Ward said. Turning to the remarks of his Latin teacher, to whom the yearbook was dedicated, Ward implicitly shared the man's belief that "the essence of learning" was something "beyond intellectual discipline." It was, rather, the pleasure of learning, the importance of general and liberal education to do any work in life, and the value of democratic public schooling. The classical or "we might say, liberal education" he had received laid "the right foundations...for any kind of intellectual career." But lest too much stress was put on the word "intellectual," Ward pointed out, "his teacher also spoke of finding work," and by work he meant "something in which one finds delight," something more than having a job or a career.

Ward first heard his calling "early in life." What his Latin teacher professed, he would often write about and as a teacher, try to represent: disciplined, intelligent thinking in whatever work one dedicated one's life to and found "delightful." ("Joyous" was the word he would use in speeches he gave as president of Amherst.) What Boston Latin stood for, according to his teacher, he would try to bring into existence at Amherst College as its president: education as defined above, fostered in an institution that did not discriminate, that was democratic, that was, no matter how private and privileged, ever mindful of the public good.

As a Boston Latin student Ward was not "dumb." He flunked a year but he once won a Latin prize, he took to stopping by the Boston Public Library on the way home from school to read in its lovely fountain courtyard, and what is not to be taken for granted, he graduated from the Latin School. But unquestionably he was, and he was known as, a "jock." The list of his other extracurricular activities listed in the yearbook is not impressive. Perhaps serving on the Mid-Winter Dance Committee his senior year bespeaks his popularity, but given the fact that his were the days before resume padding, one wonders what prompted him to become an Usher at graduation his junior year, or to sign up for the Highway Safety Committee the year before that. What obviously mattered most, what was literally first and foremost in the list of his activities, was football for four years, captain during the last one. Though not included in his yearbook entry, his team beat the highly favored team from the school's arch-rival, Boston English, and at the end of the season he was selected to be on the city's "all-scholastic" team (at left tackle). Senior year he was on the Yearbook Committee—as Sports Editor.

One surprising entry is "Literary Staff Register" his senior year, but "Staff" suggests too much editorial responsibility. What it probably refers to is the three little fictions—one page, two pages, then three pages—that he contributed to *Latin School Register*, the school's literary magazine that Santayana had started in 1881. All three are about feelings brewing under the surface. Two are about anger, in one anger barely controlled, in the other anger unleashed. The most interesting one, the shortest, is about the fear—or more, the conviction—of not measuring up. Titled "The Hero," it is about a war-time ambulance driver who is anything but. Driving along, bouncing in and out of craters in what once used to be a road, the wounded in the back, moaning and crying out in pain with every jolt, the ambulance comes under heavy fire. The groans of the wounded and "the whining of the leaden messengers of death" terrify the driver. "His nerve was completely shattered," he stops his ambulance, and runs. When he sees a mounted officer and realizes what would be his fate were he to be spotted, he dives under his ambulance—"like a rat." The next day, on the parade ground, he is singled out by the officer as exemplary of the "daring exhibitions of courage" of the unit. Here was this ambulance-driver "calmly lying under his ambulance, repairing it in the midst of battle," he says. And so, as the last sentence has it, "A hero was born." At least as far back as his senior year at the Boston Latin School, Ward knew about his anger and about feelings that would weigh increasingly heavily on him—doubts about his worth, doubts a successful man, a hero, is assumed not to have.

What may be one other manifestation of feelings that lay under the surface is more surprising: the name over Ward's entry in the yearbook is William Joseph Ward. He was not John William Ward until 1943, until he was twenty-one. The difference between William Joseph Ward and John William Ward is relatively slight, ultimately just a matter of dropping the name Joseph. It would seem hardly worth the trouble Ward had to take to make the change that he asked the Harvard registrar and the appropriate civil authorities to make two years after he graduated from the Latin School. But though the change is slight, to Ward it must not have been inconsequential. The name John William Ward wafts on more gracefully than the thumping name William Joseph Ward, but it is unlikely that he was concerned about how his name scanned. Something more serious was involved.

Name changes often accomplish two things, name changes in ethnic groups, at any rate. They may erase your father; they may also help you hide the obvious traces of origins that you know are frowned upon by those who dominate the culture. In the '70s, if you were an African-American, you might want to reverse the process by taking on an African name and divesting yourself of the name you were given, in order to announce your pride in your origins. We saw Ward applaud a black student who did

ALFRED STEPHEN VILLA

"Pancho"   Northeastern

Entered Class IV from Edward Everett School in 1937.
Fidelity Prize III, 2nd Lieut. 3rd Co. 1st Reg.

JOSEPH VITO WAITKUNAS

"Joe"   Mass. College Pharmacy

Entered Class IV from T. H. Hart School in 1936.
Football I, Camera Club II, 2nd Lieut. 7th Co. 1st Reg.

VINCENT PATRICK WALSH

"Vinny"   Notre Dame

Entered Class IV from St. Peter's School in 1937.
Cheer Leader I, Class Council, Mathematics Club I,
Highway Safety Club III, Fidelity Prize IV, 2nd Lieut.
8th Co. 2nd Reg.

WILLIAM JOSEPH WARD

"Bill"   Harvard

Entered Class IV from St. Gregory's School in 1936.
Football IV, III, II, I, Captain I, Mid-Winter Dance
Committee I, Class Day Committee I, Usher at Gradua-
tion II, Literary Staff Register I, Yearbook Committee I,
Ring Committee I, Art Club II, Highway Safety Club III,
Literary Club I, Captain, 7th Co. 1st Reg.

Page Hundred and Seventeen

Ward's appearance in the Boston Latin School yearbook his senior year

just that and at the same time declare how proud he was of *his* origins. His effort in 1943 obscures his origins somewhat, Joseph being a common Irish name, but more obviously it erased one trace of his father, John Joseph Ward. If you were Armenian or Polish, you could simply lop off the "ian" or the "ski" of your surname and you were no longer the "son of" your father. So it was in the '40s, anyway. There was nothing you could do, or needed to do, about Ward. But you could drop one of your father's names. We have little to go by in trying to understand Ward's personal life, as we have noted, but the little we do know about Ward's relations with his father, and the very fact that we know so little, suggests that the two were not—maybe were far from—close. Nor, we should add, is there anything to suggest that the family was close-knit, or that Ward felt entirely at home in it. And if he didn't, the sufficient cause is not hard to locate: his parents and his two sisters were staunch Catholics; he had not kept the faith.

There is one final detail of the yearbook entry worth noting: his picture. In it he is looking to the side and down, not directly at the camera, at us. His lips are slightly curled, his eyes, the most striking feature of the picture, are narrowed. Above him on the page, in sharp contrast, are Alfred Stephen "Pancho" Villa, Joseph Vito "Joe" Waitkumas, and Vincent Patrick "Vinny" Walsh, heading off to Northeastern, "Mass. College Pharmacy," and Notre Dame, respectively, in the fall. All are facing us. "Pancho" and "Vinny" are smiling; nothing is ever going to upset "Joe" it would seem, so calm, so confident is he. All are at ease, contented, pleasant looking. At the bottom of the page is "Bill" Ward, who is going to Harvard in the fall. You feel he's wary, maybe angry. He certainly does not look approachable.

WARD ENTERED Harvard in 1941, one of the 750 young men who were admitted from among the 900 who applied. It was not so easy as it sounds. Ward himself provided a partial explanation: he was not an outstanding student but, he said, "the Latin School prepared one so well for the College Board examinations I was admitted to Harvard." It was not just that he tested well, though. Harvard had high admissions standards and thus did not have hordes of applicants. It assumed that anyone applying for admission had pursued a rigorous course of study at their secondary schools; Boston Latin was well known for making sure that its students had done just that. Harvard would still admit many legacies, and many other young men who had attended prestigious private schools with high standards who could use the institution to assure them of a place among the elite after they graduated, but things had changed markedly since 1933 when James Conant (who was born in Dorchester) succeeded Abbot Lawrence Lowell as president, and the changes make it even more understandable why Ward got in. Conant wanted Harvard to be at a higher level of education what Boston Latin had always been at the secondary level. "Impatient with privileged sloth," his biographer has written, "Conant sympathized with the 'meatballs'—the ambitious lower-middle-class local students, the first-and second-generation ethnic immigrants who worked overtime to overcome prejudice (and quotas) so as to enter the establishment at Harvard." "Conant was the first president to recognize that meatballs were Harvard men too," according to White, a Boston Latin graduate, as we know, and a Jew. He and Ward were strong candidates for admission. Nor can it have hurt that Ward was captain of the football team and "all-scholastic," though it surely pained the Harvard coach when Ward decided to give up the sport.

That fall Ward took his first steps toward a major in Biochemistry with an eye to becoming a doctor. At the end of the year the Japanese bombed Pearl Harbor. In the previous spring, the headmaster of the Latin School, Joseph Lawrence Powers, had addressed the seniors in words that, like those of his Latin teacher, must have had a lasting impact on Ward. Powers told the young men in his audience that they were finishing "one stage in a process of self-determination," that they were now able to plan for a future in which they could do whatever their ambition, ability, and industry might incline them to do. The reason was, again, the school's most important claim to fame: "It has made no difference who your parents are, where they were born, how much money they have, or what religion they practice," he said. It followed that their sons were not just Latin School boys, but American boys, "For every American boy has the right to go as far as his brains, his industry, and his character will take him," he said. "That is true in America—and nowhere else," which led him to address the fact that once again war threatened to engulf the world: "Democratic privileges are not just something to be enjoyed; they must be preserved and defended, or they won't be enjoyed for long." And then, implicitly acknowledging that they were in fact special American boys, that they were Latin School boys, he advised them not to be thrown off-stride but rather to "go calmly about [their] plans for college." If called upon to take arms they would surely be true to the school's tradition of "loyal service and devotion to God and country," but for now it was more important that they prepare themselves to face the political and economic problems that the country would soon face: "You, and boys like you, are the people who will have to deal with them; and the solving of them is going to tax the best-trained minds your generation can furnish." Ward remembered and heeded his advice: he completed the second term of his freshman year.

The following spring Powers told the senior class much the same thing about continuing on with their education, but America was now at war and winning it was what mattered most. Ward was not there to hear him; having completed his freshman year, he'd enlisted in the Marines.

From the '30s on, it was the tradition at the Boston Latin School that every student was a member of a military organization. What they all did was, for the most part, march, march in preparation for the city-wide competition that took place each spring in Boston. "Pancho" Villa was a second lieutenant in the third company of the first regiment—"2nd Lieut. 3rd Co. 1st Reg." "Joe" Waitkunas was "2nd Lieut. 7th Co. 1st Reg," "Vinny" Walsh was 2nd Lieut. 8th Co. 2nd Reg." Ward distinguished himself. He was "Captain, 7th Co. 1st Reg." It is fitting that as a Marine he went first to Quantico, where he completed basic training and became a Drill Sergeant. After that he went to Officer Candidates School and then over to Europe as a first lieutenant.

Occasionally Ward referred to his "participating" in Allied landings in France, but clearly at a distance. Had he experienced combat at first-hand he would surely have had stories about it—what better ones could he have?—but we know of none.

There is a sketch that he wrote that features quite a different aspect of his Marine experience. It is titled "On Shining Shoes." In it he tells of dating "an Irish girl whose father was a Sergeant on the Boston police force," and of proving to him that he was "a young man of probity and character to whom one could trust one's nubile daughter for the night." How did he do it? His shoes were very well shined—not just the toes but, as the man saw when he had the young man turn around, the heels too. The Marine

Corps was run on much the same principle, Ward goes on: "For four and a half years, I shined leather," which was more important, he says, than the "few battles and invasions." A dapper man (and Ward always tried hard to be just that), living in New York City many years later, he frequents a shoe-shine parlor on Lexington Avenue—one with seven chairs, no less! So appreciative is he that in paying he would leave a dollar tip, much to the chagrin of his wife. One day he discovers that the parlor is gone, having given way to a high-rise that was under construction. No tragedy, he says; there's another stand of chairs in Grand Central Station. "Something was gone, though: spirit, pride in the group." With that he concludes, "Maybe the Corps was on to something. Maybe that was what it was all about." And then one night, soon after, he goes home and shines all his shoes.

The experience of "spirit, pride in the group," was meaningful in its own right. (*Semper Fi* would have been a handy version of "Keep the faith" during his years in the Marines.) It informed his hopes for the academic and political institutions in which he played a role or that he led. It informed his expectations of his staff as president, or his disappointment in its members when they failed to meet those expectations, when they didn't show up at a faculty meeting, for example. Perhaps it was "because I reached the age of majority while a member of the Marine Corps, where the custom was that an officer never gave a direct order, but simply indicated his pleasure," he wrote them. Maybe he hadn't made his expectations clear enough. Or "perhaps it was not much in [his] nature to be sharply directive, and may be a failing on my part. *But*," he reminded them, "I have more than once said it is my expectation that members of the Administration will be present at all Faculty Meetings." Though ROTC programs were hardly popular on college campuses in the '70s, it is no surprise that he defended them when he was president of Amherst.

The one story about an actual happening that has come down to us is about what must have been a high-point, perhaps *the* high point, of his years as a Marine. He served on the USS *Augusta*, the flagship of the Atlantic Fleet; during that time he was Head of the Marine Honor Guard that escorted Truman to the Potsdam Conference in 1945. In that role he was the Officer on Deck when Truman arrived on the USS *Augusta*. What was memorable, the climax of the story, was Truman's extending his hand and introducing himself to Ward as he came on board. His was the kind of gesture Ward would have made: I am the president of the United States, he seemed to say, but I am also just Harry Truman, just another citizen.

HAVING SERVED for three and a half years, Ward was back at Harvard in 1946. There was an accelerated program in place, as there was at many educational institutions during the war. Harvard held classes throughout the year, having added a summer session, two weeks shorter but more intensive than the fall and spring terms. So there was time enough for him to switch from Biochemistry to American History and Literature, to study under F. O. Matthiessen, Perry Miller, and eventually and most importantly, Henry Nash Smith, with Stephen Whicher as his tutor, and thus set out on the course that he would so successfully follow well into his years at Amherst.

He roared out onto his new-found field, enrolling in Matthiessen's graduate seminar on American Poetry and, not surprisingly, as he later wrote in a short tribute to Matthiessen, "It just seemed impossible for me. I wasn't understanding a thing." He wanted to drop the course. When he went to Matthiessen for his permission (which was required), Matthiessen kept asking why he wanted to do that. Finally Ward told him everyone in the class (Leslie Feidler and Richard Wilbur among them) seemed to understand what was going on "except me. I don't understand what they're talking about!" Matthiessen's response, or at least Ward's version of it many years later, was, "Neither do they. Stay the course, and trust your judgment a little more." He did, he survived, and went on to graduate with honors.

Matthiessen was the chairman of the History and Literature Program. Though he was the author of books on T.S. Eliot and Henry James, it was his magisterial *American Renaissance: Art and Expression in the Age of Emerson and Whitman*, published in 1941, that exemplified what exciting work could be done in this new field that would soon become American Studies. Unlike the "New Critics" whose exclusive attention to the inner workings of literary objects ("well-wrought urns" and the like) was beginning to dominate the study and teaching and criticism of American and English literature at the time, Matthiessen's reading of the great works of Emerson and Whitman (and Thoreau, Hawthorne, and Melville) were also readings of mid-nineteenth century American culture and society. By undergraduate standards Matthiessen was not a first-rate teacher, but he represented an ideal of the intellectual life that Ward and countless others who went on to be academics revered. He "acted out in his own life," Ward wrote on another occasion, and so "made available to his students, a commitment to the life of the mind which transcends by far the subject of any particular course." Matthiessen's left-wing politics, which were eventually the target of an investigation by the House Un-American Activities Committee, set him apart as well, as did his homosexuality, the two, it is assumed, precipitating his suicidal leap from a Boston hotel window in 1950.

The breadth of Miller's scholarship is evidenced by his *The New England Mind, The Life of the Mind: From Colony and Province in America, From the Revolution to the Civil War*, and *Errand in the Wilderness*, his book on the Puritans' mission in the New World. A more popular teacher than Matthiessen, he had the capacity, Ward wrote, "to dramatize the immense importance of ideas in the life of a culture, and could make forbidding material come intensely alive."

In 1940, Smith (and Daniel Aaron) were awarded the first doctorate degrees in the university's American Civilization program; five years later Smith came back to Harvard to replace Miller, who was going on leave. It was that year that Ward first met Leo Marx (himself having returned to the academy after four years in the Navy), who was Smith's student and his course assistant. Whicher, an Amherst graduate and the son of an Amherst English professor, was more of a specialist, the author of "the best single book" on Emerson, Ward said in 1973; but "his influence on me," Ward also said at the time, "was important far beyond our tutorial relation." In 1961 Whicher too committed suicide.

For Ward, the man of so many parts and interests, the History and Literature Program was ideal. It gave him, he said, "the most intellectual elbow-room." You could take courses in history, literature, art, politics "or whatever, and count them as courses in a single major, the study of American civilization." (Many years later he would translate his youthful enthusiasm into the language of the academy: "American Studies is not a discipline," he said. Rather, "it is essentially a point of view which insists that the meaning of an action or a text cannot be wholly understood by the techniques of a single academic discipline, but must be understood also in relation to other actions and texts in the context of its moment in time.") Majoring in History and Literature, he said, he had "caught for the first time a glimpse of the delight of making a life around books and ideas and good talk."

But though he had had a glimpse, he was not yet sure what he wanted to do with his life. Upon graduation he went into a small sweat-shirt business with a cousin, but it was quickly apparent that it did not inspire him in anything like the way the life he led at Harvard had, so he applied to the Graduate School of Arts and Sciences. Gaining admission to Harvard at that level was not like gaining admission to Harvard College, though: he was turned down. But having gone out to the University of Minnesota in 1947, Smith, the man whom Ward later said "brought [him] up professionally," opened the doors of its graduate school for him and in the fall of 1948 he gladly entered. A year later Marx came out to start teaching in the university's American Studies program.

At the time, Minnesota's English Department was exceptionally strong and lively. Among its members were traditional and venerable scholars and teachers (Joseph Warren Beach, Samuel Holt Monk, E.E. Stoll), others who were inclined, or even leading the way towards the "new" as readers and writers (Robert Penn Warren, Allen Tate, William Van O'Connor), the more socially conscious Americanists (Smith and Marjorie Turpie, "our intellectual guide" and "our godmother" respectively, Marx called them in his "Reflections on American Studies, Minnesota, and the 1950s"), and visitors not easily categorized (Saul Bellow, John Berryman, Irving Howe). One might be tempted to imagine those whose focus was on autonomous texts, appreciators of their aesthetic unity, lined up against those whose focus was on the historical context of their creation, but as Marx pointed out, the two approaches were easily reconcilable and, moreover, the readings were the more exciting for having been arrived at by both, as the work of the leaders in the field (Matthiessen, Miller, Smith, and, one should add, Marx himself) clearly showed. Graduate students might complain about the day-to-day workings of the department, or, worse, about the workings of the annual meeting of the Modern Language Association, the "slave market" at which they had to present themselves in their quest for jobs, but the voice of one of their numbers, Richard Cody (who would eventually end up at Amherst), rings with more authority than any student's complaint. "He would think to himself," he has written, "'Yet shall we ever in our lives be as fortunate as we are now?'"

For Ward, of course, what was most exciting was the American Studies program. That is all it was at the time, just a program, most of whose members were in the English Department, "its administrative home," as Marx put it in his essay, though drawing on members of the Art and History and Political Science departments as well. But as an encyclopedia of United States History has it, "The most influential institution in establishing [the] hey-day of American Studies was the University of Minnesota." Ward, one of the scores of graduate students in the field in any given year, was happy and inspired to be there when that happened.

The beginnings of American Studies must be traced back to the '30s, to the Depression, and then to the New Deal, to a time when America seemed to be off-course, the vision of its founders in danger of being lost, just as a later surge of interest in the field in the '60s must be attributed to the feeling that that vision had been betrayed by America's presence in Vietnam and racial conflicts at home. After service during World War II, and supported by the GI Bill, men like Marx and Ward turned to American Studies in order to recall and reassert what was culturally and politically distinctive about America. (It would be years before the point would be made that "United States Studies" would have been a more appropriate title.) Later, as prominent Americanists, they would go abroad as Fulbright Lecturers, defining and celebrating for others what made America "exceptional." And it is important to recognize the fact that students and professors of American Studies not only taught what they believed to be the promise of America but also represented it. The Latin School, Conant's Harvard, and American Studies were hospitable to men from diverse ethnic and religious backgrounds.

Ward was a believer, but his time in graduate school was not easy. He was short a course, so Marx agreed to read Emerson with him for credit. Again, one must be mindful of the pronounced self-deprecatory tic that he later developed, his habit of distancing himself from his own statements, undercutting his talents and his achievements, but by his account his "general, oral examination for the Ph.D. was a disaster." He had trouble with his dissertation. Once he had finished it, his examiners, coming as they did from the English and History departments, and thus inclined to approach textual evidence very differently, reached an impasse seemingly so final that Smith was forced to bar the door of the room in which they met, saying that no one was going to leave the room until his student was awarded his degree. But however unsure of himself he might have been, Ward was now certain that a life "around books and ideas and good talk" was the life for him.

AT MINNESOTA, Ward's new wife Barbara helped support him by working as a secretary. He had met her through a friend he had made in the Marines, a man whose wife had gone to Westbrook Junior College in Portland, Maine, with Barbara. Barbara was from Auburndale, a prosperous community west of Boston; her father was a dentist; her family owned a summer home in Maine, a home and a guest cabin on the coast in Lincolnville. Neither set of parents was pleased, his because Barbara was not Catholic and, to make matters worse, because she had been married before, Barbara's because he was Irish and had been raised as a Catholic. (Barbara told a friend that her parents used an old ethnic slur to express their displeasure: "The harps are taking over.")

And there was once again the question of social status. In the summer Barbara would often take the children to her parents' home in Maine; family vacation trips were always to Maine and not Brighton. There is no evidence that Barbara was concerned about the issue, but Ward could never forget it. He never had, he never would. You sense it when a friend jauntily writes him that he can tell his "proper Boston Mother-in-Law" that there is nothing "'middle of the road' about your cocktail officiating"—sense, in other words, that Ward has raised the issue himself. You can't help noticing it when Ward brings up Barbara's forbears in the letter he wrote in 1974 defending his 'illiterate" grandparents and his student's African heritage: "You happen to be wrong that I could trace the name 'Ward" back to George Washington (although my wife on her side can trace names back to the Massachusetts Bay Colony in the 17th century). Not that it matters." Maybe, maybe not.

But at Minnesota Ward's was a success story in the making. In 1952 he accepted a job as an instructor in the English Department at Princeton. His salary would be $3,200. He was awarded his doctorate the next year—

though given the expense of the trip, he did not return to Minnesota to
receive it in person—and he would soon make a name for himself in the
field of American Studies.

TWO

The Writer and the Teacher

"I prefer writer to scholar."

(Ward in an interview, May 26, 1979)

"I know that in the seminar room and in the classroom is where I truly like to be."

(Ward in a letter, February 7, 1970)

TOWARDS THE END of his life, Ward would look back on Minnesota as "a realization of...an ideal community of teachers and learners together." But in ways that mattered greatly to Ward, Princeton did not come close to realizing that ideal. Racial diversity was all but unheard of. In the '50s a young man could graduate from Princeton (known then as "the northern-most southern university in America") in a class of about 750 never having seen a black student on campus in his four years there. The one black professor, Charles Davis (also a member of the English Department), prompted not only alumni but several southern senators to protest—insofar as they were specific, to express their fear that his presence would lower Princeton's academic standards. (In 1970 Davis left to become the first chair of Afro-American Studies at Iowa University; two years later he went on to Yale.) There was little or no talk about racial diversity; there wasn't much talk, or evidence, of ethnic, religious, or socioeconomic diversity either.

From Ward's perspective, the students and the faculty were of a piece—WASPY and wealthy. Looking back on his senior seminar on Religion and American Life, for example, he said that it was populated exclusively by Episcopalians and Presbyterians from good, upper or upper-middle class American families, all of whom shared the same social values and unexamined assumptions. As for what might loosely be called class diversity, one story that Ward liked to tell is almost quaint. It was about a student who came down one evening to his apartment in what was called "the Project," the university's junior faculty and graduate student housing complex. He was delivering a late paper. When Ward answered the door, he held it open wide enough for the young man to appreciate the limitations of his professor's small quarters. The young man was silent for a moment, and then he said, "I didn't know people lived like this."

There were a few exceptions, a few kindred spirits, in the faculty. One was Martin Duberman, who was of Ukrainian Jewish descent, in the History Department, whose response to Princeton was very much like Ward's. After more than a decade at Yale, Duberman has written, "What I found in Princeton drawing rooms surpassed in formality and complacency anything I had previously known." As for the students, he was "appalled by their attitudes." They "seemed uniformly committed to playing parts from a fifties script, according to which paternal white men benignly ruled a prosperous country devoid of serious conflict." He vented in his diary: "Here they are, the members of the coming white elite, with little awareness of the social and power structure of our country, of the realities of life for the underprivileged, and most horrifying of all, with no compassion for the less fortunate. What a generation this is!" Another was Julian Moynahan, Ward's colleague in English, whose experience of the department can easily be inferred from his wife's report of his coming down from Rutgers, where he then taught, to deliver the Gauss Seminars many years later. His lectures were on Anglo-Irish literature, their title "Irish Enough: The Literary Imagination in a Hyphenated Culture." In a letter to Moynahan's wife Ward drew a fanciful, vengeful portrait of some of his former colleagues' responses. He said he envisaged "all the elegant young (now middle-aged) boys of the department shifting uneasily in their chairs" and pictured the lectures forcing the most debonair member of the department to hide behind his cigarette-holder. Princeton residents were even WASPier and wealthier. Alumni figured large in the town and, by their very presence, in university affairs. There were many of them, most of whom commuted to New York City, where they worked, typically, at very high-paying jobs. They were a constituency that could not be ignored. "Geography plays a part in my discomfort here," a former student who was teaching writing at Princeton wrote Ward many years later, "but so does the community." There is a "dreadful smugness" about it, he said. "The town's conversation [had] gone over almost entirely...to stocks and shares and tight money." The town of Princeton was a long way from Boston, the educational institution that was named after it a long way from the Latin School and Harvard.

Ward was popular among the residents of the "Project," though, and as he always would be, among students. In one image, passed on by an Amherst alumnus who was a graduate student at the time, he is clearly out of place, not a presence you would expect beside a Princeton pool. The alumnus was the lifeguard. He had his Red Cross certificate; he could use the money. What he remembers is Ward's showing up early on Sunday mornings, sitting down on a beach chair, opening up the *New York Times* and—the final touch—proceeding to puff away at a cigar. He seemed to be at ease with himself; there is no question but that he put the lifeguard at ease. "He treated me like an equal," he said of Ward.

In fact, if not socially, he was surely and securely at home in one respect. He was an emerging scholar or, as he preferred, "writer." Right from the start, during his years at Princeton his life as a writer was especially fulfilling. In 1953 his thesis was published and would go on to be an extraordinary success; one after another, his articles appeared in the *American Quarterly*, the *American Scholar*, and *Virginia Quarterly Review*, and it followed: he began to move up the academic ladder with relative ease. He didn't have to worry all that much about the culture of Princeton.

HIS DOCTORAL thesis was on Andrew Jackson, its title *Andrew Jackson: Symbol for an Age*. His advisor was Henry Nash Smith, whose influence on him and his work, he said in his Preface, was "so pervasive that it is difficult to describe....I would like to think that his mark is discernible on every page of mine." More specifically, Ward's thesis is obviously a direct descendent of Smith's *Virgin Land: The American West as Symbol and Myth*, the book that as much as any established American Studies as a new field.

It was Smith's first book, published in 1950. He was forty-four. Publishing was not yet the most important name of the academic game, or at least it was not in his mind—nor would it ever be in Ward's. But Smith could not have written *Virgin Land* quickly under any circumstances. Considering the politics, the economic situation, the social history of the West in the nineteenth century, and showing how they were reflected in texts ranging from the global visions of Whitman to the complex representations of the relations between primitivism and civilization in Cooper's novels down to Erastus Beadle's "dime novels," considering figures as different as Thomas Jefferson, Thomas Hart Benton, Daniel Boone, Buffalo Bill, and Calamity Jane, its scope seemed to one reviewer to be "epic." Still, there were complaints that Smith had left out important aspects of Western life, the most glaring (and to Smith the most regrettable) omission being "Indian" life (not yet recognized to be "Native American" life). And there was the problem of the subtitle's terms: "symbol and myth." The reviewer for the *American Historical Review* expressed the hope that "the use of these terms would not prove catching, for in less skilled hands such terms could lead to pernicious results," but catch on they did, and then spread so far as to give rise to a "school," the "myth and symbol school" of American Studies—which eventually came under severe criticism. Seeing no need to dwell on any methodological or theoretical questions his book might raise, on the very first page Smith just said, "I do not mean to raise the question whether such products of the imagination accurately reflect empirical fact. They exist on a different plane. But as I have tried to show, they sometimes exert a decided influence on practical affairs." Ward would later put his own bias even more simply: he knew it had gotten him in trouble, but the fact was, he said, "I tend to identify an historical problem through literature." After reading *Virgin Land*, and *Andrew Jackson*, we are left wondering: What is the relation between ideas and reality, between works of the imagination, or of myths and symbols and empirical or objective fact? Or, going back to Harvard, of History and Literature? If they are on "different planes," what does it mean to say they "reflect" each other? And how often, how many times, can we say an influence is "decided"? But in the '50s both books were considered prominent and promising examples of what could be done in American Studies.

Turning to Ward's work, we come upon one undeniable example of "decided influence." Like so many others, he thought that *Virgin Land* represented "a major new direction in the study of the American past"; more specifically, a review of it in the *Yale Review* pointed him in the direction of an ideal topic for his doctoral thesis. It "suggested that a study of the national appeal of Andrew Jackson might reveal a pattern of attitudes common to the general society." Or in the words of the reviewer, Jackson was "a single, complex hero-symbol" who could unite "not only Western and Southern but also the overriding national mythology." The reviewer gave no indication that there might be any question as to the relation between the "symbol-hero" and the "national mythology" and what Americans actually believed in Jackson's day, nor at the time did Ward. He just went right to work on his dissertation. He had a subject that suited him perfectly. In Jackson and in the so-called Jacksonian period, he had the origins and embodiment of ideals that he would try to establish and preserve in the educational and governmental realms in which he would work for the rest of his life. Though flawed and no longer required reading in courses, we can depend on the book as a guide as we make our way towards an understanding of the significance of Ward's life.

Andrew Jackson: Symbol for an Age is not a biography, not even a study of Jackson. "It is a study of popular ideology," of "a social construction made by others," he stated several years later. It is a study of the "symbolic figure" of Jackson, a figure not of his own making, or of his party, the Democratic party, but of America in the early nineteenth century. "The symbol was the creation of the times," Ward said in the last paragraph of the book. "To describe the early nineteenth century as the age of Jackson misstates the matter. The age was not his. He was the age's." That is how the book ends. Going back to the very beginning, to his title, Ward had chosen his preposition carefully: Jackson was the symbol not *of* his age but *for* it. He was impatient with those who said "of." They didn't see the point: Jackson stood *for* Americans in the early part of the nineteenth century; somehow they had chosen him to symbolize themselves.

In 1970, fifteen years after *Andrew Jackson: Symbol for an Age* was published, Ward contributed an essay on his book to a collection titled *The Historian's Workshop: Original Essays by Sixteen Historians*. In it he said that in his effort to discover just how and why Americans chose Jackson to be their symbol he began by trying to read everything they said about him— memoirs, magazines, newspapers, political speeches, cartoons, and the occasional anonymous song or poem. He took masses of notes and then pored over them in an effort to discover "some pattern, some lines of relationship." (Poker player that he was, he called it "the 'shuffle, cut, and deal' stage of scholarship.") Then, in the University of Minnesota library, he came upon two books, not promising sources he thought at first, but in them he soon discovered the plan of his book. One was a collection of twenty-five funeral orations, or eulogies of Jackson, the other was Martin Van Buren's *Autobiography*.

By Ward's lights, the eulogies were "ritual acts" in which speakers gave voice to "what everyone [was] supposed to feel." Upon examination, he thought all of them could be broken down under three headings, into what became the three divisions of *Andrew Jackson: Symbol for an Age*: Nature, Providence, and Will. They were, he said, the three words that defined an ideal pattern in which all the eulogies participated.

He read the eulogies in one evening. The next day he read Van Buren's *Autobiography*. The book itself seemed to him to be "one of the dullest testaments of a political leader in American history," but one word stood out: "civilization." Then and there, "the design of the entire book" seemed to have been given to him, "'given' in the sense that [he] was the passive recipient of a detailed plan and outline." The revelation seemed quite miraculous; at the same time, what was revealed is really quite simple. The word "civilization" made him realize that "Jackson's public meaning lay in the fact that he dramatized the tension between opposites in the public mind." More specifically,

> "Nature" was to be understood in relation to its opposite, "civilization." The concept of "Will" was divided between Promethean self-reliance and a humane regard for others; "Providence between the fatalism of acquiescence and the necessity for personal striving.

The pattern, the "design" of the book was, in effect, one for the life he was constructing for himself and, ideally, for others. It was of a civilization, an America, populated by citizens who were self-reliant and at the same time humane in their consideration of others. He made three separate piles on his desk and began to write. With a short first chapter, titled "In the Beginning Was New Orleans," he was on his way.

It was in New Orleans, in 1815, that Jackson led American forces to a victory over the British. The war had been going badly; cities along the coast were thought to be vulnerable, New Orleans especially so; the chances of defending it against the British seemed slim. America's confidence was at stake. So the victory was stunning. "At a moment of disillusionment,"

Ward wrote, "Andrew Jackson reaffirmed the young nation's self-belief; he restored its sense of national prowess and destiny." From among the many reports and tributes, in this first chapter Ward selects that of a Representative from Georgia, appropriately named Troup, who proposed a resolution to the House that offered thanks to Jackson and his men, chose it because it presented "in embryo the dominant conceptual strains which later characterize the fully developed symbol of Jackson."

The first strain is "Nature." The victory was, in Troup's words, a victory of "the yeomanry of the country....The farmers of the country triumphantly victorious over the conquerors of Europe," of "undisciplined militia" over "regular troops, the best disciplined and most veteran of Europe." Jackson himself would be celebrated as "Nature's nobleman," his victory over John Quincy Adams in the 1828 election as one of the Ploughman over the Professor. After his death, one eulogist would way, "Nature had made him a farmer"—though he was none of the above. Then came "Providence." Quite simply, God is on our side, or, as Troup put it, "The God of Battles and of Righteousness took part with the defenders of their country and the foe was scattered as chaff before the wind." But lest Jackson and his men be thought of as passive, their victory merely fated, there had to be the third strain—which was "Will." In Troup's words, "to be formidable...we need *but will it*. Europe will have seen that to be invincible...it is only necessary that we judiciously employ the means which God and Nature have bountifully placed at our disposal."

Ward follows the traces of these three "conceptual strains" from their embryonic state in responses to the Battle of New Orleans through the public responses to the most important stages of his military and political career—the Seminole Affair, his 1828 and 1832 election campaigns, his Indian removal policy, his fight with the Bank of the United States, to the eulogies that followed upon his death. All of them, he says in a short "Coda," possess "a dramatic unity...all three achieve realization through one figure, Andrew Jackson," and "a logical unity" as well. They are "organically inter-related." The man who is not only close to Nature but has been endowed by Nature and God with powers and with ideals that through his own determination he has realized, thereby proves that he has been providentially placed on this earth by Nature and by God to begin with. Out of these three ways of conceiving of Andrew Jackson, Ward argues, in the early nineteenth century Americans created an ideology for themselves.

After a few years and a number of "myth and symbol" studies, crit-ics came forward to question the proposition that certain myths and sym-bols, these manifestations of consciousness in particular, could be said to characterize or represent the society out of which they were said to have emerged. To take one prominent example, in an article titled "Myth and Symbol in American Studies," published in *American Quarterly*, the official organ of the American Studies Association, editor Bruce Kuklick adduces Ward's conclusion that Jackson's being seen as "God's Right-Hand Man," reflects the need of the American people to believe in Jacksonian doc-trines. Considering the ten pieces of evidence in the preceding paragraph (a hymn, an epic poem, a campaign biography titled *Pictorial Life*, five eu-logies, and two obviously slanted newspaper reports)—not voices whose sources you could confidently trace back to "the American people"—one must agree with Kuklick that, "It is fallacious to infer from the popularity of politicians and pulp fiction that the contents of speeches or books are accurate indicators of a people's beliefs."

But it was typical of Ward that he was as harsh, even harsher on him-self than were his critics. He concluded his contribution to *The Historian's Workshop* with three criticisms. The first was that his book was "static." He had used words like "embryo" and "developed," but he had treated all his evidence "as if the material constituted a single moment in time," a very long, thirty-year moment. His second criticism was Kucklik's, but couched in language that reflected greater sympathy for the "people" he had left out—the inarticulate masses of men who leave no written record behind," Ward called them. He had tried to explain why Jackson was a pop-ular hero by presenting a multitude of things that were said and written about him, but in fact, as he had to concede, "people may follow or vote for their hero for reasons quite different from the reasons that are given to them to do so" by those who *did* leave written records. And then, finally, there was the question, "Why?" Why did Americans living in the early part of the nineteenth century revere Andrew Jackson? What kind of society was it that celebrated the values one finds in an examination of the symbol of Andrew Jackson? To address those questions, Ward said, would have been to damage the "the self-contained unity" of the book he had writ-ten. But the main reason was that he just didn't yet know enough. So the answer to these questions would have to come in another book that was "in the works." And that is where the answer would forever remain—"in the works."

Politicians and writers of all stripes have their agendas, then and now. Consciously or unconsciously, cultural historians have theirs too. Ward knew this to be true. In an American Studies seminar on "Lindbergh, Dos Passos, and History" that he gave at Carleton College in 1965, when asked if he hadn't run the "danger of *imposing* a pattern on history" in his writings, he replied: "I do not think that the pattern, the shape, is there in the evidence; the pattern in the historian's account of history is *his* pattern. He creates it." And then, in an effort to retrieve some of his authority as an historian, he added: "But the pattern is potentially there in reality." In Ward's case, an imposition is nowhere more evident than in his gloss on the idea of Jackson's "Will." The victory over the British was attributed to Jackson's superior willpower; the people elected him as their president because "they saw living proof that success inevitably awaits the man of iron will." But an "iron will" was not enough. As we have seen, in introducing the concept of "Will" in his first chapter, he stresses the importance of *how* those who possess strong wills should act: they must prove themselves "worthy of God's favor by improving the opportunity he so bountifully provides."

In his book and in the story of his life the issue is of vital importance. Americans during the Jacksonian period could dwell on and believe in God's and Nature's favor. In mid-twentieth century America, certainly in Ward's mind, what a man willed, what a man did with his life, was what one focused on. Going one step further, when you couldn't believe in God or Nature, it alone was important. It was what Ward said he found most arresting and challenging about Van Buren's use of the word "civilization." The tensions in the public mind that he thought the word implied between Nature and Civilization, and between God's power and the efforts of individuals, are easy enough to understand and to live with. But after reading Van Buren's *Autobiography*, he concluded that "the concept of 'Will' was divided between Promethean self-reliance and a humane regard for others," and that the fate of civilization hinged on modern man's resolving the tension between the two. How—how in the name of God, we might ask—can that division be bridged? He would spend his professional life trying to answer that question.

"The man of iron will," or that man transposed into "the self-reliant man" and "the self-made man" (one chapter's title) is, according to Ward, a man who has always unnerved Americans. Deriving his "own standards of conduct from within," he creates "a sharp antithesis between the individual and the society." But no: "What actually seems to happen," Ward says, "is that the individual incorporates society's demands into his own consciousness and thereby is led to strive even harder because the demands of the society seem to be the demands of oneself." Or more boldly, "What was needed was not a denial of the self-reliant man, but assurance that the self-reliant man was on the side of society and not against society."

In his reading of Jackson, Ward was assured: Jackson was obviously "on the side of society." In Ward's, and in the minds and writings of most American historians, "the Jacksonian period" is almost always coupled with "Jacksonian democracy," and for many good reasons. Jackson was the first commoner to become president of the United States, the first whose origins were genuinely humble. And the means by which he became president were common and humble as well. He did not rise up through offices that he held, from having been the secretary of state, say, or vice president; he did so because ordinary (white, male) citizens nominated and voted for him, their ranks no longer restricted by the requirement that they own land. They were the men whom he celebrated in his Farewell Address, "The planter, the farmer, the mechanic, and the laborer," who knew "that their success depended upon their industry and economy," who had no political connections and "little or no share in the direction of the great moneyed corporations." They were the men who formed what he called "the great body of the people of the United States...the bone and sinew of the country." Jackson considered himself their popular sovereign, elected to use his power to defend their interests and fulfill their wishes. He was responsible to them. It followed that he opposed "nullification," or a state's right to reject any law it considered unconstitutional. Considering it controlled by corrupting business interests, it followed that he warred against the Bank of the United States. Believing that the official duties of public servants were plain and simple, and that the average citizen could perform them, he argued for the rotation of governmental officials, lest any partisan position become entrenched.

In his teaching and writing Ward would continue to seek out and to celebrate individuals who incorporated society's demands into their own consciousnesses; more generally and impressively, he tried to create the demands throughout his working life. Generally speaking, he himself wanted to succeed, to rise in the world and in the world's eyes, and obviously he did. At his best, he wanted *society* to succeed as well. So he measured his success according to his influence on the students he taught or the institution he administered or the legislation he helped bring into being, measured it by his ability to foster in individuals any and everywhere "a humane regard for others." In fostering it, he would earn the favor of the God he no longer believed in.

THE FIGURE of the "self-made," the "self-reliant" man," was grounded in the Jacksonian period. This man's existence, his place in society, became more complicated in the decades that followed, and Ward shifted his attention accordingly. There would be no follow-up to *Andrew Jackson: Symbol For an Age*. Ward turned to the individual, to Individualism, instead. It was a grander, a more ambitious subject, but in studying the fate of it in America he could generalize about ways to improve society more easily than he could by limiting himself to one historical period and to one man. Individualism would be of primary, of central, importance to him ever after. A large portion of what he went on to write about and work for was in its name, about the forms threats against it took, about how it could be preserved and extended, and thus how what America stood for could be preserved. "Eventually," Leo Marx has said, "individualism influenced everything he did"—individualism that would, by his definition, be "for society." "He quite literally believed in the myth of American society, that people can make a difference."

It is fitting that Ward wrote the entry on Individualism in the *Encyclopedia Americana*. Fitting too is what he wrote. In it he said that there have been two ways of defining the word's meaning ever since it was introduced into the English language in the 1830s, one ideally, the other historically. The first way is to assert "the supreme value of the individual and [see] society as only a means to the satisfaction of individual ends," and then to relate it to a variety of figures and movements going back to ancient Epicurean thought and the Judeo-Christian tradition. The second way is to trace the transformation of the idea in America from one that at first "denied the importance of society" to a "social ideology," a transformation necessitated by social and economic changes that made men increasingly dependent upon each other. This second way was Ward's. The form that he imagined Individualism taking is obviously his too. It is an updated version of the self-reliant man who is for and not against society:

> The growth of social organization and the interdependence of men in a complex society led to a shift away from individualism as freedom from restraint to individualism as the realization of self through participation in society. Freedom of the individual became freedom to do what was good for society.

He ended the entry with this description of the road ahead: "It remains to be seen whether the sense of primacy of the individual may still be realized in the complex conditions of modern life."

Again and again, in his classes and writings and speeches, Ward began his analyses of the historical meaning of Individualism in America with Alexis de Tocqueville's *Democracy in America* (published in 1840, near the end of the Jacksonian period), with special emphasis on the two-page chapter in Volume Two titled "Of Individualism in Democratic Countries." It was Tocqueville, as Ward argued in "Tocqueville and the Meaning of Democracy," who first posed the question, and who "still speaks to us today": He recognized "the basic structure of values which characterize a democratic society, a society which emphasizes the equality of all citizens and puts the individual first, that is, the worth, the primacy of the individual self, at the center of its vision of the meaning of the good society."

"Our fathers only knew about egoism," Tocqueville wrote. "Egoism is a passionate and exaggerated love of self which leads a man to think of all things in terms of himself and to prefer himself to all." By contrast, he called individualism "a calm and considered feeling," an enviable feeling it would seem, one to aspire to perhaps, but he was wary. It was also a feeling that "disposes each citizen to isolate himself from the mass of his fellows and withdraw into the circle of family and friends; with this little society formed to his taste, he gladly leaves the greater society to look after itself." Or, what was worse, "individualism at first only dams the springs of public virtues, but in the long run it attacks and destroys all others too and finally merges in egoism."

In America, this individual man, this democratic citizen, this potentially self-reliant and self-made man, would be celebrated and mythologized ever after. But coming from the old world, what Tocqueville saw was an unstructured society made up of atomistic individuals whose allegiance was at most to family and friends, at worst to their own well-being and no one else's, and he feared that as any society became democratic it was in danger of suffering the same fate. He did imagine that American men might find some truths in their religious beliefs or in moral laws that they did not question, that would counter their "egoism." But he put more faith in the evident, observable fact of the "voluntary associations" that Americans seemed continually to form. Like "democracy in America" itself, these associations were new to him: "There are not only commercial and industrial associations in which all take part, but others of a thousand different types—religious, moral, serious, futile, very general and very limited, immensely large and very minute. Americans combine to give fetes, found seminaries, build churches, distribute books, and send missionaries to the antipodes. Hospitals, prisons, and schools take shape in that way," he marveled. If men were to remain or become civilized, he said, if they were to become more than a collection of self-seeking individuals, "the art of association must develop and improve among them at the same speed as equality of conditions spreads." Or, in the final words of Ward's *Encyclopedia* entry, as equality spread, individualism had to mean "self-realization through participation in a greater entity."

But what remained a constant danger inherent in a democratic society, transcendent beliefs and voluntary associations notwithstanding, was what Tocqueville famously called "the tyranny of the majority." Ideally all men were equal, independent, autonomous, but what Tocqueville observed in fact were men unable to think independently, men silenced by whatever the majority of them thought. He saw mere conformists. In no uncertain terms he said, "I know of no country in which, speaking generally, there is less independence of mind and true freedom of discussion than in America." When he turned to "the immense thrusting crowd of American political aspirants," Tocqueville saw "very few men who showed that virile candor and manly independence of thought...which, wherever found, is the most salient feature in men of great character."

The problem, the challenge, facing America was how to maintain the "manly independence" of its individual citizens when they subscribed to the proposition that they were each others' equals. What would enable this democracy to avoid becoming an anarchic society of self-interested men on the one hand or a mass of orderly but spineless men on the other? What outside these men's selves might command their allegiance that did not reduce them to subjects, that enabled them to maintain their individuality? Might there be a way for the individual so to transform himself that he would be mindful of and work to create "the common good?" These were questions that Ward asked again and again for the rest of his life.

In essay after essay ("Individualism: Ideology or Utopia," "Mill, Marx, and Modern Individualism," "Herbert Croly: The Promise of Constructive Idealism," "The Ideal of Individualism and the Reality of Organization," "Individualism Today") he defended the freedom of the individual against "the organizing power of modern society." In 1969 he collected many of them in his next and what proved to be his last book, or, given his view of such collections, what he called his "non-book": *Red, White, and Blue: Men, Book, and Ideas in American Culture*. He dedicated it to "Henry Nash Smith: Teacher, Pattern, and Friend."

Insofar as it contains an historical account of the fate of the individual, it always begins with the Jacksonian period—"truly a pastoral idyll in our nation's history," he called it. His most famous treatment of the problem that individualism faces in the modern world is his essay "The Meaning of Lindbergh's Flight." On the one hand, he considered Lindbergh individualism incarnate, the self-reliant hero who was the first to fly the Atlantic alone, the "lineal descendent," Teddy Roosevelt's son said, of Daniel Boone and Davy Crockett, that type of man who "played a lone hand and made America." He did so at a propitious time, in 1927 when the nation was in need of someone to show the way out of the moral and spiritual morass into which it had descended during Prohibition; he was perfect for the part. The handsome young man who came off a Minnesota farm reminded a writer for the *Nation* of Lochinvar; his flight was "the kind of stuff which the ancient Greeks would have worked into a myth and medieval Scots into a border ballad." In sum, Ward said, "Lindbergh gave the American people a glimpse of what they liked to think themselves to be at a time when they feared they had deserted their own vision of themselves." On the other hand, as Lindbergh himself knew full well, he represented the triumph of the machine and the highly organized industry and society that produced it. He spoke of what "we," not "I," did; he told reporters that they hadn't said enough about "that wonderful motor," "this silent partner" President Coolidge called it, that "represented American genius and industry."

Turning for a moment to Lindbergh himself, Ward said that there were two Lindberghs, one private, one public, and that what America made of him was "fastened on to an unwilling person." "The tragedy of Lindbergh's career is that he could never accept the role assigned him. He always believed he might keep his two lives separate." It is a tantalizing observation. When we come to the most memorable (and controversial) act of his own life, we will see Ward claiming he could do just that. But in his essay he says no more about the private Lindbergh. His subject is the public Lindbergh. ("The Public Meaning of Lindbergh's Flight" was its original title.) Ward said that the response of the American people to him and his flight revealed that they had a problem, our problem, he claimed: "We cherish the individualism of the American creed at the same time that we worship the machine which increasingly enforces collectivized behavior. Whether we can have both, the freedom of the individual and the power of organized society, is a question that still haunts our minds. To resolve the conflict that is present in America's celebration of Lindbergh in 1927 is still the task of America."

Ward concluded his essay on "The Ideal of Individualism and the Reality of Organization" with three alternatives: use the word "individualism" only when referring to the early nineteenth century, when it had its first meaning; acknowledge that the individual is now defined by his function, his role in an organization; and bear in mind "the notion of consent," the idea that power is legitimate only when the individual accepts "emotionally and intellectually" what power demands. That is "the political answer... that is what we mean when we say that America is democratic. A democratic society," he says,

> is one in which those in positions of power, public or private, are responsible for their decisions to those whom their decisions affect. That definition

forces us, then, to ask how the organizations of our modern, complex society might be made responsible to the individual and serve the ends of a democratic society.

One might have thought that the problem was overwhelming, but not Ward. He thought that we were still responsive "to the ethical overtones of the word, 'individualism,'" that we needn't leave individuals "defenseless in the face of the organized power of modern society," and that we could discover a community in which their ambitions and personalities could be sustained and nourished.

Red, White, and Blue is indicative of the range and variety of Ward's interests and, by the same token, of how much he deserved his prominence in the field of American Studies. There are "Afterwords" to Signet editions of James Fenimore Cooper's *The Prairie*, Harriet Beecher Stowe's *Uncle Tom's Cabin*, and E.W. Howe's *The Story of a Country Town*, pieces that are evidence of the fact that Ward was very good at bringing history to bear on literature. There is a long essay on Andrew Jackson Dowling, the "Father of American Landscape Architecture," titled "The Politics of Design," in which Ward asks, "what human values, what view of man, what view of the political order, are implicit in the shape of our modern environment and in the minds of those men who play a central role in its creation." Of most interest is one on Benjamin Franklin, aptly subtitled "The Making of an American Character." In it he poses the personal question: "Who was Benjamin Franklin?" It too is tantalizing, not prompting us to look ahead to an event in Ward's life, but more generally, *at him*. For Ward, Franklin is "so many different characters....the self-made man, the jack-of-all trades...a witness to the uncertainties about social status that have characterized our society." His story is "the success story to beat all success stories." But who was he, Ward asks? We need not hesitate to say that Ward is reflecting on himself, need not because at the end of his essay he makes the identification explicit. Franklin, he writes, "not only puts the question that still troubles us in our kind of society, 'Who's Who?' He also raises the question that lies at the heart of the trouble: 'Who am I?'" Who was Ben Franklin, a man of many parts that to Ward did not form a whole? That may not be every reader's Franklin, but it makes sense that he was Ward's, a man for whom the question "Who am I?" was so difficult, and thus who ultimately so seldom experienced what Tocqueville called the "calm and considered feeling" of individualism.

Under the heading "Self and Society," Ward coupled the essay with a Voice of America talk he gave on John F. Kennedy, who, like Jackson, was a symbol for his age, and for Ward a model of individual manhood—the kind of man, we can safely say, that he wanted to be. At the heart of Kennedy's *Profiles in Courage* (the ostensible subject of the talk), Ward said, was a "sense of the courage of the single individual to be what he is....

> What is primary is the necessity to be one's self, and to take delight in that act of being....What is essential is the primacy of the self and the courage to be that self....Love yourself enough to be what you are, whatever that may be. If you don't do your own thing, if you start doing someone else's thing, then you become alienated from your own self. The rest is ashes.

"To be one's self, and to take delight in that act of being....Love yourself enough." Would that he too could have been a man who loved himself enough to be who he was and to love himself whoever he turned out to be.

WARD SPENT the academic year 1963-64 at the Center for Advanced Study in the Behavioral Sciences at Stanford. It was an enjoyable and productive year, not least because of the room in which he worked. He described what he looked out on in the opening paragraph of "The Politics of Design," his essay on Andrew Jackson Downing:

> one glass wall gave upon a distant scene, through the gnarled branches of blue oaks, over the red-tiled rooftops of the Stanford campus, to the blue and green and rust colored salt-flats of the lower reaches of San Francisco Bay, to the bare burned-brown masses of the range of mountains beyond.

He could not see, but, he went on, he could not forget

> that the Camino Real with its shrill vulgarity runs through the middle distance, that the fill and filth of cities on the shore threaten the very existence of the San Francisco Bay, and that the research plants of a war economy which have made Stanford's land a great capital asset have also pulled the population with them which threatens all the land around.

It should not go unnoted that he had a keen eye (several people have attested to his unusually sensitive appreciation of paintings) and that he was indeed a writer, setting down what he actually saw in fine prose and moving effortlessly to its significance. The landscape was full of meaning for him. He said the view from his room was "proof of the easy condition of the critic of our culture and our environment," and then he defined that condition as he understood and embodied it. There before him were the "glaring irreconcilables" that Lindbergh's flight represented: on the one hand, the pastoral setting in which a boy might make himself into a man, and on the other, the world as it had been transformed by industrial and technological revolutions. And right there was evidence of the "political and social values... implicit in [the] ways in which we have shaped our physical environment," proof of the political significance of "design," all this to be illuminated further by the historian, this time by Ward himself, who would provide insight into the "usable past" and thus "some perspective on ourselves."

He called his condition, his as the critic, the historian, and the writer, "easy," and in many ways it was at that time and at Stanford, but when Marx wrote him from Amherst, where he had been teaching for six years, to ask if he was intent upon returning to Princeton the following year, Ward said he wasn't sure. Princeton's values fell far short of his. At the moment, though, what was most important was the fact that the university's program in American Civilization that he directed was not anything like the vital force that Minnesota's program had been. Its faculty was not so distinguished; nowhere near so many students had enrolled (only 40 out of a student body of about 3,000, in the spring of 1964). No, he wasn't sure about Princeton. He would probably be happier elsewhere. Maybe Stanford. They had asked him to stay on as a professor of history. Maybe Indiana. They were interested in him and would soon ask him to come and chair their History Department. But his commitment to American Studies precluded his seriously considering either offer. Maybe Berkeley, where Smith had recently gone, but he'd be offered only another associate professorship there.

Writing from Amherst, Marx was obviously asking for a reason; from Ward's perspective, if Amherst wanted to look at him, it was obvious as well that he had reason to want to look at Amherst. American Studies at

Amherst was not just a program, it was a department, one that was flourishing. It was the oldest of its kind in the country. It had started in the '30s, when George Taylor turned to fields other than his own (Economics) in his effort to understand the Depression. Now, in the '60s, the department was again asking what had gone wrong, and many students were eager to join it in its effort to find answers. Almost 10 percent of the classes of 1963 and 1964 majored in it, and the percentage would rise steadily thereafter. Between 1966 and 1969 the number of graduates who had majored in American Studies climbed from forty to fifty-five, from 14 percent to 18 percent of their classes. So large had the numbers become that in the fall of 1967 the faculty allowed the department to limit the number of majors in a class to 30.

Colleagues were drawn to it too. Out of the faculty, under Taylor's general editorship, came a series of small volumes devoted to "Problems in American Civilization," introductions followed by selections of primary and secondary readings on specific topics, "Readings Selected by the / Department of American Studies / Amherst College," as the subtitle of each volume had it until the series was taken off Amherst's hands in the early '70s by the publisher. Symptomatic of the extent of faculty support for American Studies was the range of departments other than American Studies that the faculty members represented and the number of volumes that they edited. Twelve professors from five departments other than American Studies (almost all of them held joint appointments) produced over thirty of these volumes. The volumes were extremely popular, having been adopted in courses nationwide, exciting at the time for encouraging students to think critically, to make choices, to come to their own conclusions. The year before he went to Stanford, Ward's *Andrew Jackson: Symbol for an Age* came out in paperback. Being readily accessible to students, being eminently teachable, it too would reach an enormous audience, and by the same means as had the "Problems of Civilization" volumes.

In February Ward was lecturing at Indiana. These being the days before national searches, he was simply invited to continue on east, make a "social call" on the Marxes, and meet with Calvin Plimpton, the College's president, and with the American Studies Department, with Plimpton in attendance. Plimpton kept notes. In their conversation, after learning the facts of Ward's family situation—his marriage, his three sons, by then "ca.

eleven, nine, seven"—and what little there was to be said about his military service, he came to what Ward said about his time at Princeton. It seems that he "blew hot" with Robert Goheen, the president of the university, and that "he [was] able to apologize." Ward summarized his teaching in a way he did on other occasions. "He told me two questions that good students should be encouraged to ask—Oh yeah? So what?" Plimpton wrote. "Has lots of ideas about administration—but says not interested," Plimpton noted. But that did not put the question to rest, not in Plimpton's mind, not in his because, as he must have sensed, it did not in Ward's mind either. After a brief detour to other matters, Plimpton wrote: "I asked if he would consider presidency of Colgate." As for his writing, Ward said that he "would like to get his book finished. Individualism and society." It was like his book on the relationship between society in Jackson's day and the symbolic values ascribed to Jackson himself. It was "in the works." A few days later Plimpton contacted an outsider, a Princeton economist and administrator, who reported, according to Plimpton's notes, that Ward had had to struggle "going up to Prof—Bill less conventional and did not satisfy staunch 17th Cent. Fellows—It was very close—Middle road scholar could not stretch."

After Ward's meeting with the department, a vote was taken. Only Henry Steele Commager, the most well-known and celebrated member of the department, had a serious objection, which was ironic because it was assumed by many (including Ward himself) that when he did come to Amherst he came as Commager's heir apparent. Commager worried that Ward was "not particularly productive—thesis Jackson—is only thing he has produced—everybody expects things from him, so should we....depth as a scholar uncertain." But the department agreed to make Ward an offer. He accepted and in the fall started teaching at Amherst, a small liberal arts college (with between 1,200 and 1,300 students over the course of following decade) where at the time, teaching was more important than research.

Turning back to *Red, White, Blue*, there are two essays in a final section (titled "The Values of American Culture: The Intellectual and the University") that illuminate what Ward thought of colleges and universities, of teaching and research, during these pivotal years. The first, "The Intellectual: Critic or Cleric?" came out in the *American Scholar* in the winter of 1965-66. At the very outset he asks: is teaching "the transmission of knowledge and the values of the culture to future generations," or is it "research, the discovery of new knowledge"? He begins the essay with teaching and before he is two pages into it—sharply, arrogantly we might say—he dismisses "research." He questions how much of the knowledge that results from research is really new, and then goes on to insult (the word is not too strong) those who engage in it, indeed, to insult almost all of what had been his university colleagues, or, as he put it, "99 and 44/100 percent of the faculty I know":

> Among my own acquaintance in the profession, there are hardly one or two who have made an original contribution to knowledge, if we take the word "original" in any serious sense. I would go further and say for 99 and 44/100 percent of the faculty I know, that if they had a truly original idea, it would present such a threat to all their established and comfortable notions they would be so embarrassed by its presence they would hardly know where to put it, where in the desk to hide it away.

This sounds like the symbolic Jacksonian ploughman attacking Adams, the Harvard professor, in the election of 1828, but we are prevented from calling it out-and-out anti-intellectualism not only by the title of essay but by Ward's description of the teacher and "the field of energy we name the intellectual life" in which he labors. In *that* field the teacher

> modestly sets himself the still enormously ambitious task of assimilating what others have said, the lessons of the past, of becoming, in other words, a responsible embodiment of the tradition of the past, the man who does not presume to be an "original," who is content to write books setting forth what he has learned and how he thinks it bears upon the present.

While being aware of our being afraid of words like "conventional" and "traditional," and of "the pejorative associations we now bring to the words "amateur" and "dilettante," Ward declares that we "desperately" need what was once meant by them. These teachers will transmit the values of the culture and at the same time criticize them. They will pass on what they have learned about the past, and then with students whom they have encouraged to respond, they will criticize those values and arrive at and test conclusions about their worth in the present. His insistence on the cultural, the social and political relevance of the past, his constant search for what will work for the betterment of society, and his consistent attraction to those he thinks can lead the way or support him on *his* way, all so characteristic of his academic style, leave relatively little room, we might observe, for the disinterested pursuit of knowledge or enjoyment of the free play of ideas that intellectuals commonly experience.

In spite of the title of the second essay, "The University: The Trouble with Higher Education," Ward now includes colleges in his analysis. The essay begins with the word "Berkeley," a symbol of "the necessities and the possibilities which confront higher education in the United States today" and also of "the crucial fact that higher education is in trouble." The reason for the trouble, as Ward had said in the first essay, was the emphasis that higher educational institutions had placed on research (this time defined as "practical") as opposed to "ideal" education or "service." It is the conflict between the two that has caused student unrest from "the great urban university like Berkeley to the small private college in its pastoral setting like Amherst." Drawing on the Port Huron Statement of the Students for a Democratic Society (SDS), he rejects the idea of "disinterested intelligence or withdrawal into the academy from the heat and dust of daily life." Like them he wants faculties and curricula to be "directly related to the needs of society," the real needs of an ideal society, ones that are drastically different from the practical needs they believe higher education is serving all too well already. As he has it in his nice summation, "They want not to be prepared to play a role in society. They want to change society so they may play a role in it." There was now no thought of the disinterested pursuit of knowledge. Either your studies and your teaching contributed to its reformation—its salvation, one might go so far as to say—or, to use a loaded word, to its defense.

Whether or not Ward himself was conscious of the fact, those who interviewed him in 1964, those who read these essays in 1965-66, and those who read them when they were published in *Red, White, And Blue* in 1969 had reason to sense that they were in the presence of an administrator in the making. When they came to the end of "The University: The Trouble with Higher Education," they would have had reason to put it another way: Ward was a man who was interested in power. Here is the final paragraph:

What troubles American higher education today is the simple fact
that it has no choice between these simple alternatives. It must meet both
demands. It must serve power and yet make that power humane. Whether it
can or can not is at the bottom of what troubles American education today.

But when they had finished they might also have stepped back and wondered: perhaps they themselves *did* have a choice, perhaps they didn't
have to serve power and humanize it at the same time. In other words, perhaps they might have been content to remain disinterested intellectuals.
Or perhaps, like Alan Trachtenberg, they saw that they had still another
choice. In a review of *Red, White, and Blue*, published in the *Carleton Miscellany* in 1970, Trachtenberg imagined that rather than serve and humanize power, you might oppose it. He concluded his review with this challenge: "There is an agony of commitment implicit here, an agony I cannot
share. Where is the place for the scholar who does not wish to serve power
but to oppose it, perhaps by questioning its legitimacy? Or who wishes to
undertake a new search for America, outside the old definitions?"

But Ward lived by the old definitions all his life. He would often de-
plore the social and economic results, but he did not finally question the
old principles on which they were founded. He was not a radical. As he
often said, he was a good liberal. He believed that in spite of a man's background, he was an American like every other American, free to make a success of himself and at the same time be a member of a society of equals—a
democracy. Ward himself was a humane individual, an individual defined
ideally in terms of his service to others; he believed that others should and
could be humane individuals too. Yes, he knew about the possibility that
individualism could devolve into egoism, into selfishness, into greed; he
knew too that individuals could be regimented to the point of losing their
individuality, and he knew about how dangerous power in the hands of a
few or of an unresponsive government could be. But he was an idealist. He
thought the best of people. He was ambitious, on the make. He enjoyed
power, he aspired to it for its own sake. But he also wanted it in order to be
able to inspire individuals to create communities, to create a society devoted to causes and ideals that were greater than themselves, even as they
worked in their own interests. He thought power could be humanized.

WHETHER OR not Berkeley, symbol of the fact that higher education was in trouble, knew what was going on at Amherst, tucked away in its "pastoral setting," the *Student*, a very good undergraduate newspaper during the period, kept Amherst apprised of what was happening on other campuses. And what was happening was replicated at the College. A steady flow of prominent activists and spokesmen came to speak from some of these campuses (Mario Savio from Berkeley, Mark Rudd from Columbia), from the political left (Norman Thomas, Wayne Morse, Tom Hayden, Stokeley Carmichael) to the (heavily out-numbered) political right (Robert Welch, the founder of the Birch Society). In 1964 and 1968, a host of men running for state and national offices made the rounds of the four, and with the arrival of the first students at Hampshire College in the fall of 1970, the five colleges in the area. In turn, Amherst students and faculty left Amherst to march and to register voters. They marched in Northampton, New York, and Washington. Eight students and two faculty members went down to Selma, Alabama, to register voters and be among those who marched to Montgomery, Alabama in March 1965. Four of the students were jailed. Even before rioting broke out in nearby Springfield, Massachusetts, in 1965 students went there to tutor and register voters, at first under the auspices of the Congress of Racial Equality (CORE), then as members of Amherst Students for Racial Equality, and beginning in the summer of 1969, Amherst students, along with Smith College students, tutored ninth and tenth graders who were bussed up to Amherst to attend the Springfield-Amherst Summer Academy.

The College itself registered the shocks the culture was experiencing in a variety of ways. The students called for the loosening and then the repeal of parietal rules, and for the abolition of the requirement that they attend meetings in Johnson Chapel, meetings that were secular and short (and brutish only insofar as dogs were frequently in attendance), on a certain number of mornings a week. More important, they wanted their voices heard in conversations and meetings in which the nature and purpose of their education were being discussed. In other words they wanted to be represented on curriculum committees, at faculty meetings, and even on the Board of Trustees. In an early issue of the *Student* in the fall of 1968, the editors intoned: "We are entering a new season of politics at Amherst. It shall be called the season of committees and the year of student participation." And so they were, and so it was.

Opposition to the Vietnam War and racial injustice lay behind and fueled discontent and agitation on campus. Increasing numbers of students
joined SDS; committees calling for the end of the war or for radical action
formed. The threat of the draft lay heavy in the air. War protest was the
more intense when opposition to it meant opposition to putting one's own
life on the line or, in the case of young men of color, to being trained and
sent out to kill men of color halfway around the world.

It wasn't the case that the community was uniformly against the war. In
the fall of 1965 a small group of students seized and burned the pamphlets
that the Committee for Nonviolent Action was handing out in the parking
lot of a fraternity and let the air out of the members' tires. President Plimpton's angry response was that though their actions were seemingly minor,
the perpetrators would suffer the consequences for years to come in the
form of their guilty feelings ("They are going to be looked at by other students....Here are people who are basically yellow," he said) and the negative references that would dog their attempts to get jobs. More impressive
was his statement, quoted in the *New York Times*' coverage of the incident,
that, "The silent ones who stand idly by are almost as guilty as those who
interfered physically with freedom of speech." In November a more civilized and much larger number of students (almost 400), signed a petition
supporting the government's position in Vietnam. Three years later David
Eisenhower, Class of '70, along with seventeen other students, wrote a judicious letter to the *Student* that opposed the idea (never realized) of Dr.
Benjamin Spock's being awarded an honorary degree, not because of his
opposition to the war, but on the basis of the "possibly illegal means" he
chose to express it."

In the spring of 1966, in the most widely publicized event of these
years, Robert McNamara did receive one. Early in the morning, before the
Commencement ceremonies began, he engaged with those who opposed
the war in heated but not unruly discussion in the Chapel. The facts that
many students wore black armbands, several refused their diplomas, and
many faculty members did not stand when McNamara was awarded his
degree made Commencement more tense than festive.

Though always in danger of being drowned out by opponents of the
war, black students and their white supporters made their protests heard

as well. Admissions was a basic and burning issue, as it was in colleges and universities across the land. The numbers were clear; they needed to be improved—drastically. At Amherst in 1966, two percent of the students was black, as had been the case, more or less, for the previous twenty years. In the spring of 1968 there were as many black freshmen as there were in the three upper classes combined at the time. Other demands—for a Black Studies program, a black administrator, black faculty, and continued and increased support for summer programs—were not so successfully addressed. In February 1969 black students walked out of a meeting with the Instruction Committee of the Board of Trustees, saying that though there had been a flurry of activity the previous spring after Martin Luther King's assassination, indifference and stagnation had soon followed. Bernard Barbour, a freshman member of the African-American—the Afro-Am— Society's executive committee, read a resounding statement. The college had "reneged on its promises," it began:

> We wish to establish our utter disgust with the glaring deficiencies in the liberal education which Amherst College boasts to provide. We feel that the Amherst education does not afford black students the exposure necessary to prepare them for leadership in the black community, nor does it prepare white students to react intelligently to that leadership. We maintain that Amherst College constricts the very individual development it claims to promote. We consider it imperative that Amherst College accept the reality of a genuine Afro-American culture. The continued denial of this reality is justified only by racist assumptions.

In April the faculty voted to establish a Black Studies Department, beginning with two courses of its own, an Introduction to Afro-American Studies and a required seminar for prospective majors, and for the time being, a steering committee, made up of three colleagues. There was unrest aplenty, but Amherst would then, and for the next several years, avoid the kinds of confrontation and violence that many other campuses experienced.

Meanwhile the percentage of alumni sons who were admitted (75 percent of those who applied in 1964) declined steadily. And waiting in the wings were women. Everyone was aware that Amherst's competitors were "going co-ed." According to a poll conducted in the spring of 1969, one to which more than a third of the student body responded, those in favor of Amherst's admitting women outnumbered those who were opposed by a margin of two to one. All of which is to suggest the kinds of issues that the campus faced during what we call the '60s, and to give some sense of the difficulties the institution faced as it tried to address *all* of them at the same time and still try to go on about its educational business. Most importantly for our purposes, it is to set the stage for Ward's appearances and to see what part he played.

We may be surprised at how relatively inactive Ward was during this period, how small a part he played on campus. Not until two years after his arrival would his name appear in the *Student*, and then only on the occasion of the publication of his article on "The University: The Trouble with Higher Education." He took almost no action and said almost nothing about what was actually taking place. He was Professor Ward, the teacher, well-liked and respected by most of his colleagues, more than well-liked, revered, by some of his students. He stood somewhat apart from all that threatened to disrupt their work together.

What satisfied him most was the work they were doing together in American Studies. The department had been addressing "Problems in American Civilization" since 1948, when "Civil Rights" was among those raised in a course titled "Interpretations in American Revolution." Now it had gone a step further and offered courses, required of its majors, on what was causing the "trouble" even as they spoke, on the war in Vietnam in 1966 and in the following year, blacks' struggle for civil rights. The former was the subject of the last four weeks in a course on "Liberalism and International Disorder," the latter of as many weeks in one on "Assimilation and Pluralism in a Democratic Society." Applying the most frequently invoked standard of the day, the headline of a *Student* article describing these courses read: "American Studies: The Evolution of Amherst's Most Relevant Course." (Two years later, in the fall of 1969, the *Student* reported on how Ward had gone on to apply the principle of using the past to illuminate present problems in chairing the program committee of the American Studies Association. Among the topics that would be discussed at its annual meeting would be "The Professor and Society," "Student Activism," and "The Pan-American Impulse Among Blacks before Marcus Garvey.") Ward would have said that the department was bringing students into the public arena in the best way that an educational institution could.

His relations with his colleagues in American Studies were excellent too. He met with them regularly for coffee in Morgan Hall, the home of the department; he was the liveliest presence among them. There, along with Marx and Allen Guttmann (who had also come on from Minnesota), he, Ted Greene, Gordie Levin, Ed Rozwencz, Ellen Ryerson and others would engage in conversation about the College and about their course offerings, especially about whichever version of the introductory course many of them were teaching together. In 1969-70, three of them were on the Committee of Six, the executive committee of the faculty. The members of the department became known as "the courthouse crowd."

What did not go as well as Ward had planned was his writing. In the "Talk of the Town" segment on him in the *New Yorker* he is quoted as saying, "I thought I'd have a quieter life there and more time for writing. This wasn't true." Not true at all. Not only did he have less and less time for writing, the writing that he did do, the writing that meant most to him, his book on Individualism, just would not come together. That it might never come together became painfully obvious in the spring of 1966 at a meeting of the newly formed undergraduate History Club, a meeting organized by its president, Gordon Jones. Jones, who was writing his senior thesis under Ward's guidance, asked him to talk about the book he was working on. He invited members of the History and American Studies departments and members of those faculties from the other colleges in the Valley as well. Between 40 and 50 people were there. What took place, by Jones' account, may not be the academy at its worst but it was the academy presenting Ward with an image of himself that was the polar opposite of the one he wanted to see before him. Ward talked for about half an hour about his project, and then came the comments and questions, primarily from colleagues at the other colleges. They added up, Jones has written, to a "not very thinly veiled attack on the entire conceptual basis of the individualism project" and on "Bill's whole methodology, the legitimacy of the kind of popular/intellectual history he engaged in." In sum: "The overall tone of the remarks was harsh and patronizing, they were delivered with some relish and appeared to have been thought out in advance." The students were taken aback; Ward was clearly upset. Who is to say how much resentment against Amherst College, the most prestigious of the colleges in the area and in those days the least willing to engage in cooperative ventures, stoked the fires, but undoubtedly *he* was being attacked as an historian and intellectual. In the years that followed he would try to complete his book and thereby justify himself as an intellectual—until he could no longer.

But there was an obvious and enduring reason why Ward was happy about having come to Amherst. In the "Talk of the Town" piece he contrasted his experiences as a teacher at Amherst and at Princeton: "I'd thought I was an excellent teacher at Princeton. At Amherst, I found I wasn't a very good teacher," he said. "I was not paying enough attention to the development of the young, to the shift that the whole university was going through in the last ten years—away from expertise to being a good person. I became more involved with the students." And that led him to name a significant advantage that Amherst had over Princeton ("We're not big, we're not anonymous, and we're not a university"), and as we will soon see, to present it in terms so glowing as to be blinding ("We've never had any problems of confrontation or occupation of buildings").

Even as president, he continually acted on his belief that what mattered was the worth of each and every one of them as individuals. "The only thing that keeps me sane, believing in the worth of what I do," he said, "is the capacity of the College to keep constantly in view that it is the individual student which is the final test of what we do." On a rare occasion he might give a student a sense that he was a friend. Once, with a student who was obviously depressed (and who ended up transferring to Hampshire his senior year), it wasn't enough for Ward to hear him out. Ward surprised the student by saying that he too got depressed at times, and then telling him how he dealt with his depression. But it was a rare occasion. Ward's relations with students characteristically went one way, and that way was enough to make a student think that that man who was so concerned about him was a friend—just as those who got along with him well might have thought they knew him. A member of the last class that knew Ward as a teacher said, "I could find you thirty undergraduates who would claim to be Ward's best friend among the students." They were not inclined to give a thought to the fact that they knew little or nothing about Ward, that they weren't Ward's friends, and, moreover, that Ward wasn't interested in being their friend.

As a teacher he wanted to know about them in order to discover and bring out the best in them. When Plimpton asked him to be a faculty advisor to a fraternity, he declined, saying that the way he came to know students was their mutual interest in books. Or he might summon a student, perhaps not even a student of his, but one he thought was trying to make Amherst a better, a more democratic, college. Sam Lovejoy, for example. Descended from Elijah P. Lovejoy, who in 1837 was murdered by a mob opposed to his abolitionist writings, Sam was head of SDS. Ward wanted to know why Amherst was less stirred up than Berkeley and Columbia, a question that he surely could have answered for himself. But Lovejoy said it was the conversation, the exchange of views that he remembers, and that mattered. What he called the "intellectual bond," is also what Neil Sullivan remembers, the bond being the sounder given the fact that he too grew up in Dorchester. But months would pass before they realized they had that in common. Almost ten years after he graduated, Sullivan returned to live in Dorchester and to work first as a policy advisor to Kevin White, the mayor of Boston, and after that as head of the Boston Private Industry Council, a public-private partnership that connects youths and adults to educational and subsequent employment opportunities.

Though as a faculty member he was not actively engaged in the political life of the campus, on a few formal occasions, speaking to students in a Chapel talk or a senior assembly, or to parents and alumni, he presented himself as Citizen Ward, the Idealistic American, disheartened by what he witnessed all around him. They are worth attending to because they enable us to register his mounting frustration and anger as he contemplated the state of American culture.

Addressing the students in the spring of 1966, his second year at Amherst, for example, he likened himself to Frank Lloyd Wright, who had once begun a talk by saying that the occasion on which he was speaking demanded stirring words, promises of a better world, one that would be made so by the energies of young men like those he was addressing—and then proceeded to say that he had no such words and sat down. Ward remained standing but said, "It is hard to find cheering words about anything right now," and went on to describe what he considered to be the sorry state of democracy in America. He deplored the evidence of the "narcotic of purely private satisfaction," of individualism reduced to mere selfishness, deplored not just that failing that Tocqueville had feared, but deplored too the absence of "free autonomous institutions" that Tocqueville thought acted as "buffers between individual citizens and a powerful state," that state now represented, he maintained, by the recently exposed CIA infiltration of student organizations, unions, and journals of public opinion. And then he turned to his own personal feelings. "What is one to do?" he asked. "I honestly don't know," he said, "and that is what lies at the root of my sense of being tired and not wanting to talk."

He *had* done something in response to the Vietnam War, but his response was complicated. His years of service in the Marines, his loyalty to the Corps, precluded his being simply opposed to the war, or opposed to the presence of military recruiters on campus. But he had taken *some* action, and he spoke about it that morning in the Chapel. He had stood in silence on the Amherst Common, which is to say participated in the Sunday morning vigils, sponsored by the Mt. Toby Friends Meeting in the nearby town of Leverett, that had recently begun and that would quickly include hundreds of citizens. But contemplating what he had done seemed only to have darkened his mood. It was like writing your congressman, he said. You do it "knowing full well, as your hard-headed friends are only too glad to point out, that it is not going to change anything." And what was worse: "You know that yourself, and so suspect yourself of sheer self-indulgence and the private pleasure of feeling virtuous." "If you don't do your own thing...then you become alienated from your own self," he said in his talk about Kennedy. But now, for him, there was no "thing," no course of action that he could confidently claim as his own, and so he felt tired, alienated, depressed.

It had not worked for Wright, but what snapped Ward out of this mood on this occasion was the thought of the students, the active ones, the ones petitioning for a change of foreign policy. "I am not sanguine at all about what they will discover," he confessed, "but they serve us all by disturbing us, by not letting our weariness overwhelm us and force us into silence." They reminded the minority that it was not alone: "To remember that," he said, "may give us strength to overcome the foreboding sense of disaster and stir us once again out of our weariness and give us the courage to hope and so to speak and act."

Early the next year he took further action. Along with 30 colleagues he signed a letter that had been drafted by the Boston Area Faculty Group that was printed in successive issues of the *Times*. "Mr. President, Stop the Bombing" was its headline. It was no more specific than that.

Then the following May the seniors asked him to speak at their last Assembly. Reverting to his role as an English professor, having had copies of one of his favorite poems, Frost's "The Wood-pile," placed on every seat, he began by glossing it. The abandoned pile, there in what he called the "cold, inhospitable, forbidding world of nature," signified to him that "man asserts his essential self in creating moments of order, by asserting himself against an impersonal world which threatens to annihilate him at best or at worst ignore him." From this excessively gloomy reading (mightn't there be a self with which we are contented? and if so, would it be so bad that the world ignores us?) he went on to describe that world in impressively sweeping and withering terms:

> We live in a world of brutal and sickening international violence; we live in a society where we seem to have forgotten that men came here to create a community attentive to the uses and needs of human beings and not simply to seek immediate and gross material satisfaction; we live under a polity where amorality prides itself as realism; we live with each other in an atmosphere where love can be only an individual and private gesture and not a public affirmation.

Turning to the seniors, Ward implicitly wondered if they could do anything to revive the founders' vision of a democratic society. His conclusion seemed to suggest that the answer was *maybe, just maybe*. He said he didn't know if their intelligence and imagination had been sufficiently developed to lead them "to envision the dimension of order" that the wood-pile represented, didn't know if they had experienced "anything at all [at Amherst] which may be called an education," but as they, like the woodcutter, were leaving the place where they had worked, he offered them these words: "But to whatever fresh task each of you now turns, my hope for you is that you will turn to it gladly and with courage." Though it contained the word "courage," it did not sound much like the way he concluded his talk on Kennedy.

To take a final, an extreme example, in the fall of 1968, Ward spoke at a Parents' Day Meeting. The title of his talk, "Can We Go On Like This?: Education and Youth Today," suggests how bad things seemed to him to have gotten; the talk itself suggests how much more deeply he was affected. At one point he cited the "brutal murders of men who...tried not to go on doing business as usual," the Kennedy brothers, Malcolm X and Martin Luther King, two of them assassinated the previous spring, and then turned to—almost turned *on*—his audience. "You and I are strangers," he said. "We do not know each other."

> But, however high or low your personal standards, take a walk through your local shopping area, through the five-and-ten, through the supermarket; take a look at the junk, the sheer pile of meretricious, shoddy junk that the wealthiest society in recorded history spews forth for our consumption every day. Consider a society which is willing to spend five billion dollars every year just to change the style of its automobiles. Consider the gross fatness of our society, and ask yourself if we can go on like this.

And *he* went on: "take a drive through the center of your nearest city and look, really look, at the rot which is eating away at the heart of our urban society, and ask if we can go on like this." And on: "look at the history of the black man in America, at the ugly racism that runs like a cancer through our society, a society which prides itself on equality and opportunity for all men, and ask if we can go on like this." He reminded the parents that their annual income, like his, placed them among the top 9 percent of all families, probably among the top one-half of one percent in the world. Things had gotten worse generally, and worse specifically because of the economic inequities that such figures represented. He scoffed at his own guilt feelings, "the last self-approving rationalization of the well-fed, well-cared-for intellectual, who is not about to give up his private comfort to redress the public horror he sees all about him." And then he went after his audience. We elders, we parents, we're all the same: "we hug our guilt," he said, "with a pleasurable *frisson* of self-indulgence, and go on about our business."

As for the students, maybe like most of us they didn't want to be bothered, didn't want to think; maybe only about ten percent of them wanted to change the world they'd been given. And what if in ten years they turned out to be like students ten years ago, the so-called "silent generation?" he asked. He admitted that what he called "the vociferous ones" could be difficult, "perverse and outrageous, often a torment to live with," but what would happen if they failed to inspire us? And besides, we owed them "one measure of justice." The young were different from us. It was a hard world they found themselves in; they found it hard to live even with themselves. By the fall of 1968 Ward was clear about the War. It was "a cruel and foolish mistake," and yet "we are so hung up in our own cant that we cannot admit that we are wrong, that we are wasting lives because of a foolish pride." We say, "It is not *my* life that is going to be wasted. It *is* for that young man who feels the same way; it is *his* life; the war is for him an existential fact, and that makes all the difference." The students, their children, were being liberally educated, but unlike students before them, they had been denied "the one thing we owe them first and above all else, their legitimate patrimony, a model of life, an image of dignity, in the shape of which they may make their own selves and fashion their own life," and so Ward ended where he began, exhorting the parents "to change the kind of world we offer our sons as their legitimate heritage." There was no longer any question about it. "We simply cannot go on like this," he concluded.

It was a stirring, an unnerving performance. Though he identified himself as only a teacher among many, in the course of his remarks, standing up there in the pulpit in the Chapel, speaking for the College, he sounded, and he must have seemed, quite presidential—not like just a top administrative officer, though, but like a president from some bygone era, a president who was a preacher. Amherst was founded in 1821 to give free instruction to "indigent young men of promising talents and hopeful piety, who shall manifest a desire to obtain a liberal education with a sole view to the Christian ministry." By 1863 more than half of her graduates had become ministers, 63 of them missionaries in such far-away places as the Sandwich Islands and the Malay Archipelago, Borneo and Patagonia, responding to the call of the College motto: *Terras irradient*. Here and now, in 1968, was a man telling his audience what had to be done to save the country's soul.

MEANWHILE, AT the College and across the country, confusion often reigned. (In 1969 almost 450 institutions of higher learning either struck or were forced to shut down.) Some confrontations erupted into violence, even death, but though there were a few "action freaks" at Amherst, order prevailed. Ward would be heard from, but to repeat, the part he played did not have many lines.

In February 1969, at a meeting on decision-making at the College, President Plimpton announced that with due consultation of various groups
and individuals on campus, in the next six weeks he was setting up a Long
Range Planning Committee that would oversee the work of Task Forces,
made up of faculty members, students, and administrators, that would, in
turn, explore the following: Experiential Education; the College's Size and
Coeducation; Student Life and Physical Facilities; the Nature of Trustee-
ship, the Presidency and the Administration; Co-operative and Exchange
Programs; and Special Education Programs. The purpose of all the work
that lay ahead was, Plimpton said in a disarming formulation, to determine "how to 'plan how to plan.'" Ward was on the task force that was to
look into "Co-Operative and Exchange Programs." The College was entering the season of committees and student participation that the *Student*
had predicted, but that was not all that the season brought.

A few months later, as opposition to the war grew stronger, and unrest
threatened to turn into chaos, perhaps even into violence, the Committee
of Six met with the president and the dean, as it did weekly, and drafted
a motion that they would put before the faculty, that all college activities,
curricular and extra-curricular, be cancelled for two days to make time
and clear space for the college community to talk about its problems and
to propose solutions to them. It was called a "moratorium."

What took place on Monday and Tuesday, April 28 and 29, indicates
how nearly unmoored Amherst College was at the time. It also underscores
the virtue, the advantage, of being a small institution. In such tumultuous
times, rational discussion is more likely to take place; as a result, moor-
ings can be made to hold. Over the weekend, at a meeting in the Chapel,
filled to capacity and then some, the atmosphere was tense, but one of the
more vocal members of an Ad Hoc Committee had said beforehand, in
an interview on the College radio, that, "The Ad Hoc Committee is not
an action group in the sense that they've got a plan of action for Tuesday
night if things don't happen....You can't operate on the basis of threats. It's
childish and it's irresponsible....There has to be a commitment to rational
discourse followed by rational action," and that view prevailed.

On Monday morning at 11, at a mass meeting in the gymnasium, the
questions and proposals before the College were announced by Bruce
Morgan, a professor of religion and chair of the College Council, and four

centers were named where these questions and proposals would be discussed by students, faculty, administrators, and the several trustees who had come to the College to participate. Proposals were shaped and at a mass meeting (again in the gymnasium) on Tuesday night they were accepted. They were just proposals, just resolutions that would go before the students and before the faculty the following week. Those that were approved would be forwarded to the trustees.

Three solid steps were taken, or at least steps that were sufficiently grounded to enable the College to move on as an educational community. The first and most dramatic was a letter, drafted by the Dean of the Faculty with Marx's editorial assistance, that Plimpton was to sign and send to Richard Nixon. It was an impressive letter. It warned Nixon that campus unrest would continue "until you and the other political leaders of our country address more effectively, massively, and persistently the major social and foreign problems of our society," and ended on this high note: "If this important element in student unrest is understood, it would be possible for you, Mr. President, to redirect youthful energy toward those idealistic, creative and generous actions which reflect a concern for others." A large majority of the faculty and the students signed it. On Sunday the *New York Times* described and seconded the letter in its lead editorial; on Monday the *Boston Globe* praised Plimpton for responding publicly to the administration's position on campus disorders and printed the letter in full, as did several other newspapers. The editors of the *New Republic* printed a lengthy statement on the cover of their May 17 issue, followed by the letter. The statement, titled "Take a Hand," declared that the scholarly community had to take politics "not as a spectator sport but as a solemn duty," and went on to cite the letter as evidence that that was beginning to happen: "One expects the university to set the true perspective, to serve itself and the larger society by demanding that society see itself as it is and could be. That is what Amherst has done."

The second step was the establishment of a Summer Commission, consisting of six students and six faculty members. Its task was to come up with a new governmental structure for the College that would ensure representation for all and that would be responsive to their needs and desires, and to report on its recommendations by July 1. Ward was one of the faculty members. Though he had not been a vocal presence during the moratorium, who better than Ward to discuss and arrive at a governmental structure that would make Amherst College more democratic?

The third step implicitly acknowledged the fact that when Americans individually, or American educational and other institutions, considered and confronted their problems, for all their good intentions, they almost invariably came to what the letter to Nixon called "the unequal division of our life along racial lines" last. May 14 would be set aside as a "Day of Concern"for discussion of racial problems, May 14 because Ralph Ellison was scheduled to come and lecture that evening. His talk was bound to be anything but divisive.

The most important proposal in the Summer Commission's report was that thirty students be allowed to attend faculty meetings and to debate and vote on all issues except students' academic standing and the degrees they would receive upon graduation. Because of their presence, the newly constituted body was to be renamed: it would henceforth be the College Assembly. It was Ward's idea. Who more obviously than Ward would want power to be distributed more equitably, or, more specifically, would want students, the young, the hope of the future, to be more fairly represented? The proposal emanated from what it is safe to say were the beliefs about the individual and his relation to society, about the common good, and about education that he held most dearly. But though he was respected by most of his colleagues, few of them agreed with him that academic institutions should be democratic institutions. The faculty had to approve the idea of the Assembly, and it was not about to.

In the fall the College seemed to be going back to business as usual. But that was to spell trouble. It was precisely what the Afro-Am Society had protested against: Amherst College's satisfaction with business as usual. The most pressing questions asked by its members were about admissions and, again, the hardest to answer, about Black Studies programs—how to set one up, how to staff it, how to define it in the first place, questions that were being asked at colleges and universities around the country. The faculty had voted in a Black Studies Department, but the results were not at all what black students felt they needed.

On the night of February 18, they and about 250 black students from the area took action. A handful hid themselves in each of four buildings, Frost Library, Merrill Science Center, and administrative buildings Converse and College Halls, waited until they were vacated, then let in those assigned to each building, who proceeded to chain and lock the doors. The headline of a special edition of the *Student* in the morning—BLACKS SEIZE BUILDINGS—was the biggest anyone had ever seen. There was talk of a supportive strike by white students, but the buildings were evacuated that afternoon. The faculty met in Kirby Theater (Converse, where it usually met, was still occupied when the meeting was called), and adopted a three-part resolution: "because the ideals of an academic institution are built upon reason and persuasion," the faculty condemned the takeover; it recognized its responsibility "to address seriously the issues presented to it by the Black Community of the Five College area; and it welcomed the evacuation and looked forward to "substantive negotiations." In an editorial that was published in the *Student,* Horace Porter, an officer of the Society, responded by saying, "Reason and persuasion" are "mere cloaks for a basic unwillingness on the part of the faculty and the administration to act, in any significant manner, upon proposals that the black community sets forth." "Amherst was failing," Porter later wrote in *The Making of a Black Scholar*. "It was not teaching its students, who would someday wield significant power, to understand the true promises of democracy."

A few days later black students took out 300 of what they considered *their* books, books by black authors, from Frost Library and took them over to the Black Culture Center—and returned them soon after, thanks to Janice Denton, a black librarian whose husband Jim, a math professor, was the only black member of the faculty. (He had come from Stanford, in fact had met Ward there and, like Ward, had come to Amherst in 1964.) She knew that not enough attention had been paid to the purchase of books by black authors in the past. The chairman of Black Studies had not tapped the funds allotted for just that purpose; she would make sure that the library increased its holdings from then on. Questions about disciplinary action were held—and left—in abeyance.

The role Ward played in response to the takeovers by black students and the demands that they made was, like his role on the Summer Commission, what we would expect. He was engaged, the more engaged because these students that he wanted to be fairly represented were black, were like every person in America with darker than average skin, the victims of "ugly racism." The trustees were impressed by his involvement in their seizure of several buildings. It was the case generally, and would continue to be the case, that black students trusted him. As a member of the Committee of Six, along with Jim Denton, he was in a position to act, to mediate judiciously. Tactfully and respectfully he put himself forward, holding Denton back in the process lest Denton compromise himself in the eyes of the black students by being seen as the representative of the College whose ways they sought to change.

And then, before the academic year was over, there was another moratorium, this time in response to a call by the Vietnam Moratorium Committee and the National Students' Association for a national strike. On the night of May 3 forty students met with students from the other four colleges to coordinate their efforts. In a meeting on the 4th, the Amherst faculty expressed *its* outrage at the expansion of the war and agreed, along with 450 other educational institutions around the country, to cancel classes. It was on that day that four Kent State University students were killed and nine wounded when members of the Ohio National Guard opened fire on a large crowd of protesters. There followed days of discussions and lectures, seminars and workshops, at all five colleges; every attempt was made to learn what was happening at as many other institutions as possible; students fanned out to persuade residents of outlying towns to sign petitions, sometimes attending sessions beforehand that were intended to prepare them for receptions that might well not be as warm as they expected. Commager gave a resounding speech in the Chapel, urging the students to engage in political activity generally. At the same meeting, Marx was more specific, saying that in striking the students were already engaging in political activity. "There was a fundamental and underlying incompatibility," Marx said, "between a society devoted to war and racism and imperialism and the principles of higher education for which we all stand"; the elite in various corridors of power are connected to institutions like Amherst, and "they don't see how their way of life in this country can continue if the universities fail." Professor George Kateb, probably the most rational and respected voice on campus, said at a mass outdoor rally on the 5th that the strike had to be, that there was now no other course. There was "a very simple and academic reason": Nixon had "gone beyond the Constitution." He had waged war on another country (Cambodia) without Congressional authority. Kateb had often talked about the academy as "a haven for intellectual development," but now, he said, he had overcome his scruples about seeing Amherst enter the public arena.

And so, once again, Amherst stopped doing "business as usual" in order to be able to go on with its business. After it was all over, in his "Charge" to the seniors at commencement, Plimpton reflected back on the fact that the College had come near closing on three occasions. "Our disapproval of events in Cambodia and racism have led us to strike at the nearest and flimsiest of all institutions: a college," he said. He was rueful. He would have preferred it had faculty and students proceeded in more orderly fashion, with more faith in educational institutions and society as a whole." And he himself would have been happier just doing his job, behind the scenes if possible. And what was that job? In a *Student* interview he once said that he was "very suspicious of any man who likes what is known as administration. I don't like it myself, it's something I do. And what do I think I am doing? I think I am trying to move the ball from one place to another." He thought a leader was best described as a servant. In his "Charge" he drew on his experience as a doctor: "Perhaps it was a medical background," he said, "but in leading a man to health, or accompanying him on that last one-way journey, the good physician is in many ways a servant." He would have preferred an easier patient than the Amherst of the '60s, but there was a lot to be said for the way he served it.

Plimpton was an alumnus, his half-brother was a prominent and influential trustee, their father had been president of the Board. He did everything he could to lead the College into the future, no matter how unpredictable it seemed at the time, with respect for its tradition and prestige in mind. His very manner, the way he comported himself—his patrician accent, the quizzical smile with which he greeted what was unfamiliar to him—gave one the sense that he belonged, belonged at Amherst and in the social world from which generations of students had come, and that neither he nor the institution could be thrown off course. As a result, and most important, in the summary words of his faculty Dean, he "had one great strength—he never took the furor of opposition, lock-outs, sit-ins, etc. personally."

Commencement that year was uneventful. Plimpton's ten years, the number of years he had told the trustees that he would serve, were up. He was ready to move on. But he agreed to stay one more year while the trustees chose his successor. Opposition to the war in Vietnam would only mount, racial relations worsen, and, at least at Amherst, coeducation would become more and more of an issue. Students nationwide would become less and less like patients; they would insist on having a voice in the diagnosis of what ailed the country and in deciding what remedies should be prescribed. Plimpton's successor would have to be a very different kind of man.

In the fall of 1970 a Search Committee was formed. It was made up of representatives from the Board of Trustees, the alumni, and four students and four faculty members, elected by their peers. Francis Plimpton was its chairman, as he had been when his half-brother was elected. Ward was one of the faculty members.

THREE

The President of Amherst College

"The role of president is in part a secular substitute for the ministerial calling of the evangelical preacher of earlier days."

(Ward, "Education for What? The Liberal Arts
and the Modern World," September 14, 1975)

E ARLY IN THE fall of 1970, the *Student* reported that the Search Committee had begun the "long hunt" for a president; in mid-December it noted that the committee was approaching the January deadline it had set for itself. It almost met it. On Monday morning, February 8, at a special meeting of the faculty, Oliver Merrill, the chairman of the Board of Trustees, announced that John William Ward had been selected to be the fourteenth president of Amherst College. Such searches were simpler and went more quickly in those days than they do now, but the process by which Ward became president was unusually complicated.

The number of names of possible candidates that the committee gathered ran into the hundreds; they quickly cut it in half. After inquiries were made, the list was narrowed down to about 20, all of whom were visited by a team made up of a faculty member, a student, and an alumnus or a trustee. The committee as a whole then decided whom they wanted to interview. In December the number of promising candidates was down to three: Julian Gibbs, an alumnus, who was a chemistry professor at Brown; Dean of the Faculty, Prosser Gifford; and Richard Wasserstrom, also an alumnus and a professor (of Law and Philosophy at UCLA). Gibbs "struck everyone as very collegial and engaging," one of the student representatives said; Gifford began as the most likely candidate, but "he struck out," according to Seth Dubin, one of the alumni on the committee, when he spoke about a bifurcated presidency in which he would be the "inside" president, while someone else represented the college to the world beyond the campus, a suggestion that the committee considered symptomatic of the fact that he was not all that keen on being a college president. It turned out to be true. At his final meeting with the Committee he announced that all his life he had been in competitions, always to win, but that after having talked about what the presidency would involve almost all the previous night with his wife he had decided that this was one competition he didn't want to win—and withdrew his name. Wasserstrom then surged forward," according to Dubin. Wasserstrom was Ward's choice. "If I thought I could be that objective about myself," Ward said in the spring of the first year of his presidency, "I would say honestly that I think he would make a better educational leader for a good liberal arts college than I do myself. He is a most impressive man." Wasserstrom was also the choice of another faculty member on the committee, his former philosophy professor (the other two favored Gifford), and the choice of all four students. It is easy to see why the students favored Wasserstrom. In the words of one of them, "He was very much in step with the times, and the fact that he was not waspy and preppy and an Eastern Establishment figure made him all the more appealing....Wasserstrom clearly stood out as someone whose views and youthfulness and intellectual brilliance seemed perfect for Amherst in 1971." The committee was enthusiastic about him too, but they foresaw how the Board would respond. The Board was not entirely "waspy" and "preppy," but established in the East it certainly was. Of the 18 members of the board (all but one an Amherst graduate, many of whom were the sons and fathers and brothers of Amherst graduates), 11 lived in New York City and were members of either the Century Club or the University Club or both. It was not a group that was ready for a man so radical as Wasserstrom. He was supportive of Angela Davis when the Regents of the University of California tried to prevent her from teaching because she was a member of the Communist Party; he had defended the Black Panthers—pro bono—in a number of criminal trials.

At a meeting in mid-December, as it was becoming increasingly obvious that none of the three was going to prevail, Dubin turned back to Ward and asked if he would withdraw from the committee and become a candidate ("turned back" because he had been asked at the outset and refused)—which he did. He had impressed the committee all along. His questions and comments were to the point, he listened, his jokes and quips were funny, but in announcing his willingness to be considered, the impression that he had made was lost on the students. When it became clear how much he wanted the job they thought he had "succumbed to a kind of careerism." During the preceding years, the lines had become that sharply drawn. The students "looked upon the president as 'upper management,'" one of them said, "and the faculty as more egalitarian and accessible....[S]tudents and faculty were thrust together during the many campus protests of that era and thus perhaps felt more in tune with one another's sympathies than they might have been with the trustees and the president. Hence in announcing his candidacy Ward seemed to cross over to the other side."

Ward's name was passed on to the Board along with those of the other three. They were all interviewed by the Board in plenary session, and on grounds that at least one member described as transcending the interests of any one constituency, it chose Ward. Walter Gellhorn, a professor of law at Columbia said at Ward's memorial service that "Bill unbendingly exhibited the qualities of intellectual integrity that marked his whole career.... In the end, all the trustees then in attendance knew that Bill Ward was a principled person, moved rather than immobilized by thinking about complexities."

The Board's decision was also based on its knowledge of Ward's position on campus, the very position we have seen that he did indeed occupy, the one that the students described—and thought he had abandoned. However well Plimpton had handled the campus protests, the Board had had enough of them. Ward was obviously more "egalitarian and accessible" than Plimpton; he had maintained a steady course, had acted judiciously, during the crises of the '60s. It seemed that under him the College would be in good hands; it could finally go back to "business as usual" and stay there. Francis Plimpton adduced Ward's commitment to racial justice and went on to say that anything that was seen as a diminishment of a commitment to black students would be dangerous. (He could well have had his own political commitment and principled activity in mind: in May the year before, as president of the New York City Bar Association, he led a group of young lawyers down to Washington to lobby against the war.) The views of David Truman, another member of the Board, had to have been exceptionally influential too. He was Dean at Columbia when it was experiencing far greater upheavals than Amherst had, and he had recently settled in as president of Mount Holyoke, another of the five colleges. What was perceived to be Ward's ability to maintain order must have mattered a lot to him too. Moreover, it was obvious to everyone that the talk about coeducation that was heating up wouldn't proceed very far without including discussion of Five College cooperation.

Ward had resisted similar overtures before, "four or five times before," he said in a letter to Commager. He might have appeared to be presidential to audiences he addressed; he *was* presidential material in the eyes of other academic institutions, liberal arts colleges in particular—Colgate (we assume, from the question he was asked when he came on to interview), then Reed in 1967, Bowdoin in 1968, and presumably others. He told Commager about these offers and gave his reasons for refusing them:

> I am not sure anyone knows himself well, but so far as I do I do not think I would enjoy being a college president or do very well at it. I tend to get too impatient with other people ever to be an administrator. But, more importantly, I simply enjoy my life the way it now is. Out of sheer selfishness, if from no more exalted a motive, who would give up the delights and the self-determination of the professor?

In February 1970, when Plimpton asked him to serve as his Dean of the Faculty while Gifford was on leave, he refused, saying he belonged in the classroom and, what was more, he didn't think of himself as an administrator. He said he grew impatient at meetings, they got in the way of what he really wanted to do, which was to teach and, as he often put it, to maintain his sense of himself as an intellectual. He wasn't interested in administration, but then he added, "Not now anyway."

Less than a year after explaining to Plimpton why he didn't want to be the acting Dean, the reason he gave Plimpton's half-brother for not wanting to be considered a candidate for the presidency was just the one about continuing to be an intellectual, but this time *this* Plimpton didn't have much trouble loosening his grip. In what Ward called "a very funny note," Plimpton simply observed, "I am amused that you find a contradiction between being an intellectual and being a college president," which was enough to clear Ward's way to the top.

But in fact, as president he obviously had less and less time for the intellectual work he wanted to do. (And it should be noted that he was a prodigiously hard worker, beginning his day at seven, sometimes as early as four if he felt he was falling behind.) In 1970 Ward had published a long and excellent review of Alexander Berkman's *Prison Memoirs of an Anarchist* in the *New York Review of Books*. Perhaps he could be not just an intellectual but a *public* intellectual, yet in February of 1972 he had to admit that he couldn't possibly fulfill his next assignment: "The pace of my life has quickened and thickened incredibly," he told the editor, Bob Silvers. A year later he simply forgot that he had agreed to review a book on Tocqueville. He did manage to contribute a paper at a conference at the Hastings Center on "The Future of Individualism" that same year, but it became harder and harder for him to pretend to himself that he was alive intellectually.

The dynamic went the other way as well: what he took to be his failings as an intellectual drove him into administration. In a paper on "Jacksonian America: A Generation of Interpreters" that he gave at the meeting of the Southern Historical Association in 1978, he said specifically: "I sometimes think, in all seriousness, I decided to become a President and an administrator because I knew I was not smart enough to answer the problem. The problem is this: what are the relations between the expressed ideals of a culture and the social and economic forces at work on it." Nor was he ever able to bring his many writings on individualism together in another book.

Just after he was named president, he talked again about the challenge of teaching at Amherst, going to an extreme this time that could be explained, if not justified, by his frustration as a writer: "One thing that has been driven home to me by students here," he said, "is that the bright guy who comes to be a scholar doesn't know what it means to be a teacher." But now he questioned his standing as a teacher too. He thought that there was a limit to how long one could sustain oneself in the classroom. He often told students to choose courses on the basis of the professor who taught them; once, more precisely, he advised catching professors at their best—the third time they taught a course, say. After that their excitement, and thus their effectiveness, would be on the wane. Since his time at Princeton, Ward had given his Toqueville (i.e, his Jackson) course many more than three times. More generally, as he was leaving Amherst, he was asked why he took the job of president. He said that he had been teaching for twenty years and that his wife had said he was showing signs of getting bored; when he started out as president, he cited her again: "My favorite reason when I don't want to go on at length is Barbara's comment: she writes it off to incipient male menopause." Once he agreed to be a candidate, there was no doubt about how he felt about the job. As he said in a radio interview a few days after the announcement, "I really hoped they would name me. I really wanted it."

There are many reasons why, not just negative reasons, not just as compensation for the gradual erosion of his sense of himself as a teacher and a writer that he had built up since he was first inspired to be an academic, but strong, if not indisputably positive, reasons. For one thing, having heard so much as a member of the search committee, having heard much more than he would have in an isolated interview, he came to the conclusion that he could do a good job himself, maybe not as good a job as Wasserstrom would do but a good job nevertheless. And then there was, simply, obviously, and in Ward's case very strongly, the sense of his own importance that would come with the job. Just after he was elected, he made the point himself: "Nobody in this society cares what John William Ward says, but they will probably attend with great care to what the President of Amherst College says." Thereafter, he would often say, "I can just pick up the phone...." Moreover, after he was gone, people would still care. In the middle of his presidency he warned a former student who was beginning an academic career that one "peril" of the profession was "the fear you are all too soon and all too easily forgotten." Another man might not think being a forgotten college professor was such a terrible thing. Ward did, and so it followed: he liked the thought that he would be remembered as having been a college president. In a word, he suffered from what Milton called "the last infirmity of noble mind." He wanted fame.

Everyone knew this side of Ward. In a letter to a young man who had worked in the Development Office when he was president, he told of his return to Amherst on the occasion of his successor's inauguration in 1979. He and Barbara stayed with George May, the college's comptroller, and his wife, Annie. When they turned in at the end of the evening Barbara asked her husband if it was hard for him to "walk through all that." He said no, but he had to confess that he had "a curious feeling": "It may not be a good comment on my character," he told her, "but I like to be important." Ward wrote that she nearly fell out of her single bed laughing; then, having got hold of herself, she said, "My God, you're fifty-six years old, and only now can you give voice to what anyone who has ever known you has always known." In the morning, when their hosts asked what all the ruckus had been about, Annie too doubled up with laughter. Ward's conclusion was one he came to again and again: "As I always said, we know ourselves slenderly."

In becoming president, Ward was arriving at the climax of the story that he had told and written about and presumably internalized for years and years as a professor of American Studies. He had exaggerated the part about rags (and Barbara would point this out to him), but there was no denying the riches he was about to enjoy. And he had done it all—had made it—on his own, made it with none of the privileges or advantages that men like Plimpton or Gifford had started with. What's more, he had overcome an obstacle that even his forbears, Ben Franklin, Horatio Alger and their kind, hadn't had to face: he was Irish. As a writer and a teacher he hadn't felt especially resentful. He hadn't brought it up in a long while, but it surfaced when he entered the new world of administration. "If my last name had been that of my mother, Carrigan, or my father's mother, Casey," he said just after he stepped down in 1979, "I don't believe I would have been named president of Amherst." If we are inclined to doubt it, or to attribute his remark to bitterness, we should recall that Ward became president in 1971. The question of a candidate's religion was in the air. Not even Jack Kennedy had dispelled it. Before naming a former Catholic as president, the Board wanted to know about Barbara, so they sent one of their number to ask Marx: was *she* Catholic too?

But poor or not, Irish or not, he didn't quite know what to make of the fact that he was the president of Amherst College. One man recalls being at a dinner party at which Ward "whooped with delight," having just heard that he had been selected. Horace Porter recalls his strolling into his junior seminar the week of his election, sitting back and (as he had many years before at the pool in Princeton) lighting "the longest cigar I had ever seen," and announcing, "Before anyone says anything, I'm it!" Yet at the time of the announcement, when he repeated the words, "I'm it" to Ellen Ryerson, he did so, she said, "with a bit of a haunted look." (Just that little pronoun—"it"—this time seemingly so depersonalized, so exposed and fragile.) He was not like Plimpton, who was and would forever confidently be Plimpton, and who, as president, would also be Plimpton the administrator, making sure the ball continued to roll. He was like Ben Franklin, the first of "the self-made men, the jack-of-all-trades," who, we may recall, Ward considered "an exemplary American because his life's story is a witness to the uncertainties about social status that have characterized our society, a society caught up in the constant process of change," the man, Ward said, who "raises the question that lies at the heart of the trouble: 'Who am I?'" He himself had no easy answer. What Hannah Arendt once called "The calm good conscience of some limited achievement" (conscience, she explained, being "con-science...to know with and by [one's] self") was not enough.

Uncertainty about his background, his relations with his family and their religion, and about his place on the social scale made matters worse. More than one person referred to him as "rootless." When he became president he could define himself as the hero of the story of the self-made man, of the American success story, but still, who was he, what he called "the authentic self," now that he was president? More specifically, he could never be sure about the relationship between John William Ward and the president of Amherst College. On the eve of his departure, in an interview, he spoke of "the most serious difficulty he faced, "a constant source of human discomfort" that he experienced. It was when

> you are in office there's a danger people will not treat you as a human being; they see you as simply as an office. But that's inevitable. There's also the danger which is personal—that of losing touch with, not trusting, your own feelings and judgment. You're caught in the center of that tension between role and self always.

Ward makes the first part more of a problem than need be. It is a fact. As Ward said, it's inevitable. People may not see you "simply" as an office, but in their dealings with you they are bound to respond to you, in some measure, as the man who occupies the office of the president. Though he might have solved the second part of the problem, he never did. What about the president? How does he define himself? How does he present himself? How does he come across? Writing in the 17th century on "Great Place," Francis Bacon gave this piece of advice: "Be not too sensible [i.e., sensitive] or too remembering of thy place in conversation and private answers to suitors; but let it rather be said, *When he sits in place, he is another man* [his emphasis]." For Plimpton it wasn't a problem. The self, the person, was not absent of course, but it was in the wings, and the surer of itself for being there, letting "another man" be front and center. Not Ward. To him, that "other man" was extremely important, he was a source of great pride. "Every time I drive in from the East, on Route 9 from Belchertown, and start down that long hill, and look across the Valley to the College high on the hill," he confessed to a *Student* interviewer, "it never fails to astonish me to realize I am the president of Amherst College."

He—Bill Ward—wanted recognition. It was the case from the very beginning. But he couldn't leave it at that. He was *too* sensible of his place. One of the stories he delighted in telling was one with which he began his first Convocation speech. It was about the 5-year-old son of a neighbor who, when told by his mother that Bill Ward was now president of the College, said, "Not really!" Well yes, he really was, but as he said, he was caught in the tension between his role and his self. He thought Lindbergh's "tragedy" stemmed from his inability to accept his role, and from his belief that he could keep his person and his role separate. We might say Ward's problem was that he *couldn't* keep them separate, he couldn't just accept and divorce himself from his role as president. To Jill Conway, whose presidency of Smith overlapped with Ward's at Amherst, and another fellow president in the Valley, "Chuck" Longsworth, the president of Hampshire College, it was *the* problem. When he was in a conflict, Conway said, "he couldn't hold on to his private being," couldn't keep it in check. By the same token, he was "never at ease with public commitments." In Longsworth's words, "Bill was unable to shed his persona as an English professor and adopt the role of president. We knew perfectly well who he was in a role he could never accept." Of course a president's person, the beliefs he has, his thoughts and feelings, must determine how he comports himself in office and the decisions he makes, must do so whether they are in evidence or not. On the other hand, though it might be winning, the merely personal might also be distracting, even unattractive; it certainly makes him vulnerable.

Most importantly, right from the start, he wasn't sure about who he was in relation to the faculty now that he was president; as a result, by the end, the faculty proved to be by far the most difficult constituency he had to deal with. True, as a faculty member he had been elected to the Committee of Six and to the Search Committee, but committees were one thing, those who elected him were only a majority of the faculty, and among them maybe not a majority of the elders. His being their president was another. "Why not me?" Ward's trusted colleague Ted Greene imagined some saying when Ward was elected. It was rumored that at least one of them thought that he should have gotten the job. More generally, there was the simple fact that, as Conway pointed out, "Bill had been there. The faculty would not give him enough space." Whether the things they knew about him were good or bad, everyone knew too much about him. He couldn't understand why his former colleagues treated him differently. "I don't know why I have something of a strained relationship with Leo and Ben [DeMott]. They were my best friends. It makes me sad," he once confessed to John Esty, an especially sympathetic member of the Board. (And it must be said, as we will clearly see, the idea of his thinking Ben DeMott was one of his "best friends" does support his claim that he knew himself only "slenderly.") To make matters worse, so ingrained was his belief in the potential good in every man and in the persuasiveness of his own good intentions and ideals that he appreciated neither the limits of his power to win over those on the faculty who for whatever reason were opposed to him, nor the fact that some of them just didn't like him. Again, Barbara tried to set him straight: "You don't even know when you're being insulted," she once told him.

He was caught. He wanted everyone to work together for the good of the institution, he wanted to work with them as an equal, to inspire everyone the way he inspired students and, as we will see, junior faculty by his personal example—not because he was president, a man more equal than everyone else. But he was. Esty's response to Ward's confession was, "You're a different breed of cat now." Another president would have let that be the last word. But Ward was not just another president.

INAUGURATION DAY, October 23, 1971, was a glorious fall day. Spirits were high, the costs were relatively low (a fact that was gratefully noted by several trustees), the introductory speeches mercifully short. Merrill, the chairman of the Board, said that in turning to "an eminent historian...

Ward the day he was inaugurated as president of Amherst College

for leadership," the College was turning to one "who knows that as we better understand and judge our past, so may we hope the better to form and design our future." In his remarks, Ward's former mentor, Henry Nash Smith, spoke of the needs for strengthening the humanities and for balancing fidelity to tradition with openness to innovation. And then a brass ensemble played—more like blasted out—Aaron Copeland's "Fanfare for the Common Man," chosen by Ward as the perfect musical expression of the democratic ideals that he would try to realize as the new president of the College. After a brief silence, there were stirrings and murmurings. Then Ward came forward, and before turning to his prepared speech, applying his own common touch, remarked, "I always wondered what a fanfare was." It was a little disingenuous, but it got laughs. In the speech that followed he set forth his goals and his hopes in impressively lofty terms. Just before he left Amherst eight years later, he said in an interview that when he took it, he "didn't have the faintest idea of what the job was like," but as is clear from his speech, he did know from the outset what he wanted to accomplish while he was on it. The title of his speech was "The Spirit of This Place: The Necessity of Freedom." We ourselves can think of its being titled "Democracy at Amherst."

He began by citing the many things a college could be said to be—a place, diverse people, a tradition, a set of functions—but for him it was, "Most of all, though, a college, a good college, is a spirit, an ethos, a body of ideals and values." And then he quickly added that it was not for him, not for any man, "even if he has the great good fortune to be the President, to define the meaning and essential values of the College." To do so would be to deny others' "capacity for rational and emotional self-determination," to deny them their freedom and their individuality, by which he meant their ability to "transcend irrationality and base self-interst." Recognizing the frailty of human beings, you could not give any one of them unchecked power over others; "those in positions of power [had to] be responsible to those whose decisions they affect." So it had been during Jackson's presidency; so it would be in his. Ward made the connection between the political and the educational explicit: "To use the language of one of our own cherished documents, power must be with the consent of the people." He pointed out that as he spoke, calls for "democratic freedom" were being heard throughout the land, from those who sought public representation on the boards of "our great corporations," from "oppressed people, most especially blacks locked in the ghettos of our cities," from women, and from students who wanted to have their views on "what constitutes an education" heard. These were all "the attempt of people to gain some effective voice in the determination of what happens to their lives."

Turning to the students, he said he did not think that their perceptions of what the faculty had established in the curriculum as their education had been sufficiently attended to. But he went on to describe their situation not in terms of institutional structure but more grandly, in terms of "the existential conditions of personal freedom....freedom from the restrictions which surround a child into the freedom of becoming your own self." What was required of them was that like citizens in a democracy they become "self-governing." Educationally, they were responsible for their own work. Socially, they had to extend the freedom they enjoyed to all others. "To be free and to be subject of no one else's will means you may not turn others into objects, to use others to your own ends." Free they had to be "because there is no other way to test that the student realizes what it means to be an aware and rational and decent and humane person." Drawing towards the end of his speech he admitted that "the state of freedom he described assumes an outrageous hope," but it was also "the hope of what constitutes the nature of a free and democratic society." "If we cannot make that hope work here," he asked, "what hope is there?" And he concluded, idealist that he was, "If we can make it work here, it might catch on."

In the years that followed, at commencements at Amherst and other institutions, at convocations, in speeches to parents and talks to undergraduates, he focused his attention on the idea, the hope, that students could learn to be humane people and, even at their age, democratic citizens, and on what he believed to be the means of realizing those high hopes. "The means determine the ends," he wrote in his annual report to the Board in 1973. "In education especially, where professors and students are teachers and learners together, the means are themselves the ends." If the educational process went forward the way that Ward imagined it should, the institution in which it took place would thereby be a democratic community; for its part, the College should "ceaselessly strive" to "turn out for the work of the world graduates who have the emotional will as well as the trained intellectual capacity to create a social order closer to the very ideals which define education at its best." The ideals and values were at one and the same time those of a democracy, informing the ideals that Amherst College sought to live up to, and of Amherst College, whose graduates, having realized those ideals, were therefore prepared to go forth and be leaders in the continuing effort to democratize America. He was a man of his time and he wanted Amherst to be a model for those times.

From the outset, Ward's efforts to democratize were efforts to equalize as much as possible, to do so not only in the life of the mind at Amherst, in having teachers and students "thinking independently together," but in the administration of the College, in personal relations, and where it is most difficult, in the dismal realm of economics. Immediately upon being elected president he resigned his professorship in History and American Studies, something professors appointed to high administrative offices seldom, if ever, do. He wanted his exchanges with the Board to be open and frank, he explained to Merrill. He didn't want to have a fall-back position. He wanted the same kind of exchanges with the faculty, by which he meant all the members of the faculty, not just those colleagues with whom he had worked most closely and thus whose advice he might be most inclined to heed. He thought he might even prove he was not unduly influenced by those who were, or were assumed to be, his friends by going out of his way to oppose them. And of course he wanted the openness of discussion with students that he had enjoyed as a teacher to continue, even though he was now the president. He wanted that above all: "The one thing that concerns me most," he said as he set out, "is maintaining the close contact that I've been able to have with students as a professor. I would hope that I could keep to an absolute minimum the distance imposed by the Presidency between myself and students."

In the same democratic spirit he sought to narrow the distance between the salaries of faculty members. Generally, he decried the fact that Americans lacked "the political will to achieve the equality it celebrates in its ideals," could not, for example, "with the greatest wealth in all of human history...realize a minimal standard of decency for all its citizens as a matter of political right." He thought that at least educators ought to respond to a higher calling than one that bade a man go forth and accumulate wealth. He protested too much about his humble origins, but he was not rich and never lived among those who were. As a graduate student he felt that if he and Barbara ever had as much as $10,000 a year they would consider themselves lucky. He was right about himself when he said that he was "innocent of money." But his concern about the salaries of the junior faculty was based on more than his egalitarian beliefs. He understood and was sympathetic with those who were untenured, especially when, as was the case when he became president, the academic market declined and most institutions of higher learning took advantage of the decline by keeping salaries and benefits relatively low and hiring those who were coming out of graduate school only as adjuncts and part-time teachers.

He increased the salaries of the junior faculty by larger percentages than he did those of their tenured seniors. And so there is not a present senior colleague who was untenured when Ward was president who does not speak of him in glowing terms. With them, his gregariousness, his seeming openness, his geniality, coming as they did from a man who might be expected to appear what he in fact was—a superior—were irresistible. In turn, what Ward admired most in these professors was a certain temperament, a presence that he imagined was effective in the classroom. (Recall his disparaging remarks about the "99 and 44/100 percent of the faculty" he knew who, if they ever had "a truly original idea" would "hardly know where in the desk to hide it away.") In his job interview with Ward, a Spanish professor was asked whether or not he wanted to write "academic books." When he said no, Ward approved. Not long after, Ward agonized over breaking the tie of the Committee of Six and thereby denying tenure to an obviously popular teacher on the grounds that he had done little or no scholarship. He couldn't understand why one mathematics professor received tenure rather than another, the better mathematician rather than the one Ward thought was more personable.

He imagined—imagined, if not trumpeted—another step towards the democratization of education, one that also involved money but that was more radical than just narrowing the gaps between salaries. Not only did he think college and university teachers' salaries should be more nearly equal, he thought teachers at the lower levels of education should be paid more than all of those teachers, no matter how highly they were paid. He stated this belief in the spring of 1974 in a letter to a graduate of the college who had asked him if he might "jot down in an informal way some of [his] thoughts on the future of secondary education." Ward did indeed have some. He replied that because secondary teachers did not have "the respect of society (and therefore little self-respect)," and because they didn't have time to remain intellectually alive because of the number of students and the extra-curricular activities they had to be involved in, their teaching loads should be cut in half and their salaries doubled. We oughtn't to put "our social capital" into "graduate Ph.D.s like me," he said. We ought to use it to get people who could train and develop young minds so that we could be "self-initiated" by the time they came to places like Amherst and could use faculty members as resources. (He was not just trying to make a former student feel good about entering the world of secondary education; it was not the only time he made the argument.) It made good sense if you thought the purpose of education was to sharpen the minds of future citizens, but of course most Americans set their sights much lower when they think of the rewards of education.

In his efforts to democratize the spirit of the College, the further down the pecking order he reached, the more the people he met there liked him. At the bottom of the pecking order were the students, thirty of whom, as we saw, would have sworn that they were Ward's best friend among their peers. And among those peers, applying a slightly different formula, those who were the farthest from the norm were the most appreciative of the way he treated them. There was the 27-year-old freshman, for example, who had graduated next-to-last in his high school class and who had wisely decided that he wasn't going to try to get an education until he really wanted one. The president's welcoming reception was "a deer in the headlights moment" for him; after he introduced himself to Ward, Ward said to him, "Oh yes, I've heard about you. You're the old guy. Welcome. You're where you belong. Enjoy yourself." It was, the young man said, "an incredibly valuable thing for me to hear....Almost instantly I felt at home." Or the student who came from Malaysia, who was walking on the campus, deserted at the time, when Ward stopped his car and offered him a ride, telling him to sit up front. Ward would have loved this man's recollection: "Coming from a hierarchical society where a College president will certainly not talk to a humble student, let alone give him a ride, I was very favorably impressed by William Ward and the egalitarianism of America."

It wasn't just Ward's manner with individuals, though. He wanted the student body to be as one not only in its quest for learning with each other and their teachers, but as a community. In the beginning he said many times that he was sorry that morning chapel had been abolished. There were so few occasions when the community came together, so little opportunity for him to speak to the entire student body. The evening assembly meetings that had replaced attendance at chapel were not enough, it wasn't a good time, the meetings were voluntary. He often gave talks at them though, even as the numbers of those in attendance dwindled.

He expected that all faculty members would attend their meetings. (It was tacitly understood to be a requirement.) Whenever attendance seemed about to dip below the level required for a quorum Ward was obviously upset. The one evening when it did in fact, Ward knew why. He knew that many, too many, faculty members were at a reception for a visiting dignitary, and he knew where. So he excused himself from the meeting, went into his office, and called over. Those who had shown up at the meeting sat and waited with Ward until their delinquent colleagues filed in.

He had many names for what he would be as president. He thought the times called for more than just "administrator"; it wasn't even on his list. The nearest to hand were "teacher" or "seminar leader," the obvious ones in his case, though not the first that come to mind when one thinks of a college or university president. "I continue to believe that the President should be an educator and, like a good seminar leader, should lead by naming the questions which require an answer," he wrote in his 1973 report to the Board of Trustees. But those were not the only labels. Ward wanted being the president to be and to mean more. He said in one of his Thursday evening talks, and then again at the inauguration of the president of Whitman College, that he found that "the role of president is in part a secular substitute in the modern world for the ministerial calling of the evangelical preacher of earlier days." Another word that he used for this role was "stewardship"; he believed in "the doctrine of calling." In 1973, in his Charge to the Seniors at Commencement, he could have been talking about himself—indeed, predicting his own future—when we said, "One must do the best with and develop to the utmost one's gifts, one's capabilities...but always remember that the ultimate test of one's individual worth is the degree to which one advances the common good, the commonwealth, as we still say here in Massachusetts."

By now we know full well that the doctrine he preached was the doctrine of democratic citizenship, and that he wanted Amherst not only to do "a superior job in training critical intelligence," but more explicitly, "to train the mind to further a decent and humane life." But we might well be surprised at the lengths he went to in inveighing against examples of what he thought was *in*decent and *in*humane life. Early in the fall of 1975 he began a Thursday evening talk by announcing that there would be three such evenings a term. There was a wide variety of things to talk about; there was a need for "communication," but not just "communication." He had a "felt sense or the need for what the old language called 'communion,' that is a sharing and a partaking together." He mentioned buildings and the renovations that were in progress, then the responsibility that everyone should feel about the College, and from there to what were to him unnerving examples of its absence in student behavior—broken cues and racks, and water fights. And in faculty behavior as well: he'd seen one member crush a cigarette out on a rug. Not worth mentioning, we might say, but the evangelist in him saw these as instances of "a pervasive problem in American cultural values." In a talk in 1977 it was smashed chandeliers and defaced walls, and the problem was not something so vague as "cultural values." The man who grew up in Dorchester and Brighton was speaking when he said, according to the *Student*'s account of the meeting, that the problem was "'a spoiled, privileged, well-off group of people' who have the attitude that because I pay dues here I can do anything and the working class population will clean it up."

Looking back, the treasurer of the College, Kurt Hertzfeld, said that he and Dean Gifford begged Ward not to take on every issue, to rise above some, but to no avail. The president's Irishness intervened, Hertzfeld said, by which he meant Ward's impatience, his temper. In the most startling of his outbursts, though, Ward's fury welled up from the Catholicism that was rooted in him as well. In 1973, in the November 8 issue of the *Student*, in the middle of the debate over coeducation, there appeared, spread out before you as you read the paper, a two-page article titled "Sleazing." It was written by one "Homonculus," which turned out to be "the embryological spirit which resides in the sperm." The definition of "Sleazing," and the manner in which it was presented, can be exemplified in short order. The piece began, "So you want to screw...well then don't believe any of that NO COED bullshit, because here in the Pioneer Valley there's more hymeneal wilderness than you can shake your stick at. Every weekend is a veritable parade of public [sic?] delight and you can cash in at slit city if you only know how." A lengthy series of tips about places, sartorial signs, and types for those who would learn, leads to this conclusion: "Remember, THERE ARE 6,000 OF THEM LOOKING FOR ONLY SIX INCHES.... Never before have so many existed for the pleasure of so few."

The editors wanted it to be controversial and it certainly was. Almost 50 letters responding to the article appeared in the issue of the 15th, more than had been written about coeducation since the editors had come into office nine months before. Ward did not wait that long. He denounced the article in a College Assembly meeting on the12th, calling it "juvenile," "re-pellant," "deeply immoral," "inhuman," and he chastised the editors for publishing it. He did allow that it may have been written in an effort to sway the debate in favor of coeducation (which it surely was), but if so, it was a "politically and ethically infantile" attempt. Maybe it was meant to be funny, but to him it was only sad. Whoever the author was, his life with women was "empty and insecure" and his anonymity cowardly.

Ward couldn't step back, not as a reader, not as president. But most of those who wrote letters could. They referred to Jonathan Swift sever-al times: Ward's attack made as much sense as accusing the author of "A Modest Proposal" of eating babies. Of course the issue wasn't that simple. No baby could object, but women could and some did. But others did not. One woman summed up what was the most common response: "Sleazing is a satire, its object coeducation," and added, "Surely, with the intelli-gence which put us in the Valley in the first place, we can see the irony, the wit, and the humor." Trying to sound archly British, one student probed more deeply. He wondered what nerve of Ward's had been struck: "Slea-zing, good sir, is an outrageously funny article, and presents a 'politically and ethically infantile' comment only to those whose mental attitudes are of the same disposition."

However slight or shaky was his knowledge of himself while he was president, in his first year he gave wholly of the self that he knew—most dramatically and famously at the end of his first year. On Thursday, May 11, 1972, he, along with hundreds of others, committed an act of civil dis-obedience in protest against the war in Vietnam. In doing so he explicitly and consciously raised the question of who he was in relation to his role as the president of Amherst College. His answer was one that no other college or university president gave.

WESTOVER

THE SPRING of 1972 was no more tranquil than the three that had preceded it. Though the forms they took and the degree of urgency of each obviously differed, the issues were the same: the war in Vietnam, and on campus, black-white relations and the question of whether or not Amherst should become a college for both men and women. But as the spring wore on, it was Vietnam—Vietnam consuming thousands of lives, making a mockery of America as a democracy, even posing the threat of nuclear war—that provoked the most frustration and anger and vehement calls for radical action. Though they would not be forgotten, the others could wait. Accordingly, in the spring, none of the protesting was directed at the institution itself. Yet it was more institutionally based than it had been before. Opposition to the war was nationwide but Amherst students were less concerned about protests beyond the Valley than they had been during the moratoria of 1969 and 1970. "No outside standard guided us, no national coordinating center dictated our course of action, even informally," the *Student* proclaimed in late April. "This year found us suddenly undivided, as a college, and as persons."

One reason was impossible to ignore: Amherst College was in the flight pattern of planes the size of a football field that regularly flew over the Valley. They were B-59s, going in and out of Westover Air Force Base in Chicopee, a little over thirty minutes away, transporting heavy equipment to Vietnam. You couldn't miss them, you saw and heard them regularly; when you did, you were likely to stop whatever it was that you were doing, and whatever your thoughts, they inevitably turned for a moment to the war. There would be marches in New York or Washington, protests on campuses and around the Valley, protests that took the form of blocking traffic on bridges that cross the Connecticut River, for example—13 demonstrations between April 21 and May 11, resulting in 450 arrests, to be exact. But no one needed a "national coordinating center" to explain how to register opposition to the war most dramatically. There were plenty of alternatives around the Valley. The most obvious was to block traffic going in and out of Westover Air Force Base.

Ward could back up his opposition to the war with much more authority than most. In 1964 he had organized a course on American foreign policy that concluded with eight weeks on Vietnam. That was an introductory course in American Studies. In the spring he turned the Vietnam segment into to a full semester's study of Vietnam; it was then that he came to the conclusion that it wasn't just the war or the fear of a Communist takeover that he objected to; it was the fact that America's policy in the region was just plain wrong. He realized that what we were fighting for, the freedom of the North and the South to choose their governments in internationally supervised elections, was precisely what had been set up in the Geneva Accords in 1954 and then sabotaged by the United States (which had not been a party to the agreement) because President Eisenhower and Secretary of State Dulles feared the Communists would win such an election in the South and then one country after another would fall into the hands of the Communists—like dominoes. Ironically, Ward had argued for Nixon's election as president in 1968 because he thought that "as a new hand" he had more freedom to change the direction of American policy in Southeast Asia. He applauded Nixon's overtures toward China and the Soviet Union. Recognizing that France's long involvement in Vietnam was a failure, Charles De Gaulle had protected French troops by simply withdrawing them. Perhaps Nixon would do the same. But no. "Now, after eighteen years of waste of blood and treasure, we seek precisely the conclusion we had in our hands those many years ago"—with the proviso, still, that the government in the South had to be non-Communist. Now Ward was firmly opposed to the war. As a professor in charge of an American Studies course on U.S. foreign policy, and then of a course on Vietnam, he had analyzed and discussed and criticized American foreign policy in Vietnam and he had signed a letter of protest. As a citizen he had taken part in vigils on the Amherst Common on many Sunday mornings. But that's all he had done in opposition to the war—talk and sign a letter and stand silently.

Earlier in the spring of 1972, what little agitation there was on campus was over coeducation. With the campus relatively quiet, there seemed to Ward to be nothing to prevent his and Barbara's taking the vacation that they had been planning for a year, so in mid-April they joined a group of Amherst alumni on a chartered flight to Paris.

On Sunday, April 16, Nixon ratcheted up the war by ordering the bombing of Haiphong, the major port in North Vietnam, and Hanoi, the capital. No place in Vietnam was off-limits, he declared to the North Vietnamese. Meetings and protests sprung up all across the country. At Amherst, the *Student* called for an all-college meeting in the Chapel the next night. The meeting, attended by between 400 and 500 students and a few faculty and staff members, lasted about two hours. It began with a slide presentation of the automated electronic air war in Vietnam and ended with the students voting overwhelmingly for a two-day strike at the end of the week, one that would be voluntary for both faculty and students. In the meantime, on Wednesday afternoon, there was another meeting, this time outdoors, in front of Chapin Hall, with Charles Trueheart, the editor of the *Student*, presiding. A variety of activities during the strike were proposed: fasting, campaigning for peace candidates, going to a rally in New York City on the 22nd, boycotting companies that manufactured weapons, a midnight vigil in front of the library with a coffin draped in black, and, of course, "sitting-in" at Westover. Nothing was ruled out, but, "If you only do one thing, do Westover," the *Student* said in its announcement of the alternatives. Gifford said he would call the president to inform him of the students' plans.

That evening the Committee of Six met, its deliberations summed up in a statement that Gifford wrote:

> I hope that the next two days will encourage constructive concern and commitment in opposition to a brutal war which now has again been senselessly extended. Individual students and members of the faculty who wish to participate in political or moral action will, I trust, be free to act on their consciences. I am sure many will join with me in supporting serious activities of protest which do not prevent others from continuing to teach and learn on Thursday and Friday if they wish.

About 150 students fasted, subsisting on milk and juices for five days, the vigil was observed, the New York march joined, a statement issued calling on the College to divest itself of securities in ten major military contractors in the aerospace industry, and among the 100 demonstrators arrested at Westover on Friday morning were 22 Amherst students—arrested, fined ten dollars, and released with suspended sentences. (Before the second week of May was out, there would be 15 demonstrations at Westover, many of which included Amherst faculty and students. On May 11 the arraignments of the hundreds arrested that day were postponed because of the backlog of the nearly 500 cases that had come before the court since mid-April.) On Sunday, April 23, at a relatively sparsely attended third all-campus meeting, the strike was officially declared over.

That week small groups of students barged into about twenty classes and demanded that their opposition to the war be heard. Some professors consented, some folded the war into the class's discussion, some refused. A disciplinary process involving the dean of students and the Judicial Board that would hear seven students' cases began; after much debate about that process, the cases were dismissed. They and what they signified would not be forgotten, but for the time being, what the alumni magazine's retrospective report said was true enough: "a casual visitor to the campus would not have known that a 'strike.' or any other activity for that matter, was in progress." There were some on campus who said that Ward need not have interrupted his vacation; there were others who criticized him for taking one in the first place. Having decided to return, and having double-checked with Marx about his decision by phone, he arrived back in Amherst on Monday, April 24.

Soon after, another item appeared on the College's agenda. As they declared the strike over, those who had attended the third meeting also voted to call on the president and the trustees to examine the College's investments not only in corporations that furthered the war effort but in those that did business with countries that oppressed minorities. About 100 students, mostly black students from Mount Holyoke and Smith as well as from Amherst, but some white students as well, responded by picketing in front of Converse Hall in protest against the College's financial investments in South Africa. Ward responded by addressing a College meeting on May 4 on the subject of "The Ethics of Investment." He proceeded judiciously, one step at a time. Citing Thoreau ("Trace a dollar to its source and we are all corrupt"), he said that "a pure portfolio is a fantasy." He then made a point he would make soon again: he did not want to turn an educational institution into "a social agency," yet an educational institution was not "a neutral space with no social responsibility." Furthermore, taking an action that implied that the faculty and students had a collective voice would inevitably affect the climate of the College and inhibit the free expression of individual views. On the other hand, "certain social and moral responsibilities" still followed from "acceptance of the maximum return principle as primary." Finally, if an investor saw that a corporation was contributing to "grave social wrong," after having tried to change its policy by action and found that there was nothing he could do, he could, as a last resort, "disinvest."

All of this escalated (the word was in the air) into the faculty's declaring, as its resolution had it, "that Tuesday, May 9, 1972, is a Day of Concern at Amherst College for a discussion of the issues raised by the Afro-Am Society. All regularly scheduled activities will be suspended for that day." How this came about represented, Ward said in a "Message" to the College in the *Student*, "simply, Amherst at its best."

Shortly after the demonstration in front of Converse, the Afro-Am Society asked that the College set that Tuesday aside for discussion of racism everywhere, and insofar as Amherst was implicated, its need to strengthen the Black Studies program, its admission and subsequent advising and counseling of blacks, and its need to do something about what they considered the racism inherent in intercollegiate athletics, and racism in general. Seven members of the Society were invited to the faculty meeting called for Monday morning, May 7, to consider their request.

Ward began his summation of the meeting in his "Message" by invoking once again "the spirit" of Amherst. He reported that those present were "teachers and learners together, ...committed to education, to the importance of mind, to the worth of as intense and full an awareness as we can possibly achieve," but, he reminded his audience, "Our experience here together is larger than what is organized in the curriculum. We profess humaneness, not just subject matter." The black students had spoken "out of a felt sense that there are social, political, and ethical issues which transcend any one assignment or classroom, or course." They were right, and right too in insisting that it was "the work of the College to do all it can to define and engage such issues," right in realizing that "the task is educational, that the proper tools for the College's work are discussion and debate."

That was what Ward had come to the meeting prepared to say, "fashioned," he went on to confess in his "Message," "to reach an opposite conclusion" as a result of a meeting Saturday morning the 6th with the Committee of Six and representatives of the Society, at which it was agreed that there was no need to call off classes. But as Ward reported in his "Message," the faculty meeting convinced him to reconsider his "obligation." "I wish that all who are part of Amherst College...whoever cares for the intellectual and moral quality of this place, had been able to share what took place in the Red Room of Converse Hall." Having presented their case, the Society's representatives left; the faculty and those students on college committees who regularly attended faculty meetings (one result of the 1970 Moratorium) then engaged in what Ward called "an intense and dramatic acting out of the ideal that persuasion, the fusion of mind and feeling, really does in this place count." The process leading up to a three-to-one vote by the faculty in favor of calling off classes for a day was nothing less than the democratic ideal brought into being in an educational institution. Ward couldn't have been more pleased.

He concluded his account of the meeting by saying that he was sure that anyone who was at it came away with "a deep sense of obligation to listen to the voices of students who say things are wrong here and to learn together with them." It was now time "to translate that ideal into action." The next day, speeches in the Chapel in the morning and in the afternoon and evening, discussions on specific topics led by members of the Society in designated places, went as planned.

As Ward had said, calling a strike because of the war in Vietnam was different. That very day, May 9, Nixon announced that he was ordering the mining of Haiphong Harbor, as well as other harbors and inland waterways, in an effort to cut off supply routes to North Vietnamese troops fighting in the South and to prevent supplies of any kind from entering North Vietnam itself—and a call went out for another all-campus meeting. That night while Ward was at one of the meetings planned by the Afro-Am Society, a student called his house and left word with Barbara that he and other students hoped that Ward would write a letter, presumably one like the one Plimpton had sent to Nixon three springs before. When Ward got home he tried to write one.

Wednesday afternoon an estimated 800 people crammed into the

Chapel. Ward had not called the meeting but he opened it with a statement that he had told no one about, "for fear of cautionary advice," he later said—no one, not even Barbara, who heard what he had to say for the first time that afternoon. His statement was radically different from Plimpton's letter, but two days later it would be reprinted in the *Times*.

Once again he began by invoking "the spirit" of the College." "Let us make this place, Amherst College, as good and decent and human a place as we can. If we stand appalled at the cruelty and the indecency we see around us in the world, let us not give them a place here among us." He began, he said, as the president of Amherst College. He also said that that was the voice his audience wanted to hear, the voice that they had heard many times before. But admitting to being "tense and uneasy with the act of dividing [himself] in two," he said he would also speak in his own voice. From the start, he had not wanted that second voice to be silenced: "My hope, as president, has been not to lose myself in the role, the office, to retain a sense of my own self while still president."

He then went back to the student's phone call and now answered it by exclaiming: "Write a letter! To whom? One feels like a child throwing paper planes against a blank wall." Had he written a letter he might have been cheered, been thought to be "a pleasant and sympathetic fellow." "But the mines are laid," he said; he went on to rail against "this bloody war" that had gone on for 18 years. He quoted what he had said on Parents' Day three years before about this "cruel and foolish mistake, that we got into on a false ideological premise." But "Voices louder than mine have been saying as much for a long time," he pointed out. "What are we protesting?" he asked, and then went on to answer his own question, to answer it as "'Bill Ward,' self and citizen," noting again that, "as I said when I took this office, I do not intend to disenfranchise myself or lose my rights as citizen because I am president."

The harbors had been mined; Nixon had ruled out withdrawal, saying the only way to get to the negotiating table was to apply more and more force; Kissinger had been reported as saying "nuclear confrontation is an acceptable risk, preferable to the present land war in South Vietnam" if the blockade failed. But what was done was done, Ward said. What he protested against was what might come next, but he had come to the conclusion that there was no way to do that, which was to say, "What I protest is there

is no way to protest. I speak [out] of frustration and deep despair...," and
he reached a conclusion few if any expected:

> I do not think words will now change the minds of men in power who
> make these decisions. I do not. Since I do not, I do not care to write letters
> to the world.
> Instead, I will, for myself, join in the act of passive civil disobedience at
> Westover Air Force Base.

Almost everyone in the Chapel stood up and cheered.

When the cheering had died down, after the member of the "coalition"
who was chairing the meeting asked for responses to the fact of the blockade, one student said he felt the pressure of conflicting demands on him—
as a citizen, a student, a person. He was "aware of the problems, and yet
[was] powerless to do anything about them." He asked two members of the
faculty, one an authority on Russia, the other on foreign policy generally,
what they thought were the likely consequences of Nixon's recent escala-
tions. But before either could answer, Marx, emerging from the front of
the audience into the aisle, declared, "For the first time in my knowledge,
the president of a college has offered to lead us in an act of civil disobedience. This is an extraordinary opportunity for people who have lost control of their lives. I don't know what we are waiting for. I assure you that if
nothing else it will get extraordinary national publicity." Another faculty
member stood up and, concurring with Marx that Ward's action would be
national news, urged that the demonstration take place the next day rather than Sunday, as had been planned: the mines had been laid; they were
to be activated at six in the morning. One of the faculty members called
upon to predict what might happen as a result of the blockade eventually got to speak. Ward spoke again, saying this time that "as president" he
would "preserve a space of freedom" for people in the College. There was
to be no coercion, no attempt "to force people to act the way you think they
should act." Gifford read a letter that he had written to Nixon that began,
"Your remarks on the night of May 8, 1972 reveal assumptions which were
thread-bare and self-deceptive five years ago. Without consultation with
Congress you have again brought us to the edge of despair and big power
confrontation," a letter he said anyone who wanted to should sign. Everyone was worked up, there was no order in the house. All that was clear

was that scores and scores of people from the College would be going to Westover with Ward in the morning.

Right after the meeting, the faculty met and adopted a motion saying that it believed that President Nixon's actions had created a global crisis and that the faculty would allow students to take whatever political action they saw fit after they had made arrangements with their professors for completing their course work.

Word traveled quickly to the other institutions in the Valley. The *Times* estimated that "some 1,000 students" from Amherst and other area colleges went to Westover early Thursday morning to sit down in the road and thus block the entrances through the two main gates of the air base. Ward was among them. Barbara joined her husband, as did Gifford, five members of the Committee of Six (an immediate family member of the sixth was dying), about twenty other professors, and, it is estimated, about 400 Amherst students.

It was a fine spring day. The atmosphere was heady, so nearly carnivalesque that at one point Marx, who had been arrested with five colleagues the week before, on the second anniversary of the shootings at Kent State, at what had been a very solemn occasion, felt compelled to remind everyone that people were dying in Vietnam. Ward himself was harder to read. Given what he later said—"Sitting there in that circle, I didn't really know what to do. What a crazy world this is"—one might surmise that this was one of those times when he knew himself "only slenderly." Eventually (the *Times* said "nearly two hours" later) the demonstrators were led into busses (a few had to be dragged) and driven to the Chicopee jail, where they milled around in the yard until the court officials, already overburdened by the many previous demonstrations, decided to postpone their arraignments, and released them. (A fund was later set up by a handful of faculty members to help the city of Chicopee defray the costs of the Amherst contingent's actions.)

Ward's arrest was immediately headline news. He later claimed to be surprised by the reaction to what he had done—"'flabbergasted' by the commotion," as he put it. Countless newspaper accounts of anti-war protests and demonstrations and actions across the land consistently either began with a reference to Ward's action at Westover or ended with one. The publicity would be relatively short-lived, but the effects of Westover at and on Amherst College were not.

Although they were by no means of one mind, on the whole the students were supportive and proud of what Ward had done. In his Commencement issue, Charles Trueheart wrote a long appreciation of Ward's first year titled "The Blooming of the President." In it he focused on what he called Ward's "personal confusion with his roles," from his response to Copeland's Fanfare at his inauguration, to his changing his mind about the Day of Concern, culminating in his performance in the Chapel on the afternoon of May 10: "President Ward walked from the room, his chin on his chest, much the way he had begun his term of office, shy. He left Johnson Chapel the extraordinary man Amherst College, albeit unconsciously, had been waiting for." Ignoring what Ward had in fact said about his audience's expectations (that it was not Bill Ward but the president of the college that they wanted to hear), Trueheart wrote, "It was Bill Ward we had wanted to hear all along. Because if it is Bill Ward who is heard, then it is also each individual in the community, rather than The Professor or The Dean or The Student." As for what hundreds of people thought was Ward's understanding of his roles as person and president, Trueheart asked rhetorically, as did Ward: what if all of us had "lost our precious right to act as human beings?" Trueheart concluded that by raising the question, "he becomes extraordinary."

Of course not all of the faculty approved of what Ward did. Among those who went to Westover some went more in support of him than to register their approval of what he had done. Professor DeMott wrote a controversial account of Ward's action in *Change* in which he reduced Ward's act of civil disobedience to his way of maintaining his authority on campus. In an earlier piece on the 1970 moratorium that he published in the same magazine he had it that Plimpton had been forced to send the letter (which he hadn't even written) to Nixon by the faculty, and had thereby lost *his* authority. Professor Hadley Arkes and others maintained that by breaking the law, Ward had made it more difficult to prevent unlawful behavior on campus. Witness what had happened to the cases of the students who had disrupted classes. Most persuasively, in a letter that was published in the *Alumni News*, Professor Hugh Hawkins objected to what had transpired at the Wednesday afternoon meeting. The atmosphere, the loss of control by those who had called and chaired the meeting, and above all the effect of the exhortation of so influential a figure as Marx, "were diametrically opposed to the spirit that we should seek at this college." The same was true of the faculty meeting immediately after, one that began with somebody announcing that the president had just received a "unanimous standing ovation," and then went on until dinner time, with "students audibly and impatiently waiting outside." In objecting to the coercive nature of the afternoon meetings, Hawkins cited three examples of students whose work had been side-tracked as a result of the sit-in, the most telling example being that of the student who was told that the oral examination of his thesis was to be postponed because some of his readers had gone to Westover—especially telling because his thesis was on the potentially coercive effect of acts of civil disobedience. As for Ward's claim to be speaking in the second half of his statement as Bill Ward, the private citizen, given the occasion, an all-college meeting in the Chapel, Hawkins asked, "How could your action not be that of 'the President of the College?'" And then he asked another disarmingly simple question: "If your conscience told you that you must perform an act of civil disobedience, why could you not do so without making a previous announcement?" Going back to Ward's oft-stated determination to protect the institution from "an excess of passion," Hawkins concluded by saying, "As I see recent events, you have increased passions and weakened the opportunity for free exchange of ideas within the College." When he repeated his objections at a noon-hour assembly in the Red Room in the fall, Ward's response was Ward at his best, Ward wanting every individual's voice to be heard. When Hawkins finished he said, simply, "Then I'd have to say that was not Amherst's finest moment."

In a letter in which he reviewed Ward's first year as president (a review that Ward had requested), Bruce Morgan, who had moved on to become the Dean of Carlton College that summer, described Ward's act of civil disobedience as one "of the highest principle and courage as well as sound national judgment." "I went," Morgan wrote, "partly because I wanted to support the President in what I knew was going to be a difficult situation, but I also went as an act of conscience, given moral support by a person I admired and who simply, at that point, seemed to have more courage than I." He didn't think his own academic freedom had been "violated by anything [Ward] did or said," but he did add, "I ran into a considerable amount of flack from some very fine seniors in my class the afternoon of the sit-down."

The response of the alumni was mixed. In a list of what they had been confronted with in just the last two or three years, a list contained in a memo to the College's top administrators from the Alumni Office, Westover was the next to last. (The last, the sixth, we will come to soon.)

1) Moratorium
2) 1969 letter to President Nixon from President Plimpton
3) 1970 "black takeover"
4) 1971 election of non-alumnus, former faculty member, as president of the college
5) President Ward's Westover arrest
6) President Ward's recommendation for coeducation at Amherst College

Being well aware that the annual alumni fund drive was suffering, Ward wrote a letter to all the class agents in the fall, thanking them for their work on behalf of the College and acknowledging that he had made their work a lot harder.

But later, by the Alumni Office's calculation, alumni defended Ward two to one. Many did so in gendered terms. Hiram Haydn, the editor of *American Scholar*, said, "He had the guts and the vitality to say openly that he was not just an office, but a man...with a so often lacking respect for what it means to be a man." "We must allow a man to remain a man when he becomes a president," a young English professor wrote. "If we deny him his manhood upon taking office, when that time comes, we will have no man: we will have an office." But there were faithful contributors who declared that so long as Ward was president they wouldn't give the College another cent. Some called for his resignation. Many simply deplored his opposition to the war, but to many more, his injection of himself into his office was what they found intolerable. He had used the College, *their* college, for his own personal and political purposes. The objection spoke loudly to the exceptional loyalty of Amherst alumni—and to the fact that Ward was not one of their number. By the time the summer issue of the alumni quarterly came out, nearly a thousand letters had been received. You didn't have to be a sociologist to predict the results. Many sympathizers came from men in education, the ministry, and medicine, very few from businessmen and lawyers. More men who had graduated in the '30s, '40s, and '50s disapproved than approved of what Ward did, but the difference was not nearly so great as the reverse among the men who graduated in the '60s (135 to 11), those at Amherst at the time (25 to 1), and (a nice statistic) those from classes that graduated between 1888 and 1909 (9 to 1). As for their willingness to give to the College, the 1973 drive did fall $93,000 short of its goal. But Amherst alumni *are* exceptionally loyal: two years later it set an all-time record.

Perhaps the most interesting response from an alumnus was that of Stansfield Turner, who wrote Ward saying that he had a problem with what he took to be Ward's "black and white distinction," and that he was "trying to make up [his] mind on where [he stood] on this issue as an Amherst alumnus." Turner's response was the more interesting because at the time he was president of the Naval War College in Newport, Rhode Island. (He would later be head of the CIA.) He asked Ward to come down for a day set aside for a symposium on "Why Students and Faculty Oppose the Vietnam War," and Ward did, accompanied by six faculty members and five students. It was an undramatic occasion, much to the disappointment of some among the Amherst delegation.

The reaction of the trustees was, Ward told Morgan, "remarkably good." Ward had called Oliver Merrill after his arrest and advised him of his action, which, Ward said, "after due reflection...in fairness to his own conscience, he was required to take as an individual." Merrill responded by saying he thought that "the decision was for him to make and that he should do what his conscience and judgment deemed best." The trustees met soon after to discuss what Merrill nimbly referred to as Ward's "indiscretion" and to agree on the wording of what would be the "Statement of the Trustees of Amherst College." It said the trustees respected Ward's right to make "these personal decisions and the considerations of conscience which motivated his actions," and concluded, "Their high regard for and confidence in him continue." It also made the following points: it was the policy of the College not to take a position on political questions; every member of the Amherst community had a right to express his opinion and to take what he thought was appropriate action; and this included the president, though of course it was "more difficult for him to dissociate his position as an individual from his office." (And so it was. Nobody gave a second thought to professors' getting arrested; a college president, theoretically committed to defending the neutrality of the academy, was something else.) There were those on the Board who disapproved of what he had done, not just on principled but on practical grounds. The chairman of the Investment Committee is said to have walked into a subsequent meeting and announced, "This guy is bad for business "—which he certainly was at the time. More generally, the trustees' hopes that there would be no protests within or against the institution had been fulfilled during most of his first year, but here they were, at the end of it, faced with more general "commotion" than anyone, including Ward himself, had foreseen. When Ward met with the trustees for two and a half hours there was "vigorous and sharp give-and take," he said, but no suggestion "that they had second thoughts about my being president here. I was even braced for that!" His session with the trustees must have been sobering, but firing him for protesting against the war in Vietnam? One cannot imagine their doing anything but stand behind him. On the other hand, one does not imagine they ever got over what he had done.

In getting arrested, Ward had become what one man called "an iconic resister." Several groups sought his support for their protests, the National Campus Alliance for Amnesty, the ACLU, and Redress, for example. He was sympathetic, but he held back. It was easy to inform the ACLU that he was speaking for himself and not Amherst College. Mention of his affiliation would be "for the purposes of identification only." Redress was a group that was going to petition Congress "to reaffirm that we are citizens and not hostages to usurpers of power and authority" by exercising "its constitutional authority of control over the armed forces...and by ending all military and economic appropriations for a war the Congress did not vote for and the American people do not want." Ward had originally intended to join them in presenting their petition, but when they expressed their intention to go beyond a presentation by committing an act of civil disobedience in the halls of Congress, though he realized that one could present the petition and withdraw, while others proceeded "to bear further witness," there would still be a connection, a necessary if not sufficient link in the logic of events, he said. "The pressure of recent events has made me intensely aware that the hardest thing for me to do is to maintain confidence in my self and to choose on the basis of my own thought and feeling what I finally choose to do," he wrote Robert Jay Lifton and all who were members of the organization, to tell them that he had finally decided not to participate. He thought of but then changed his mind about signing a pledge for "Hostages for Peace," a group that planned to go to Hanoi and Haiphong and declare themselves hostages "to protect Vietnamese citizens and American prisoners of war from American bombing." (Ward's name appears on a long list of possible supporters of the "hostages" that Mary McCarthy drew up, a list that includes James Baldwin, Ramsey Clark, John Kerry, Coretta Scott King, and, for a reason that we have noted, Francis Plimpton.) The explanation of his reticence is simple: he wanted to keep his job, or, as he put it in a letter to Henry Nash Smith, "That act of civil disobedience last spring ran me out toward the edge and I knew that another step or even a tactless word in defense of it would push me out there all by myself."

Some college and university presidents explicitly distanced themselves from Ward's position, saying that though they would do all they could to support lawful student demonstrations, they would not implicate institutions or attract attention to themselves by speaking out on Vietnam or any other political issue. Some respected his raising the issue by getting arrested and wanted to explore it with him. John Coleman, the president of Haverford who had spent a year working as a ditch-digger in Atlanta, a salad and sandwich man working in a Boston restaurant, and a trash collector in College Park, Maryland, and then written *Blue-Collar Journal: A College President's Sabbatical,* went further. In an op-ed piece in the *Times* he said that Ward, along with Father Theodore Hesburgh of Notre Dame, was "on his way into the leadership circle." But he warned that he would find it "a lonely place" once he got there. "The presidents of yesteryear are gone," he said. A few years before the cry had been "Keep the peace, if possible." Now it was "Get us out of financial trouble—but don't change in the process." Coleman's conclusion was, and still seems, about right: "Administrators now administer. They don't lead."

What was to Ward the ideal response, or occasion for responses, occurred the weekend in early June when alumni returned to the campus for their reunions. On Saturday morning, June 3, 650 alumni filed into the Chapel to hear him talk about Westover and to ask questions. One alumnus summed up the meeting in retrospect by saying (again the word) that it took "'guts' to face the alumni as you did, especially after having heard, sometimes rudely, about the lack of 100% support for your action." The

discussion was "enlightened" and "left little doubt that each of us ben-
efitted by the open and free exchange, and that the College is in good
hands." To Ward it was like the faculty meeting that led up to the Day of
Concern, what with "the hard discussion and the decency on both sides."
At the end, Francis Plimpton read the Trustees' Statement, after which the
alumni gave Ward a standing ovation, one that must have been every bit
as satisfying, if not more so, than the one he had received just over three
weeks before in the same room.

He tried to make every exchange about Westover resemble that one as
much as possible. He traveled to meet with 31 alumni associations the following year. And all along he answered nearly 2,000 letters, sometimes,
to be sure, plugging in the same paragraph when his correspondent raised
a question that scores of others had raised.

Almost everyone had an opinion, quickly made up his mind, and was
sure how he felt about what Ward had done. Ward himself, though, spent
an endless amount of time defending and trying to explain his action to
others—and to himself. His skepticism about self-knowledge carried over
into doubts about knowing why he did what he did. In a long letter he
spoke to an alumnus's question as to whether or not he was "absolutely
certain" about what he had done:

> I would be foolish indeed if I said that I was absolutely certain about almost
> anything, let alone my own motives....Since I am skeptical of others, I am
> skeptical of myself and would say that there is no doubt in my mind that
> particular moment, the context in which I acted, and a complex of personal
> feelings, especially frustration, both played a contributory part in my
> decision to do what I did.

Everyone else's reaction was relatively simple.

Just before taking office, in an interview in the *Student*, Ward set forth
the issue with little sense of how important it would be. "The liberal fiction
that one does not speak for the institution, but is still free to speak for himself does seem to me to be a fiction," he said. Period. But then he went on
to say, "I don't intend to disenfranchise myself or become mute because
I'm President of Amherst College." Rather than attempt to conjoin the two
positions, though, he backed off: he said that whatever he thought or whatever he did before, as president he thought he would "probably be a little

more careful in deciding matters like that. So there's a problem in even speaking for myself." He went on to say that the war and the fact of racism in America mocked "the values that education professes to stand for: rationality and humaneness," but he'd have to be "convinced that this really does affect the internal workings of this one particular institution before [he] felt that Amherst College bore the responsibility of taking a stand." That might have been taken to mean that he would go so far as Plimpton had and sign a letter to Nixon—if he was really convinced. He ended by repeating what he had said in his talk about investments: he didn't want "to turn an educational institution into a social action agency or political lever," yet he didn't think one was "a neutral space with no responsibility to society" either, and that, in sum, "this matter of institutional or collective responsibility" seemed to him to be "one of the most troublesome ones to try to define or speak sensibly about." This time it would turn out to be more obviously just that. Though he would never arrive at *an* answer, he continued to speak and write sensibly and often about the question.

To begin with, he took pains to be clear about acts of civil disobedience, about what one was and about what justification there was for one. In his notes for a lecture on "The Meaning of Passive Civil Disobedience" that he delivered in the fall after his arrest, he listed several criteria. Such acts were: illegal and intentional, openly committed, nonviolent, conscious (i.e, not impulsive or thoughtless), and intended to protest or frustrate a law or policy by the government or some of its officers. All of these were important, but subsequently he laid particular emphasis on the fifth. An act of civil disobedience was illegal, but the person who committed it accepted the rule of law, which meant he accepted the consequences of his illegal act. This was his way of answering those who said that in breaking the law he had made it difficult if not impossible to fault those students who had disrupted classes. They were charged with "the grave offense of the violation of academic freedom" and had done so believing some higher end was being served. If they were to be true to their "conscientious and thoughtful reasons for so doing," they too had to "suffer the consequences" of their actions.

As to when or why one would commit an act of civil disobedience, at his request Professor Kateb wrote a piece titled "A Word on Civil Disobedience," that appeared in the summer issue of the alumni magazine. In it he updated what he had said in defending the moratorium in 1970. More than opposition to a policy was at stake. "Without consulting Congress, and in the absence of any specific authorization, [Nixon had] further extended an undeclared war." He had acted unconstitutionally; his administration was ignoring the people whom it existed to serve. "But a minority refuses to abdicate its judgment; it will not grant automatic obedience." "Civilly," as responsible citizens, a minority had disobeyed the law. To have been obedient would have meant "the end of democracy, not conformity to its moral principles," Kateb concluded.

And it would not go without Ward's saying that his was an *act*. Soon after his arrest, he prepared two statements, one titled "Civil Disobedience," the other, justifying his action, titled "The Demands of the Office of President." In the former he recalled his response to the student who wanted him to write a letter. He meant action to speak louder than words, and more, "to be a symbolic and tutelary word, that is, educational, to remind people that civil implies 'civilized,' and to recall anyone who would listen to a standard of civilized behavior I fear has been forgotten if not lost." He had in mind his Thoreau, who in *his* "Civil Disobedience" had pointed out that there were "thousands who are *in opinion* opposed to slavery and to the war, who yet in effect do nothing to put an end to them." "There are nine hundred and ninety-nine patrons of virtue to one virtuous man," he wrote. Words, letters, petitions, high-mindedness were ineffective. "Even voting *for the right* is *doing* nothing for it." So Thoreau went to jail for not paying his taxes—i.e., for not supporting a government that was at war with Mexico and that countenanced slavery. Seeing that *doing* nothing meant supporting the government's policy in Vietnam, Ward got arrested. "Action from principle, the perception and the performance of right, changes things and relations," Thoreau said. (In the fall Ward gave a freshman seminar, titled "A Majority of One," on Thoreau. It was the only course he gave after he became president.)

Ward hoped that his action was to be "educational," that it would remind people what it meant to be "civilized," which was in this context not only to be individually "unflinching" in one's pursuit of a truth, but to be a responsible citizen, or, more largely, to preserve democracy. Ward ended both of the statements that he prepared by saying, "I think that the major item on our political agenda is to ask the difficult question how we might

extend the idea of citizenship from the single self to the anonymous institutions which characterize our society and which exercise power in it."
In a paper that he wrote in March 1973 titled "Should College Presidents
Take Stands on Sensitive Public Issues?" he said that "if we tell students,
as I have for many years, that their education is not only to train their
minds but to prepare them to lead decent and humane lives in whatever
social role their intelligence qualifies them for, we had better not implicitly teach them at the same time that it is not possible to act on that ideal."
The answer was easy. In his statement about "The Demands of the Office
of the President" he raised a much more difficult question: how do you
extend the idea of citizenship from the single self to an anonymous institution? The task of addressing and coming up with an answer lay ahead—
and would stay there.

And there remained the most interesting question that his act of civil
disobedience raised. No, we better not discourage students from acting.
That's clear enough. Let's set aside the question of an educational institution's role. Now what about the president of their college? Or, more point-
edly, what is he going to ask, to demand of himself? In his last interview
in the *Student*, in the Commencement issue of his last year as president,
he made it sound as if the question had not been a difficult one after all.
There was no longer any point in going back over his answers and his arguments: "It was easy for me as President to sustain both the demands of
the role of President and the demands of a political actor, as hard as it was
for others to accept the division of office and citizen." But right after he
was arrested, he summed up his reasons for doing what he did in equally
cryptic terms, terms this time worth going back over. He said he did it because he felt that "the sheer proximity of Westover and the urgency of the
cause made the act of civil disobedience personally necessary." The first
reason is clear and sound enough; the second isn't. One way of glossing it
is to say, *There just came a point...*, and then try to explain how it came to
that point, try to explain the "urgency." It was undoubtedly caused by Nixon's escalation of the war just before his arrest, but there is also the fact,
the more illuminating fact of the evolutionary process that culminated in
Ward's becoming an activist.

We have seen that during his years as a faculty member he was relatively inactive. He argued that students should be represented (if not vote) in

a newly establish College Assembly, but he figured little if at all in efforts to bring about change outside of Amherst. Before he came to Amherst he was, if anything, even less motivated to do so. In the winter 1957-58 issue of *American Scholar* Ward published an article titled "James Gould Cozzens and the Condition of Man," a copy of which he sent to Marx. Marx's response is important. He liked the writing, it was getting "better and better," but Marx was "amazed and chagrined at [Ward's] apparent enthusiasm for the book and this man," and he went on:

> The state of mind he exalts seems to me finally indistinguishable from a high-toned sort of life-adjustment. And it is accompanied, often, by the same sort of smugness and complacency. All the modern man can do, you say, is live in the world and accept *what is* with skeptical and ironic good sense? Jesus! Given the world as it stands in 1957, what hope is there for our children if we all follow this injunction?...We haven't any ideals left, except this clever rationale for adjusting ourselves to our own inevitable doom. I say our own because I think we are shaping it out of our fear and embarrassment at having once believed in something.

Marx said that he was going to write Hiram Haydn (who would 15 years later praise Ward for his "guts" in getting arrested) to see if "we can't get a discussion going on this point"—without the personal feeling, of course, which I have only because I regret how wide a gap has opened between us." (There would be no discussion, only a letter from Marx about the piece, suitably toned-down, in the next issue.)

Over the years Marx continued to protest against the decline, and with the Vietnam War, the rock-bottom state of American culture; in doing so he became a more and more forceful presence at Amherst, his influence stemming from his unwavering commitment to his beliefs. He resigned from the committee of the Fulbright Commission that selected scholars and lecturers (of which Ward was one) that represented the United States and therefore, by implication, its policies. He was consistently chosen to speak at all-college meetings—on the war, on racism in the country and at Amherst. And yet he wisely knew when to work behind the scene, to suggest and inspire rather than lead. (The idea of Plimpton's letter to Nixon was his but he knew it would gain more support if Gifford wrote it.)

It was obvious that Marx influenced Ward. He had taught him and, in effect, brought him to Amherst. Ward consistently referred to him as his best friend. Ward, though, wanted to be seen as his own man. In a letter he wrote soon after he became president, Ward quoted Marx as saying, "I wish this honeymoon were over so people could get down to brass knuckle business." Ward confessed that he too was "a bit uneasy that the beginning seems so smooth." In the spring, when Ward acted, the gap between them narrowed appreciably, but he did all he could to prevent it from closing. "I love him," Ward said in his letter to Morgan, "But that does not blind me to his own faults and does not make me unaware that others will impute more to his influence than is the case. I have talked with Leo himself about his unfortunate use of language and easy referral to me in public, and although he is wistfully contrite, I doubt very much if he will change greatly in the future. All I can do is to continue to act as best I can and leave the record to establish what some people will not believe by my word."

In 1976 Marx left Amherst to teach at MIT. Amherst's best days were over. He feared—with reason—that it would fall back into what he called "an 'administrative' view of education, and some order for order's sake." As he said in a *Student* interview in February, in the intense atmosphere of the so-called '60s the students were more challenging, less passive. "It was a time when students couldn't envisage settled careers. So they were not as dependent on the good opinion of the faculty for getting into graduate school. They were less acquiescent, which was healthy," and then he added almost wistfully, "but temporarily as it turned out."

But Marx's was not the only voice that Ward heard when he made his decision to go to Westover. Just after his arrest he received a copy of a book on Gandhi by Louis Fischer, who had been a colleague of Ward's at Princeton. It was a gift from Fischer's son. In thanking him, Ward said that he had been thinking of his father a lot over the past few weeks. The day he got arrested, he said,

> I remembered a day many years ago when students at Princeton rioted and, late at night, I went a roundabout way to avoid the mob and went safely home. Louis was deeply disappointed with me, that I would not with my presence act for what I thought was right. All of which is to say that Louis himself and Gandhi, because of Louis' work, were much on my mind as I came to the decision to present my body and not just my words in opposition to policies I abhor.

And then, finally, there is Ward's growing impatience, culminating in his impulsiveness, at the time, the kind of impulsiveness he once wrote about in a piece titled "Anarchy and Authority in American Literature"—that seminal moment in American history and literature when Huck Finn declares, "All right, then, I'll *go* to Hell," the moment when he too becomes "a majority of one."

In his interview for the College's Oral History Project, Ward said it was naive of him to think that people would understand. *He* knew what he was doing but, taken by surprise, others wouldn't, though they might immediately jump to conclusions. But when asked if he would do again what he had done, he said Yes, but that it would have been harder, that he would have moved "much more prudentially." Just what else he might have done back then, or how differently he might have done what he had done, he didn't say.

There is one answer that is at least plausible. If he really wanted to separate himself from his office, he could have told no one what he intended to do, slipped away, and gotten arrested—on his own. When he was booked it probably would have been revealed that he was the president of Amherst College, but that might have been irrelevant in the Chicopee police station; he would have paid whatever penalty was imposed on him and returned to campus. He would have left Amherst and been arrested as Bill Ward and then returned to assume his role as the president of Amherst College. The news would have broken almost immediately; it probably would have been the more compelling given the circumstances. But what is more important, the distinction between his roles would have been clearer to others and probably to himself as well. He might have been clearer about how he felt when he was arrested. Standing in the Chapel of Amherst College he then would have been who he was—undeniably Bill Ward but undeniably too, the president of the College, the latter, under the circumstances, being the more obvious. It is the answer that Hawkins put forward and that Morgan did too in his letter to Ward: "From the standpoint of the institution," Morgan wrote, "it appeared to me later that you could have achieved a greater degree of freedom as a person if you had gone to Westover without announcement and it had become known after the fact." As it was, Ward went ahead and did what he was often criticized for doing—namely, inserting himself, his person, into his role.

Yet the circumstances were extraordinary. Ward was convinced that constitutional democracy had broken down. And so the ideal citizen had no choice but to defend it by committing an act that asserted his individual freedom, the foundation on which democracy in America had been founded. He had to rebel against the rule of its law as it presently stood—or in protest against its absence—in order to restore it to its original state.

In getting arrested, Ward in his person did just that. That, and yet more, *as* more. He also did it as an educator, as a teacher, which is how he defined himself as president. He had said many times that Amherst should not inspire students with ideals and then just leave them thinking that there was nothing that they could do to bring them into being or to defend them when they were threatened. Now, more specifically, if a man was convinced that the ideals on which the constitutional democracy of his country was based were not only threatened but violated, he had to have the courage to defend them with his disobedience.

In stating his intention to do so on that Wednesday afternoon in the Chapel, Ward said he was speaking first as the president of the College, as the person he assumed the students wanted to hear, and then as Bill Ward, the private citizen who was going to act. He insisted on the distinction and would continue to do so ever after. The moment, the times, were hardly conducive to clear thinking, but in retrospect we can say that he was not giving himself enough credit. The students *had* come to hear the president, and though neither they nor anyone else in the room had ever heard a president like him before, the president was the man they heard right through to the end of his statement.

COEDUCATION

WARD WAS arrested in May 1972. In the following fall, he and Amherst College turned their attention to what had been an issue before he became president, and that he had attended to during his first year in office, but that in his second emerged as the most pressing question before the College: should it cease to be an institution that had educated men and only men for a century and a half and become one that would educate women as well? "It would be difficult to name a single decision more important since the founding of the College," Ward once wrote, and for a spell, almost everyone agreed. Amherst's fate seemed to hang in the balance, and arguably it did, in the sense, at least, that it is hard to imagine what would have come of Amherst had it not "gone co-ed." But few other institutions— to be precise, only two others (and they were in the Valley)—would or had to take note of what Amherst decided. Almost all other colleges and universities in the country were either going coeducational or were already coeducational, most from their very beginnings. Those who argued that society had a stake in what Amherst decided based their argument on that fact: there were almost no all-male colleges left in America; by remaining a single-sex institution, Amherst would give young men a choice. It was Amherst's social responsibility to do just that. But ultimately one could be sure of only the fact that Amherst's decision had momentous implications for Amherst's future.

Almost exactly a century before Ward's arrest, at the Semi-Centennial Celebration of the College in the summer of 1871, the issue had occasioned "an animated and exciting discussion by distinguished alumni on the admission of women," according to L. Clarke Seelye, the first president of Smith. The Governor of Massachusetts, Alexander Bullock, said that he was "cordially in favor of making the experiment of admitting our friends heretofore excluded, to the privileges of the classes, if they shall desire it, and shall establish the usual qualifications," and went on to announce that he had sent to his "associates of the Board of the Trustees" the "humble offering of a scholarship endowment, with the condition that its benefits shall be appropriated to a woman upon the basis of equal fitness in the examination." He was a gentleman; he welcomed the softening influence of women. He cited the example of Raphael, whose pencil, it was said, "melted whenever it approached a woman or an angel." Henry Ward Beecher, Amherst Class of 1834, defended coeducation on solider grounds and in terms that should embarrass no one: "Amherst is for a universal education," he said. "If a man be black, and is fully prepared, or if a woman is fully qualified, its doors will open to them. Amherst should lead in this march to progress, and if she does, it will not be the first time that she has led in progress and philanthropy." But whatever discussion followed ended when Smith was founded four years later.

By the '60s, almost all American college and university students attended coeducational institutions (as many as 97 percent of them, Ward once said) and recently, institutions with which Amherst compared itself for one reason or another began announcing that they too would become coeducational: Wesleyan in the spring of 1968; Yale, Williams, Trinity, and Princeton over the course of the following year; Bowdoin the year after. Amherst, it seemed, would not do any such thing. Nor would Mount Holyoke or Smith. In the fall of 1971 both announced their intention to remain single-sex institutions.

Amherst, in cooperation with other institutions in the Valley and beyond, did take small steps to bring young men and women together in classrooms and even, temporarily, as residents on campuses, steps, though, that at Amherst could be seen as efforts to make "going co-ed" unnecessary rather than to promote it. In the fall of 1967 55 women took courses at Amherst, 120 did so in the spring. In the fall of 1969, 23 women came to spend a term at Amherst under a Twelve-College Exchange Program; no sooner had they arrived than they petitioned to be allowed to stay for the whole academic year, and permission was granted.

Coeducation was undoubtedly an issue at Amherst. How could it not have been? There were signs of "women's liberation" in every walk of life throughout the country. Not long after the publication of Betty Friedan's (a Smith alumna) *The Feminine Mystique* in 1963, to pick a powerfully symbolic moment, the Women's Liberation Movement took hold in the Valley. Women's Centers were established at the University and in Northampton; women's consciousness-raising groups sprung up. Their influences were felt in the town of Amherst, among wives, and in families. Adlai Stevenson's pronouncement, at Smith's Commencement in 1955, that the "political task" of the graduates was "to influence man and boy through the humble role of housewife" seemed a part of ancient history.

In the fall of 1969, as we have seen, President Plimpton began to put together a Long Range Planning Committee, consisting of two trustees ("Spike" Beitzel and George Peterson), three faculty members (Professors DeMott, Fink, and Kateb), three students, and two administrators, that would include among its Task Forces one on Size and Coeducation.

The Committee hoped that the Task Force would examine the interrelationship between size and coeducation and the financial implications of various courses of action. In February 1971 the Task Force reported on its findings and deliberations but made no recommendations. Two months later, in its final report, the Long Range Planning Committee did. The section on "Coeducation" was short and to the point. It began with an acknowledgment that when the committee first met, like a lot of people at the time, a majority of its members thought the whole idea of coeducation was a fad. In a poll that the Task Force had conducted, the students favored coeducation 65 percent to 27 percent, the faculty 57 percent to 34 percent, but what excitement the issue originally generated had died down. "Nevertheless," the report went on, "the majority of the LRPC has become convinced that admission of women to Amherst is not a matter of secondary importance." The minority opinions were relegated to a footnote: one member of the committee felt that Amherst should remain an all-male college, "complemented by association with all-female colleges," a second that the goal of coeducation could be achieved by enlarging the student exchange program. Only a footnote's worth, but those two positions would be strongly defended until the issue was finally settled in November 1974. The argument that Amherst should remain all-male to preserve "educational diversity" nationally was wittily dismissed as having "an appealing quaintness," rather like the preservation of the guinea "as a unit of account in Britain" and the resurrection of "competitive birling in Northern Maine."

The committee answered the question of size in a paragraph: the College should expand its enrollment to 1,500 in order to admit 300 women as full-time degree candidates; more women should be admitted in the future without an increase in the total enrollment; this should not be done "timidly," lest women admitted in token numbers be made to feel isolated "objects of almost voyeuristic attentions on campus." These numbers and the means by which they were arrived at constituted the definition of Amherst's size that was agreed upon two and a half years later. The burden of the report was a strong endorsement of coeducation.

The first argument for coeducation was a principled one: "To exclude equally able women is arbitrary....discrimination by sex involves a distinction which serves no plausible educational objective." Put negatively, "legalities apart" (and legislation that would become "Title IX" hovered over discussions of the merits of coeducation), "a college has the moral obligation to establish how the exclusion it would practice—in the student body, faculty, or curriculum—furthers its announced ends." Dismissing the possibility of there being such an argument, the committee asserted that, "the wider and more various is the campus experience, the better the study (in and out of the classroom), and the more comprehensive the learning is likely to be." Furthermore, "the case for coeducation is that it enhances, not so much the classroom, but Amherst as a place."

And here, in describing *its* idea of the ideal "spirit of the place," the report ascended to a level that committees and task forces seldom if ever reach: Amherst was a place apart, a place where "certain conditions of leisure and intimacy and space obtain"; the "qualities of personal relationship that can come to exist in a community created are more hopeful than those that obtain in the general world; and much of the education Amherst has afforded its students has lain in nurturing feelings of intense personal concern of one human being for another." Since women are "central in human concern everywhere beyond the College," the committee asked that the College "use its resources—its leisure, space, capacity for conversation—to try to adumbrate a generous relation between the sexes, to encourage people of opposite sexes to know one another in an environment free from intense competitive pressure and free (or freer than elsewhere) from the calculated urge for sexual gratification." It acknowledged that, "The matter at stake here is difficult to speak of," certainly in a committee report anyway, but it pressed on nevertheless: "Nothing is easier to mock than what Lawrence once called 'the courage of tenderness.' Yet it is perhaps not sentimental to consider the hope of nourishing precisely that kind of courage lies close to the center of the case for coeducation at Amherst." By this point, any reader who was at all familiar with what motivated Ben DeMott as an educator had no doubt that he had written the "Conclusion," just as anyone who had spent any time with him knew that only he could have cited the guinea and "competitive birling in Northern Maine."

The section on coeducation ended not on a high note, though, but with a long paragraph, lifted from their task force's report, one that distinguished between "the limited and perhaps more selfish interest" of exchange students and the kinds of commitment a degree candidate makes to his or her institution, a comparison that led to this resounding conclusion: "For this reason the admission of one woman to candidacy for a degree at Amherst might have a more drastic effect than the presence of one hundred women as residential exchange students."

And Ward all this time? In a piece titled "Looking Backward" that appeared in the College's yearbook in 1975, he said he had been aware of the work of the Long Range Planning Committee, but that he couldn't remember being engaged by the question of coeducation. In February 1971, in the radio interview that followed his being named president, he obviously knew he had to become engaged, but he wasn't at all sure what he thought: "The presence of women and men in a normal atmosphere is a socially desirable thing. Whether you reach this state at Amherst College through coeducation, I really don't know." Then in June, just before taking office, he said in another interview, "I don't think I would want to defend coeducation on the grounds that it improves the intellectual and educational tone of the place, although I do think it has an effect in that area." As for the question of "the proper social ambiance," did Amherst have to go coeducational to reach it? "I honestly don't know enough to answer that question," he said. In 1975, looking back, he said that he remembered the Class of 1969 with special affection. There were extraordinary students in it; they were the last class that was all-male. At about the same time, he also remembered his response to Boston Latin's becoming a coeducational high school in 1972: "I found myself grumbling about what they were doing to my school."

From a less personal perspective, he was unpersuaded by arguments about the positive effects of "women's liberation." In 1976, commenting on his proposal for a book to be titled *An Examination of the Nature of Masculinity*, for example, he told Robert Fein, a former student, that he was skeptical about the idea, received at the time, that "women are more in touch with themselves than men." "Perhaps, although my unscientific empirical knowledge does not seem overwhelming on that score," he said. He was skeptical too about the place of "personal affect in a specialized, highly contractual society." The *lack* of it might well be highly functional. Women were no more in touch with themselves than men; ergo, they were equally suited to succeed in modern society. "In the kind of world we live in," he reasoned, "most of one's associations are fleeting and impersonal and it may be that the women's movement is a sign of the fact that women are moving into the world of instrumental human relations," not a sign that that world was going to be improved by their greater presence in it. It was a minority opinion at the time, but one that was in keeping with his view of the way of the world, and one that might now seem prescient.

He became president on July 1, 1971. One of the first items of business on his agenda was responding to the Long Range Planning Committee's reports and recommendations, which he did in October. In his conclusion he focused on coeducation, an issue, about which, he confessed, he was "deeply ambivalent." And so he was, though we might also read his confession as disguising the fact that what thought he had given to it had inclined him toward a conclusion that he knew was not popular on campus. He went on to say, though, that what *was* clear to him was that the section on coeducation was the least persuasive of all the sections of the Committee's report. There was so little empirical evidence, so little analysis of Amherst's particular situation. What surprised him, he said, was that the committee had so quickly abandoned "the high ground" of its argument that the sole basis for "discrimination among applicants is quality of mind and imagination, the desire to pursue 'academic excellence,'" in favor of an argument about "the symbolic importance of the place of women at Amherst." He questioned whether, "in the case of gender, Amherst must go coeducational to reach a desirable social goal." And so, because "no constituted committee or group exist[ed] on the campus with sufficient breadth of representation to consider the many ramifications of the issue of coeducation," he intended to create a Select Committee, made up of trustees, alumni, faculty, and students with himself as chairman. It would be what he called "a seminar on coeducation," designed this time "to put me on the spot," he said. It was a response that could only have confirmed whatever doubts and regrets DeMott had about Ward's ascension to the presidency of the College.

Obviously Ward's ambivalence and his caution were in part those of the man who had just become the president of Amherst College, responsible to the trustees who had hired him. He couldn't afford to take the position of his oldest son, David, who had said to him, "If you think this is a first-class educational and intellectual place," well, whether women should be part of it or not was "no longer a question." Nor could he view the issue from an historical perspective, as did Marx and other faculty members, who said when the question first arose that in ten years people

would look back on the answer and see that it was as obvious as the decision to give women the vote. One of these critics was a student, the others
were teachers. Ward couldn't be so sure of what was best for the College
as they could. If he even had an idea of what would be best for it, that idea
wasn't, couldn't be just his. It had to bear some relation, as yet to be determined, to that of the Board of Trustees.

Another way of putting it is to say that the student and the teacher
might easily base their answer to the question of coeducation on principle:
we're going co-ed; now let's figure out how we are going to do it. In effect
he had done that when he sat in at Westover. He had argued that he had
acted personally, on principle. But as president of Amherst College, questions about *how* the institution might become coeducational, *if* it could,
questions about implementation, had to figure largely.

About one thing he was certain, though: What mattered most was the
process. Of that he was sure from the beginning; at the end, looking back
on his presidency, it was what he was most proud of:

> I think the greatest achievement was handling the process of the
> question about the admission of women. I take great pride in the fact that I
> had the stamina to hang in there for four years and just keep defining what
> was at issue; that, to me, is more important than the decision itself.

Nothing could confirm his commitment to the process more than the two
memos he wrote in the summer of 1972, one that made the case for "A
College for Men," the other the case for "A College of Men and Women."
The former ran to seven pages, the latter nine. After it was all over, one
trustee, Ted Cross, said to him, "Especially remarkable was your ability to
write the most convincing paper I have seen against becoming a college
for men and women."

It took three or four or even five years, according to when you think it
started. Some thought it took ages. Some imagined that he was dragging
out the process in order to drown the subject altogether. Some thought he
let it go on for so long because he wanted it to become *his* issue rather than
one that had been raised in the Long Range Planning Committee appointed by Plimpton. It was indeed a very long process, but it illuminates how
the views of an educational institution's constituencies play out in the decisions of its trustees. And it had its dramatic moments.

At its meeting in early November, 1971, the Board discussed whether or not to approve of Ward's plan to form a Select Committee, and if so, to name its two representatives. According to the minutes of Al Guest, the Secretary of the Corporation and formerly the College's Alumni Secretary, the discussion began with a short statement by William Liedtke. He believed that there was little sentiment among the members of the Board for coeducation and so proposed that establishing a Select Committee be postponed for two years. Willard Wirtz, the former Secretary of Labor under Presidents Kennedy and Johnson, and at the time the only member of the Board who had not gone to Amherst, then went to the other extreme: "There is an issue on which the Board should take a position now," he said, "which is, in essence, that 'sex is not a valid element to take into account for determining the educational structure of the College.'" "Mr. Wirtz wished the Board to take a stand on this principle," the minutes continue, "and believed that without such statement, the appointment of the proposed Select Committee would be only a delaying tactic. He believed that it was up to the Board to decide whether implementation of some plan of coeducation should be delayed but that the adoption of his position as stated above should take place now." He proposed an amendment to that effect to the motion to approve the formation of a Select Committee. In the discussion that followed, Ward said he thought both proposals were unwise and that his desire to form a committee ought not to be seen as a means "to defer action." The secretary recorded that John Esty, who had been dean of freshmen at Amherst, and later the headmaster of the Taft School when it went coeducational, "believes in coeducation for Amherst," and that George Peterson, whose extraordinary senior thesis, *The New England College in the Age of the University*, the Amherst College Press had published in 1964, "favors the position and the motion of Mr. Wirtz." So the vote on the amendment was three in favor, nine opposed. Wirtz declined to be considered for the committee. Merrill then cautiously said, "the two trustees to be appointed should perhaps not be committed to either of the two views." The Board's response was to appoint one man, Bob McKean, who was uncommitted. Liedtke was the other.

The faculty elected Rose Olver, the first among them who was female, having arrived in 1962 as an instructor (the rank at which a faculty member began in those days) in the Psychology Department, and Ellen Ryerson, who was in American Studies, two of the four women on a faculty with about 135 members. (Although it may be of only indirect relevance, it is worth noting that nine years earlier, when Olver was hired, Plimpton inquired about the salary of her husband John, an assistant professor of chemistry at the University of Massachusetts at the time. In determining what she should be paid, Plimpton had to make sure that she was paid less.) The students elected Joan Dorman, an exchange student from Smith, whose father had gone to Amherst and who herself would eventually be Assistant Director of Admission at the College for a few years, and a junior, Dirk Roberts. Dorman and Roberts were on record as being in favor of coeducation, as were all of the other 14 students who ran for election to the committee. The two alumni chosen by the Executive Committee of the Alumni Council were Miner Crary, Class of 1942, and Winston Hindle of the Class of 1952. The Dean of Admissions, Ed Wall, was named the committee's secretary; Ward, of course, was to be its chair. The lines for and against were clearly drawn from the outset: the students and faculty (and Ed Wall) for, the Board and the alumni against.

And there was another line, one that had always been there but that would become increasingly important in the debates that followed: the line between those who were and were not on campus, those who were educating and being educated at Amherst and those who were watching over the College and its administration from afar—the trustees and, distanced even further from what was going on at the College, the alumni.

The first meeting of the Select Committee took place on February 2, 1972. It started (one can easily imagine it) with Ward's handing out an "Outline," a syllabus in effect, that in its almost three and a half pages covered "aspects," "issues," "matters," "factors," "queries," and "models" bearing on coeducation. It was proof that Ward was intent upon exhausting all possibilities. The committee would meet every two weeks thereafter, on Thursday evenings, with the final meeting taking place on May 11, 1972. They received reports from the treasurer, the registrar, the alumni office, the development office, the head of buildings and grounds, and other administrators at the College. Position papers were written, polls were taken. In March the Committee sought the views of three women from institutions that had recently become coeducational. One of them, Sheila Tobias, who as assistant provost had presided over Wesleyan's transition to coeducation, is remembered for having made the irrefutable, simple (and humbling) point that women had no need for coeducation at Amherst. It was Amherst that needed coeducation lest it become an anachronism.

Before Ward went off to Paris that spring, thinking that the issue was not all that pressing, and knowing, in any case, that he did not yet know enough on which to base a decision, he announced that he would not come to his conclusion about coeducation until the fall. The Committee submitted its report in July. It was "a concise summary of the major issues which an argument for or against coeducation must confront," a summary that (again) seemed to exhaust all possibilities—"The Legal Context," "The Size of the College," "The Admission Pool," "Five College Cooperation," "Alumni Support," and "Finances." Like the Task Force on Size and Coeducation, it made no recommendation.

Responses to the Select Committee's report were solicited. Predictably, the vast majority of the 200 or so that came from students and the 500 or so that came from alumni were, respectively, in favor of coeducation and opposed to it in about equal proportions. Only twenty-five faculty members commented. The faculty's views were well known; there didn't seem much point in reiterating them. The minority, numbering consistently in the twenties, would hold steady, but it should be noted that ten of them were in the Athletic Department (coaches still being members of the faculty) and five were in the Music Department, the fear of Amherst's losing its reputation as "the singing college," obviously a college in which men did the singing, being as strong as the fear of losing games. Untenured males might well have opposed coeducation too: arguably, with a change they would be less likely to receive tenure, because women would implicitly be preferred.

Ward was scheduled to discuss his recommendation with the Board at its meetings in New York on the weekend of October 27-28. On the second of the month, having gotten word that people were saying he had come to his decision, he reacted strongly, saying in an interview, "I cannot help feeling offended. The answer to the question of coeducation is not a simple moral judgment. I have not allowed myself to formulate a decision." He added that he would decide and send the Board his recommendation two weeks before its meetings at the end of the month. What he recommended was that 1) "Amherst College become a liberal arts college for the education of men and women," 2) that women be admitted as transfer students in the academic year 1974-75, and as entering freshmen in the fall of 1975, and that thereafter the freshman class "be composed of men and women and that admission to Amherst College be without discrimination on the basis of sex" and 3) that beginning in the year 1974-75 "the College expand gradually in size to approximately 1,600 students."

At the heart of his recommendation was the section titled "Reasons for the Admission of Women." He repeated what he had so often said: the goal of an Amherst education was "to develop disciplined intelligence and to foster decent and humane values." But he went on this time to distinguish between the two. "A place of learning," he said, "is built upon qualities of mind and imagination. Sex, religion, ethnic origin, and race do not enter into it." There was no need to distinguish between the sexes "for the purposes of learning, in the sense of discipline of mind and quality of imagination." But "if the other sense of learning, the development of decent and humane persons is an educational goal," then, he would now argue, the quality of education at Amherst could be improved with the addition of the "one element" that it currently lacked: "an excellent social environment for learning." And circling back to what he had said about social change, Amherst would be fulfilling "its responsibility for the achievement of a better society" by admitting women as well as men. The experience and lives of women were changing; they were becoming an increasingly important part of the future of American society, "especially in the managerial and professional life of our institutions." The changes required "institutional change and a change in consciousness," as they had two centuries before. If "liberal learning mean[t], in the enlarged sense of the phrase, a humane sense of social responsibility," as Ward had so often said it did, Amherst had to change: "Responsibility for the future means that the students Amherst now sends into the world must be men and women." He got no more political than that, he didn't talk about Democracy in America, but the implications were there. Giving women the opportunity to come to Amherst turned out to be like giving them the vote, recognizing them as citizens.

Before an overflowing audience in the Chapel on the following Monday, Ward told of his meetings with trustees, made his recommendation public, and informed the audience that the trustees hoped to conclude their review and respond to his recommendation at their meeting at the end of January, though they gave themselves the option of not doing so until their April meeting. There was nothing surprising about the responses of those on campus. The trustees met in November and December. There was nothing surprising about their meetings either—except in one respect. But finally not even it is surprising. The November meeting took place at the Century Club in New York. The Century Club excluded women.

The Board met first with the presidents of Smith (Thomas Mendenhall) and Hampshire ("Chuck" Longsworth), and the Five College Coordinator, North Burn. (David Truman, the president of Mount Holyoke, was on the Board.) The members of the Select Committee were to join the meeting later. Having received advanced notice of where the meeting was going to be held, the three women on the committee, along with Ed Wall, had written Ward asking him to spare them the embarrassment of having to patronize a place that excluded women and to see if the Board could choose sites for future meetings with more sensitivity. The selection of the venue makes it clear that no matter how much the experience and lives of women had changed, there was a limit to how much "institutional change" the Board could countenance. (Only many years later, as a member and a private citizen, would Ward oppose the club's exclusion of women.) On the day of the meeting, the three women sat in the lobby for a while, after which they were taken up to the fifth floor where the meeting was being held—in a service elevator.

At the meeting itself, without actually opposing Amherst's becoming coeducational, Mendenhall and Burn said Five College cooperation would suffer. Longsworth, an alumnus who had been Plimpton's assistant for several years (and would become a member of the Board and eventually its chairman), thought coeducation would strengthen that cooperation and, according to Guest's minutes, furthermore thought that coeducation was "right" for Amherst and that "the question should be resolved on moral terms." He went on about the fact that Amherst was excluding "half the world's population" from the privileges of an Amherst education and all that it presumably does to benefit the world," while considering itself "to be one of the best, if not, in the view of the biased, the best small college in the world." "How, in good sense and good conscience, can that continue to be justified?" he asked.

Everyone else whose contributions to the discussion are recorded followed script. The faculty and student representatives dwelt on numbers, as did Wall, who said that the pool of applicants, both male and of course female, had increased with coeducation at Williams. In response to a question from one of the trustees, about "the effect on breadth and depth of student relationship in a college of larger size," Ryerson said she would rely "on the capacity of persons as individuals to establish relationships," and Roberts "expressed the belief that the sense of community alluded to by former students [i.e., almost all the men in the room] does not now exist." Olver, who later said that her experience on the Committee was what turned her into a feminist, pointed out that were Amherst to remain all-male it would give pause to a woman applying for a teaching position. In light of what he thought would be "the substantial 'hidden cost' of co-education" alumni disapproval above all, Crary recommended that the decision be delayed, after which there followed a discussion of costs and "availability of funds," and a call for "a reordered set of figures on costs of different models and faculty student ratios."

The Board then went into Executive Session, during which—if it hadn't already—the writing began to appear on the wall. Ward said he could work with any of the Board's three alternatives: stay all male, become coeducational, and postpone the decision. The meeting ended with Gellhorn's saying there was no "moral" or "right" thing to do and that there were Five College possibilities that needed to be explored further.

In letters he wrote Merrill, Esty said that he was suspicious of everyone's "applying rational and objective scrutiny to ineffable and irrational things," scrutiny that was appropriate to analyses of a budget, for example, but not to "the quality of human relationships between men and women." Nobody was looking into what actually went on between young people on campus. He was worried about the "messy" situation of non-academic life. His own undergraduate experience and that of his ten years as Freshman Dean confirmed his belief that "Amherst Men are inclined to be boors socially." (In less than a year "Sleazing" would appear. The year before, *Carnal Knowledge*, a film that traces the obsessions of two men [played by Jack Nicholson and Art Garfunkel] with their sex lives from the time they were roommates at Amherst in the '40s through the '60s, came out. Many people noted that it was set at the College for a reason.) Esty was also troubled by what he called "the hidden agenda." Mendenhall and Truman had talked about Five College cooperation, but not about their all-female institutions. Of course they were worried. There was nothing wrong with that. And there was no telling how much the old adage, "Dated Smith, married Mount Holyoke," applied to how many members of the Board, but it was a significant meaning of Five College cooperation that was never mentioned. Esty said he admired Liedke's saying that when he (Liedke) had started on the Select Committee he was against coeducation but that he moved toward it as a result of his experience on the committee, but, he said, "I just can't quite get over the hump." (Nor did he.) "It's a simple statement but I trust it," Esty wrote. "I can't believe we got at the full range of thoughts and feelings of all the guests or staff or Trustees sitting around that big table at the Century," he told Merrill. "The woman next to me was ready to explode!"

At its meeting in December the writing was again quite clear. Ward began by saying that he had not based his recommendation on a "moral" or "right" basis, went on to report on the students' and faculty's votes in favor of coeducation that had been taken since the trustees' last meeting, and suggested a gradual increase in the student body, "first perhaps to 1,500." But then Merrill took everyone back to square one. Referring to a memorandum that he had circulated, he summarized its five points: (1) the case for coeducation had not been made, (2) Amherst has women in classes and on the campus, (3) small size should be preserved, (4) alumni support would decline, (5) a delay would provide vital time for a sounder judgment on the merit.

All of the comments that followed were predictable, with the possible exception of Francis Plimpton's, who, the minutes read, "believes the issue is sociological"—namely, "There is a strong notion in human relationships for the equality of women, a natural relationship." William Hastie, the first black federal judge, Dean of the Howard Law School, and governor of the Virgin Islands under Roosevelt and Truman, made the point more forcefully: "The fact that my college-age daughter would never be able to go Amherst," he declared, "seems to me an injustice!"

Ward had no trouble reading the signs. On the last day of the year he wrote Merrill about the agenda of the January meeting. Merrill was probably correct, he said: "It will be difficult to achieve a consensus on either side, yes or no, on the question of coeducation at Amherst. That probability means your position on delay, for these and other reasons, will prevail." He went on to say that when that probability became a certainty he would be ready to work with the Board on the best possible case for it, defend it on campus, and work for it in the years to follow. The College shouldn't get "embroiled in the same discussion within a year or two; he thought six might be "the magic number," might provide "a sensible space of time."

By the time the sharply divided Board turned down his recommendation, Ward was, of course, in favor of coeducation, but Esty has described him as planting his feet firmly on the periphery of their meetings: "He would present the issue before us, maybe make a recommendation, and then retire from the fray of discussion....Bill seemed to think the elegance of his opening argument would carry the day." There are many ways to explain Ward's position—or his reluctance to engage once he had made his position known. Overall was his strong belief in the process, a process, one in which he didn't think his voice should be more influential than anyone else's.

It must also be said, though, that having recently made it widely, nationally, known what he thought was right on Vietnam was not going to make him very persuasive this time around. But Westover or not, there was the fact that he was the only man in the room other than Wirtz who had not gone to Amherst. Neither those other men nor the vast majority of alumni were about to forget their memories of an all-male Amherst or relinquish the privileges that could follow. (Their having daughters who would stand a better than average of being admitted seems to have made little difference—Hastie's declaration notwithstanding.) Paul Bragdon, an alumni Trustee throughout Ward's presidency, has spoken of Ward's "deference" towards the Board but also of his own feeling that he should let Ward have his say and then support him—and that the Board should have supported the president as well. Bragdon knew whereof he spoke: he was having a far easier time of it as the new president of Reed College. Years later his conclusion was that the Amherst Trustees "made a hash of coeducation."

When Ward announced the Board's decision to a large audience in the Chapel the following Monday afternoon, he was, in the *Student* reporter's words, "pensive and tired." Ward said he regretted it but that it would be

childish to be angry and arrogant to presume he should have his way because he was right and those who differed wrong. He had learned not to
waste energy over what had been decided and he urged others not to either. Then he listed the alternatives that were before the Board and said
that the one they had chosen was necessary given the division that existed
among its members. Before the meeting was over Ryerson asked Ward
if the trustees' deliberations had convinced him that coeducation was
not the best thing for Amherst after all—he sounded that weary—which
prompted an emphatic No.

Angrily (and as presumptuously as a mortal can sound), the editorial in
that issue of the *Student* opened with, "Father forgive them for they know
not what they do," and ended with the declaration that, "Students will find
it difficult to interpret Trustee inaction on coeducation as anything but a
rule by fiat and authority, made by a degree of men largely out of touch
with the campus community and unresponsive to its needs." The students'
and faculty's response was that the trustees had little idea of what went
on at the institution that was in their trust, and that they ought to come
and see—and listen—for themselves. The faculty passed a resolution that
"urgently request[ed] a meeting with the Board on the campus before its
April meeting, for consideration of the Board's decision on coeducation"
by a vote of 86 to 26. Having gathered almost 750 signatures, the Student
Assembly voted 16-2 to ask the Board to come to the campus to discuss its
decision with members of the student body at the same time.

At their meeting with the trustees, most of the students' efforts went
into describing what life was like at an all-male educational institution
that welcomed females only as visitors. Roberts cited the disadvantages
of having only males in, say, the course on "Eros and Love." "There are
obvious social reasons for coeducation," he said. "But either you don't understand these or you are not listening." Women cited incidences of verbal abuse. Merrill said that of course he knew attitudes and manners had
changed since the days when he was an undergraduate (and the tone of
the meeting certainly confirmed that this was so), but he did not think that
"the monastic atmosphere suggested that women were in any way inferi-
or to men." Genuinely perplexed, he asked the students why they didn't
just stop abusing women. Roberts' answer was: "Mr. Merrill, as long as
the black man is drinking from another fountain, you're going to call him

a nigger." It was ritually acknowledged that the analogy was not exact—
and then often used. It was later used by an exchange student from Smith
when the question of principle came up. Sounding like Thoreau, or Ward
channeling Thoreau, she wrote in a letter to the trustees, "Principles, as
we all know, are not principles if we do not act upon them. If I own slaves,
I do not dispose of the moral issues involved by saying 'My plantation will
lose money if I free them.'" It was used at the faculty's meeting with the
trustees. "Blacks and whites studying and living together learn things they
could not learn in the classroom," was one professor's version of the analogy. "The same is true for men and women, they can learn as they should
only by learning and living together."

The questions of who knew what about the "reality" of life at Amherst
and of the relation between principle and implementation dominated talk
about coeducation for at least the two years between the trustees' rejection
of Ward's recommendation and their acceptance of it. At their respective
meetings with the Board in April, the students raised the latter but dwelt
more on the former; the faculty did the reverse. Professor Greene began
the discussion by referring back to the faculty's resolution urging the trustees to meet with them, pointing specifically to the apparent contradiction
between their stating that it was morally imperative that women have
equal access to higher education and then continuing to violate that principle. "What, indeed, *is* the Board's view?" he asked. Merrill repeated that
the Board was sharply divided "as to whether the decision should be made
now or later," which seemed to suggest that timing was all that was issue,
that the Board *was* committed to the principle. But their Statement had
also said that, "Despite agreement on principle," the trustees were "divided on the application." Their concern was that "the change to coeducation
might imperil the educational quality of Amherst College...not because
of the admission of women but because of changes required to make that
possible." Maybe the same educational and social benefits could come
from Five College cooperation. So the Board *wasn't* committed to the principle—as it applied to Amherst, anyway. There were two principles really:
the general one about nondiscrimination and a specific one about making
sure that nothing was done that would hurt Amherst. The Smith student
had it right: it was the slave owner's dilemma.

The analogy became closer when, according to the minutes, Merrill told the faculty, "Almost all alumni he had talked with are opposed." It became even closer when Peterson said, at the trustee meeting with the students, that the only real obstacle was fear of losing alumni support. Possibly the overstatement of a supporter, but Merrill himself provided an amusing bit of evidence that shows how powerful the trustees thought the alumni were. Trustee meetings traditionally started with a prayer. At the one that took place after the day the favorable decision was made two years later, to the prayer that he offered Merrill tacked on, "And God help us with the alumni." The students weren't the only ones who thought the issue was so important as to warrant getting God involved.

The response of many on campus was: what more do you want? The answer was, in effect, more of the same, more about size, more about Five College cooperation, more about buildings, more about admissions, more about other institutions. "We need more facts," as Gellhorn put it, "All the Board has said is, 'Why don't you try harder? We're not going to do it for you.'" In September, at the College, a plan emerged. There were committees in place that could work on most of the issues. The one area that hadn't been explored was the experience of comparable institutions in the years since they had become coeducational. Professors Greene and Gordon and two students were appointed to a Visiting Committee. Only its news was fresh. Or better said, when it reported that the coeducation issue was stale, the last barrier erected by those who were adamantly opposed to it fell. The report was exhaustive and incontrovertible. The committee produced a "Master List of Questions about the Experience of Other Institutions" that contained approximately 175 items; they then spread out in pairs to Williams, Dartmouth, Trinity, Haverford, Bryn Mawr, Princeton, Bowdoin, Wesleyan, and Yale (in that order), ending up with a visit to Wabash, the one institution that had decided to remain all-male (for financial reasons). Not a question that was on Ward's handout at the first meeting of the Select Committee went unasked; the answers, tentative at this point, were similar to those that had been worked out over the months and months that had followed. The Report's 74 pages added up to the conclusion that "the experience of admitting women to these former's men's colleges is now considered beneficial on all counts by the institutions themselves."

To Ward, as we have seen many times, process was paramount, and hard though it may be to believe, it wasn't over. The Board wasn't going to decide until November. In the meantime, the Board wanted "information and considered assessment of gains and losses to the College for each of four possibilities": namely, the status quo, coeducation with no change of size, coeducation with 1,600 students, and with 2,000 students, with all the usual factors taken into account. In May the committees were to circulate drafts of their final reports to the Executive Committee of the Alumni Council, to commentators, the Faculty, the administration, the Board, and then the president; over the summer he and his staff would gather together and where necessary supplement the reports and provide a Casebook on the four alternatives. In the fall the material in the Casebook would be discussed by the various parties, after which it would be forwarded to the trustees, and in November they would decide. (Ward had 1,500 copies of the 380-page Casebook printed up. He apologized for the expense but said that it was politically necessary.)

In October the faculty reaffirmed its support of coeducation with another lopsided vote—95 to 29. At its meeting the atmosphere seemed already festive. Most memorably (and to some senior faculty members, unseemly), before the vote nine women stood up in the back, opened up the raincoats they had on, and displayed the t-shirts they were wearing. "Keep Abreast of the Times—Vote Yes" was emblazoned on them. On October 18 the Executive Committee and Commentators of the Alumni Council met with the Board of Trustees at the University Club in New York and informed it that "on a reasonably close vote" they recommended that "Amherst should not change to become a full residential institution for men and women."

The next day the trustees met in Amherst. After another extended discussion of items that had been explored in the Casebook, George Shinn, who had succeeded Merrill as chairman, went to the heart of the matter: "Should Amherst become a college for men and women?" he asked. Then "Spike" Beitzel reframed the question: "Is anyone against Amherst going coed on a matter of principle?" Shinn came back with: "Whether or not the Amherst trustees were in favor of co-ed as principle is the question," and again, "Yes or no. Can you perceive of a model that would be acceptable to you for co-ed at Amherst?" A straw vote was taken: 12 could (a few minutes later, when two absentees were spoken for, the number was 14), three could not. "I think the next logical step," Shinn then said, "would be to go back and focus on models." Principle had preceded and prevailed over implementation. The last item of business was how the Board would announce its decision after it had taken a formal vote on November 2.

Some on the Board shared Ward's pride in the way the decision had been arrived at, but it has to be said that it was not arrived at in so reasonable a manner as his ideal would have had it. At the beginning of October, the director of development forwarded a letter to Ward that he had received from an alumnus with this note attached: "To my knowledge this is the first letter we have had from anyone indicating that he had changed his mind. At least we now know it's possible." A lighthearted gesture perhaps, but at the end of the trustee meeting on October 19, Cross was not joking when he said, "A good deal of the trustees feel that they have been pressured into this co-ed idea. The decision has been extracted in many ways."

Ward's own response is perplexing. It reminds one of his response to being arrested at Westover. ("I really didn't know what to do. What a crazy world this is!") "I felt nothing at all," he said:

> What stands out vividly in my memory is that when the vote by the Board on the admission of women was taken, I felt nothing at all. I discovered what post-parturition means. I felt no pleasure, either with the decision or with the fact it finally had been made. I had no feeling, no affect at all. I was simply empty.

He went on to tell of a reporter who said he looked "so cold and so grim he was sure the Board had voted against coeducation," and to say that it was not until the middle of the following week that "a sense of pleasure made itself felt." We might write his response off to exhaustion, but not even he was willing to do that. "I was reminded again," he said, "how slenderly we know ourselves."

There was Westover, coeducation, and the greatest success of all, being elected to the presidency (which he had once announced with a "haunted look"). It's as if at these times he was like the would-be heroic ambulance driver of his little Boston Latin story—diving under his vehicle in fear. Fear of success, we might call it, or, more specifically in his case, fear that he didn't measure up, even when he had.

THE CURRICULUM

WARD WOULD always be remembered as the president who was arrested at Westover Air Force Base and, editing the facts of the case, brought coeducation to Amherst. (The two photographs below the portrait that hangs in the anteroom of the College's archives that is dedicated to his memory illustrate the point.) But at the outset, he imagined a very different future for his presidency. In his first official appearance before the College, at Convocation, he declared, "The first and most essential question before us this fall is that of the curriculum." He intended to focus attention on how the College could accomplish the educational mission that he had written and spoken about so often, which is to say to focus on the curriculum. But history intervened. The College's attention was diverted. The curriculum would have to wait. The story of how it came into being, and what it was that emerged, is not so engaging as the story of Westover or coeducation; moreover, Ward's role in it was limited. It had to be. The curriculum was the faculty's business more than his, but indirectly it bears on the story of his presidency. We must attend to it for a moment.

Almost since its founding in 1821, Amherst's concern about its educational offerings was exceptional. The faculty's 1826 report on the curriculum was one of the first of its kind; many were to follow; between 1938 and 1977 alone, there would be ten such reports. No curriculum was so distinctive, so demanding and, it followed, so fondly recalled, as the "New Curriculum," which went into effect in 1947. It required that all freshmen take year-long courses in Physics and Mathematics, English and the Humanities, European Civilization, and a Foreign Language (or, if they tested out successfully, a course of their own choosing), followed by another year-long course in American Civilization that was required of sophomores. It takes very little digging to discover in that curriculum the roots of alumni resistance to change. (And now, a half a century later, when so much *has* changed, it is still invoked by alumni as the ideal means of educating a man.) In 1966 the "New" curriculum was replaced by a *new* curriculum, one that required only that students take three "Problems of Inquiry" courses, one in each of the traditional divisions, the Natural Sciences, the Social Sciences, and the Humanities, during their first two years at the College, and fulfill a "distribution requirement" consisting of two

two-course sequences, one in the division in which a student majored, and a three-course sequence in another department, along with the language requirement.

But in the '60s and '70s curricular requirements at colleges and universities throughout the country would undergo scrutiny and eventually, loosenings. Only Amherst and Brown went so far as to abolish requirements altogether. The so-called "P.I." curriculum lasted four years, after which "colloquia, freshman seminars, and multi-variants of courses to be called Inquiry" were offered but not required. In 1971, when Ward began as president, other than the vestigial language requirement, a student had only to take thirty-two courses and complete a major in order to graduate. In 1973, the language requirement, and the following year, the physical education requirement, would be dropped. Without requirements, being therefore "open," it was nevertheless a curriculum in the minds of some. Students still had to take thirty-two courses and fulfill the requirements of a major in order to graduate. Even Ward went so far as to say on one occasion, in a talk on "The Curriculum and Politics" that he gave to the parents in the fall of 1972, that the "open curriculum" was "the embodiment of the ideal of a free society." But to most alumni and trustees, and to many faculty members as well, it was not the same thing as Amherst's having a curriculum. Nor was it really to Ward. However much his and everyone else's attention was diverted by the events we have been describing, he continued to assert that at Amherst College, the curriculum was of the first importance.

Thus in his report to the Board of Trustees on the academic year 1972-73, he said that, "Without a clear sense of all the necessities imposed by our educational goals, it is difficult to be fully responsible to any other major question of policy." Accordingly, though he alluded to coeducation, he did not mention it by name. It was not that "other aspects of the College" were not important, he wrote, but he wanted to make clear what he thought was the essential philosophy of the College. The college performed a "social function." A great majority of the graduates went on to careers in law, medicine, education and other professions. So too did graduates of universities. But as he had said in his Inaugural Address (which he then quoted), "I believe and feel deeply that the end of education is to train the mind to further a decent and humane life." So it had always been at Amherst. The means had changed but there had "persisted a commitment to the notion that education at Amherst is devoted to both mind and—dare one still say it?—character." He acknowledged that it might "take a secular act of faith today to believe that the College can still commit itself to both intelligence and humaneness," but he would keep that faith.

A little history will underscore just how difficult the task would be. In 1821, in *his* inaugural address, Zephaniah Swift Moore, Amherst's first president (and the first of five minsters who would preside over the College until 1890) said, "Intellectual discipline is important, but moral and religious discipline is infinitely more important." Under the fifth, Julius Hawley Seelye, that discipline was intended to result in the sterling character of Amherst graduates rather than in their future as ministers, but the priorities remained the same: the College "will ever regard the personal piety of its pupils as of far higher importance than all other attainments," he declared. The president who led the college into the twentieth century, George Harris (also a minister) said, "culture is the primary object of education," and that the "College's goal was "to train men for service in democracy." It was in his era—more specifically, under the influence of the most powerful member of his faculty, Charles Edward Garman, professor of philosophy—that the ideal of "character" became of primary importance. In the second half of the nineteenth century, as Thomas LeDuc tells us in *Piety and Intellect at Amherst College, 1865-1912*, "evangelical fervor" having "subsided, men came to place less emphasis on conversion and more on conduct." Garman's teaching (again Le Duc) "balanced the ambition of youth with altruism.

> It was saturated with optimism and hope. On the one hand, it rescued from the threat of social confiscation the individualistic tradition of America; on the other, it told men that they will realize themselves fully if they serve one another.
>
> The doctrine of stewardship, or service, was the climax of Garman's course and the heart of his philosophy.

Again and again, Ward would gesture towards the "decent and humane life" he wanted the students to pursue. As we have seen, he saw himself as "a secular substitute in the modern world for...the ministerial preacher of earlier days." But well over half a century had passed. In the '70s one had rhetorically to *dare* to talk about "character" and about the value of stewardship and service.

In his Report to the Board, Ward went on to say that if the College couldn't prescribe a curriculum based on certain subjects as it had a century before, or on certain specialized skills, as it tried to do in the required "P.I." courses, "perhaps it might return to its origins" and find direction from the words of the College's first president, Zephaniah Swift Moore. He didn't cite Moore's words about the primacy of "moral and religious" over "intellectual discipline"; rather his words were about kinds of intellectual disciplines, about "the mental habits, the qualities of mind and imagination," that ideally a student had acquired. They ranged from the ability to express oneself with intellectual precision and emotional force and a sense of what it means to be responsible, to a question of self-awareness and the ability to step outside oneself and be empathic to others who were separated in time and space, to a sense of mastery and the capacity to enjoy life. He spoke once again of his overriding concern that contemporary culture did not provide "an unambiguous sense of what it means to serve the public good" and of how he always sought to alleviate that concern: "The historical circumstances of our time...drive us back to what we never should have forgotten, the centrality of the process by which we reach the ends implicit in what it means to be a liberal and humane person." If the student could develop the mental habits that were those of a liberal and human person, he would know how to serve the public good. Having acquired those habits as a learner among fellow learners, he would go on to be a democratic citizen. He cited the words of another president of the College, the fourth, William Augustus Stearns, "The public conscience must be educated or we are lost as a nation," cited them too with some hesitation. "In our sophistication," Ward said, we might "smile at the moral earnestness" of the man, but he went on to ask, "Can we say him wrong?" No, we might reply, but we might still go on to ask: could one really imagine an educational process, or a curriculum, that could inspire students to go forth and illuminate society in the present, secular age?

In his Convocation Address in the fall of 1973 he urged the faculty to make "a serious effort to examine and assess their present offerings and requirements." The first result was a Committee on Educational Policy proposal in December 1973 that would make them even less responsible for the process than ever before. They would not impose any structure on the curriculum, they could not require anything, they would only advise. The students, on the other hand, would be required to submit annual statements to their advisor defining their goals and stating how the courses they intended to take enabled them to fulfill those goals. The structure of the curriculum, in other words, depended on the relationship between students and their advisors. Early the following year, the faculty turned the proposal down. It wanted *something* more than that. A year after the Board's decision on coeducation, in November 1975, the CEP came up with as little as it had two years before. It concluded that the College's curriculum in its present form, if it *was* a curriculum, was basically sound. It offered students a few guidelines, but again it was assumed that students would work out ways to broaden and deepen their education beyond their majors. And again, the faculty rejected the CEP's conclusion. Then, that same night, by a vote of 78 to 25, they voted to create an *ad hoc* committee that was to come up with a proposal for a new curriculum in two years. Ward was delighted. A week later, he began a Thursday Evening talk he gave in the Chapel on "Liberal Education and Modern Society" by saying that the faculty's vote was "the most important vote taken by the college in recent years," and, then going out on a very shaky limb, added, "and I do not exclude the decision to include women in the life of the college."

In the spirit of yesteryear, the students wanted to be represented on the *ad hoc* committee. In February almost half of the undergraduate body signed a petition calling not only for that (which the Committee of Six rejected by a vote of 5 to 1) but for representation on the Board of Trustees and for a voice in the election of non-student trustees (proposals which the Board all but ignored). That same month, a two-page article in the *Student* assessing Ward's presidency after five years made an undeniable point: "The Honeymoon is Over" was its title. Ward was no longer "the Westover President"—"everyone's friend." He was now "'The President,' first and foremost an administrator, which has won him points among trustees and alumni, but has resulted in an evaporation of his student following." The trustees and the alumni wanted if not what they remembered as a curriculum, at least some order, some discipline. On *this* issue anyway, they could approve of what Ward was doing and, as everyone knew, it would follow that they would happily contribute to the Alumni Fund.

The faculty had agreed at least to try to answer the question of what it meant to be a liberally educated man or woman; the *ad hoc* committee submitted its report early in 1977. It proposed a curriculum that would be "introductory" in that it gave students "an idea of the essential nature of the academic life they were entering," and "distributive" in that it gave students "exposure to some variety of subjects and intellectual styles." The former would be accomplished by requiring students to take three courses designed as "critical introductions to liberal studies," three "ILS" courses, in their first year. Each would be planned and taught by a small group of faculty members, and would fall into one of three categories: "Sign, Form, and Meaning," "Nature: Observation and Theory," and "Social Life and Social Change." No course was to last more than three years. (Perhaps Ward had repeated to the committee what he said when he decided to be a candidate for the presidency about how long a course could retain its freshness.) The "distributive" function would be accomplished by the "adjunct program," which required that beginning in the second term of their sophomore year students elect four courses (three outside their major) united by a theme or question of their own devising, that they complete the four courses by the end of the fall term of their senior year, and that by the end of the spring term they complete a short written description, appropriately titled, which met with their advisor's approval.

Writing about the importance of the curriculum in his 1972-73 report to the trustees, Ward had made the point that it was the faculty's responsibility and that, "Nowhere do I know a Faculty more willing to sit together in meeting and debate as a corporate body on issues which are of importance to the life of the College." In its response to the *ad hoc* committee's report, the faculty was as good as his words. No greater proof that the College was, as it was proud to claim in those days, "a teaching college," no more convincing evidence of the faculty's willingness to meet and discuss the important issues facing the College, need be adduced than the fact that the curriculum was discussed in six meetings, six three-hour evening meetings, that spring. In those meetings questions of staffing the new courses, of increased advising loads, of "distribution," and of what was of most importance, the number of ILS courses that would be required, arose. At one of them Ward pleaded with the faculty to approve the curriculum, "approve *some* form of curricular revision," according to the *Student* report, "citing outside expectations that Amherst will be among the leaders in the nationwide search for an effective liberal arts curriculum," citing too the "up-coming capital fund drive" which he, at least, could not ignore. In its sixth meeting, the faculty approved a motion to require two ILS courses, the adjunct program and a pattern of distribution recommended but not required by the committee.

The very fact that there was a new curriculum met with some trustee approval, but not much enthusiasm. There was no core, no required distribution. Ward concluded a forward to a 1978 reprint of the original committee report by saying that "to the degree that Amherst College remains true to the worth of the process of education as its chief and central purpose, one may confidently predict that seven years hence there will be another committee on the curriculum seeking once again to discover new ways to embody a traditional ideal." He called it "a modest conclusion." In fact, it turned out to be slightly *im*modest: the ILS curriculum lasted only five years if you include the year of planning. Suffice it to say, he had scored a "modest" victory.

Under Ward a new curriculum came into being, but it was only half of what he envisaged. In no uncertain terms the committee's report was dismissive of what he often said about preparing students to be humane or contribute to the common good, and the faculty certainly had no such ideals in mind when it finally accepted a version of what the committee proposed. The report said outright, "If Amherst has a distinctive role to play in undergraduate education, it cannot arise from some imaginary... consensus about what 'all graduates should know, or what the future requirements of good citizenship will be, or what the world needs from its educated minority." It was a glaring omission, an unambiguous declaration.

But Ward never ceased to imagine that the students in the institution over which he presided could be made to aspire to such heights. He never did, though somewhere—deep down—even as he continued to argue to the contrary, he had a gnawing sense that you just might not be able to educate men and women to be "gentle and humane." Perhaps there was something about "human nature" that precluded reaching that goal by *any* means. In his Convocation speech in the fall of 1977 he had confessed, "in my less sanguine moments, I am attracted to the bleak assumptions about human nature and innate depravity held by the Calvinistic founders of this place." Four years before, in his annual report to the trustees, he had turned to his forebears, Reverend/Presidents Moore and Stearns, for inspiration and support, but now he had to confess that in his darker states of mind he was drawn to nameless others whose preaching emphasized the undeniable fact of man's Original Sin. And as we have seen, the more evidence he came upon of what he considered Amherst's failure to produce more humane persons, or the more evidence of what he thought was students' lack of "character," their indecency—the "Sleazing" article, students breaking pool cues, faculty crushing out cigarettes on the rug—the darker were his moods.

In the spring of 1976, only 25 students showed up at a Thursday evening assembly in the Chapel. Ward brought them back to his house for what the *Student* called a Thursday Evening Chat. "What's going on?" he asked, and then ruefully observed that something had been missing over the previous four years. Students were now more competitive and "somewhat self-centered"; what was missing was the "social commitment of the sixties," he said. Students' commitment to others, to each other, to the community, the *polis,* had been replaced by individual students' commitment to their individual comfort and careers. Marx had spoken to that fact before he left Amherst. Years later, in an article on "The Making of the Liberal Arts College Identity," Hugh Hawkins noted that between 1970 and 1987 the proportion of entering college students who embraced "being well-off financially" as their goal rose from 39 to 76 percent "as later generations turned sharply to self-interested and economically focused goals." Who could deny that on the whole, over the course of the Ward years, the students had become less concerned about others, in that sense less humane, but not because somehow their "natures" had changed. History took place at more of a distance; it didn't impinge on their lives as much. In the fall of 1976, in a "Case Statement" for a capital campaign, Ward noted that 88 percent of those who had graduated the previous spring had gone on to "advanced professional training in law, business, medicine, government, and the learned professions." And then immediately thereafter he said, "In the tension between its educational and social purpose, Amherst College finds its essential purpose: the liberal education of men and women to play a responsible part in our complex society." Assuming that was its

essential purpose, perhaps those who were going on to "advanced professional training" could fulfill it, but it seemed undeniable that in the terms
that had informed Ward's thinking for years, a strong undertow was car-
rying American culture back from the ideal of democratic idealism to egoism - selfishness—and taking Amherst and her students along with it.

RACE

WESTOVER, COEDUCATION, and the curriculum all involved Ward
in more or less political situations, ones in which his beliefs and sympathies and inclinations had to be defined and acted upon with an awareness
of what the students or the faculty or the trustees thought, an awareness
of what was possible, even if, as was the case of the most momentous of
his decisions he ultimately decided to do what he thought was right and
to miscalculate or ignore the consequences. When racial relations were at
issue, though they were, of course, politically loaded, he could, and did act
on his own, confident that the political chips would fall his way—if in fact
he even thought much about the political consequences of his actions. To
put it another way, in attending to Ward's responses and actions during
the racial crises that occurred during his presidency, we can clearly see
him as the humane person that he was.

Coming from where he did, he was always sympathetic toward those
who were not considered, or who did not consider themselves, part of
the dominant culture—in a word, the Others. Ironically, as we have seen,
he was not an exceptionally strong defender of the Other whose position
Simone de Beauvoir famously defined and described in *The Second Sex*.
Women had their privileges, they could be dominant themselves, if only
complicitously. On the few occasions when gayness was involved, when
his friend Martin Duberman came to give a lecture at Amherst, for example, or in the case of a faculty member who crossed the line with students,
he was supportive and applauded what was right, sensitive and judicious
in handling what was not. Coming from Dorchester and Brighton, he was
consistently and continually sympathetic towards those he thought of as
members of the working-class and with the Irish. As he was making his
way up the academic ladder, and later, as president of Amherst College, he

became more and more sympathetic with blacks, his sympathies running the more deeply because as an Americanist he knew more about the history of blacks in America than most. Recalling his letter to the black student who was reclaiming his heritage by changing his name, we may go further and say Ward identified with them: "May both of us hope that generations from now men and women may look back on us with pride," he wrote.

There was little or nothing he could do about them when he was at Princeton—they just weren't there—but at Amherst, first as a faculty member and as a member of the Committee of Six there was a fair amount he could do, and as we have seen, what he did was influential in the trustees' selection of him as president. There was of course much more that he could do—that he *had* to do—when he became president. In his dealings with racial issues he clearly brought his ideals to bear. He acted out of his humane concern for others and at the same time for the good of "the place" over which he presided. He was at his best, even when—how could it be, given racism in America?—it was not enough.

On one occasion during his first year as president, invested with much more authority than he had ever had before, his very presence, his being Bill Ward the president, was effective. Some time during that year the members of the Afro-Am Society planned to take action once again, in fact once again to take the same action that they had taken in the year before: namely, to occupy several buildings on campus. When word of the time and place of the planning meeting somehow reached Ward, by whatever leak, he had to do no more than walk over to the Black Culture Center where they were meeting and enter it unannounced in order to bring about the end of the planning. He was the trusted authority.

And as president he could see to it, or entrust others to see to it, that the demands that had been on the Afro-Am Society's agenda at least since the Day of Concern in the spring of 1969 were met. First and foremost among them was the creation of a Black Studies Department. It was on the agendas of black student organizations at colleges and universities across the country in the '60s, an item was impossible to address successfully. There were all those institutions competing with one another for faculty who didn't exist in anything like sufficient numbers precisely because of what blacks were fighting against: a society, that society's educational system in particular, that had failed to admit and produce more than a handful of the teachers and scholars that everyone was looking for. Moreover, black students were asking for a kind of education that institutions like Amherst had not traditionally sought to provide. They sought knowledge that they could apply in service to their community. Their commitment sounded a lot like what Ward and his predecessors had so often spoken about, but they meant commitment, real commitment, to *their* community, to black communities in Holyoke and Springfield, say, or to whatever black community they came from—nothing so vague as "the community" or "the common good," or "democratic society." They'd heard enough of such talk; they knew where they stood in relation to those vague entities. On the other hand, given their demands and the lack of any precedents they could turn to in their efforts to see to it that those demands would be met, they had no clear idea of what *their* curriculum would look like. Members of the Board were hesitant. An important field, yes, but was there really a need for a separate department? For their part, though, throughout these years, Ward and the Amherst faculty and administration worked consistently and hard to honor their commitment to Black Studies. Though it would take time, and though there would be setbacks, eventually a Black Studies Department would be firmly in place.

Asa Davis, who had attended the Harvard Divinity School and then earned his Ph.D. at Harvard, and had taught in Nigeria for nine years, came on from San Francisco State to be the chairman in 1970, the year after the faculty voted unanimously in support of the establishment of a Black Studies Department. William Cole in Black Studies and Music and the poet Sonia Sanchez were added the following year, the latter soon succeeding Davis as chair. Both left before standing for tenure, the former for Dartmouth, where he encountered virulent racist treatment, the latter to become poetry editor of *Muhammed Speaks*, but by 1977 the department would number five and have enrollments totaling 135 students, close to the average of the previous five years, and by then it would be part of a Five College program that offered 50 courses. Black Studies was bound to succeed. Efforts to give black students what it thought was the best education possible was an important part of Amherst's heritage.

If not the first (histories differ), Amherst was among the first colleges in the United States to graduate a black student (in 1826). Its alumni include William Henry Lewis, the first black all-American football player and subsequently the assistant attorney general of the United States, Dr. Charles Drew, whose work lies behind the preservation and banking of blood, Charles Hamilton Houston, "Mr. Civil Rights Lawyer," as Thurgood Marshall called him, and William Hastie, the first black federal judge (Chief Judge of the Third Circuit Court of Appeals), Dean of the Howard Law School, and Governor of the Virgin Islands under Roosevelt and Truman— Hastie, whom we heard speak out in favor of coeducation as a trustee, Hastie, whom Ward called, in review of a biography of him, "one of the great men of modern American history. Not one of the great black men—one of the great men."

The College was fortunate in having as its Dean of the Faculty Prosser Gifford, a man who was exceptionally well-qualified to bring Black Studies into being. Gifford and Ward came from different worlds. They were never close; they never worked closely together. When asked to describe their conversations about the curriculum—Ward wanting one, Gifford having drawn up one of those lists intended to help advisors guide students in their choices of courses—Gifford replied that they had never talked about it. But Ward could confidently trust Gifford to lead the effort to establish a Black Studies Department at Amherst and confidently leave it to Gifford to run the meetings that led to the Five College program. Gifford had received his Ph.D. in African History at Yale (his thesis was on the economic and administrative history of the Rhodesias from 1914 to 1953) and had taught courses there and at Amherst. He knew as well as or better than anyone around that Black Studies had to involve people of African ancestry in Africa and the Diaspora: he had lived in Rhodesia in 1963-64. Ward was free to concentrate on the society that was Amherst and the individuals who made it up.

After Westover, most of those individuals ceased to be politically active. The war seemed to be winding down: in 1973, a cease-fire agreement was signed in Paris and the draft ended; in 1975 the last American troops left Vietnam. But racism in America was systemic, it manifested itself everywhere, it wasn't going to go away with the end of a war or the passing of a piece of legislation. Nothing could inspire collective action on the part of the student body as a whole, but though their attention might be temporarily deflected, black students were determined to change the pattern of history—by action if necessary. When an "incident," an instance of racial injustice, or what was perceived to be an instance of racial injustice, occurred on campus, their attention would immediately snap back into focus, as would Ward's. He did not hesitate to speak and act for the institution. During his time as president there were three that were specially— profoundly—upsetting.

The first was not an "incident" but a tragedy. On the afternoon of Wednesday, September 12, 1973, a black student, Gerald Penny, having been at Amherst for at most two weeks, drowned in the college pool. He was trying to meet one of the last of the college's requirements for graduation, which was to swim four laps and thus pass a swimming test, or, failing it, just take a swimming course. A significantly disproportionate number of black students ended up doing the latter, some putting it off until their senior year. The requirement was a sore point among the black students— swimming being loaded with racial implications—not the less sore when someone was sensitive to those implications and acted accordingly. When the swimming coach asked black students if they were telling the truth when they said they could swim, he was considered by some to be a racist.

Penny had come to Amherst from St. Augustine's, a highly selective black Catholic high school in New Orleans, known for its strict discipline (corporal punishment was not prohibited until 2011); he had been second in his class, a student council representative, highly motivated, well-liked. He had been offered full scholarships by Notre Dame and Penn and Xavier (in his hometown) as well as by Amherst. It was said that the preceding evening he was concerned about the test. He must have been more than concerned, he must have been scared: he couldn't swim (it was the one undeniable fact of the matter) and it wasn't clear to him, or to anyone else it seemed, what happened if you failed the test. Some said that the test didn't matter all that much, but not having shown up the first time it was administered, Penny had received a note from the Athletic Department which seemed to suggest that it mattered a lot. It informed him that he had to take it by the 14th, and that if he didn't—"If you fail to take the test your name will be turned into the Dean's Office and you will receive a FAIL for the first unit of physical education." Nothing about the course.

What was a highly motivated, well-disciplined, successful freshman to do? As Ward said in his report to the trustees, "He wanted to do what was expected of him and did not demur." So while others, fifteen or twenty others, a faculty member (Marx, as fate would have it) and his wife, three young girls (daughters of professors), and some students enjoyed the relief from the heat, and while (perhaps) the lifeguard was explaining the test to another freshman, or was in the glass-encased office and (perhaps) didn't have a clear view of the end of the pool, Penny jumped in. One witness's account had him completing a lap and beginning to swim a second; the lifeguard's account had him completing almost two laps. Penny's father would have none it: there was no way his son could have swum more than ten yards, he said. After however many yards, Penny sank to the bottom. One witness noticed but thought that whoever it was might have been practicing holding his breath. The County Medical Examiner estimated that Penny remained at the bottom of the pool for between three to eight minutes before anyone realized what had happened. The lifeguard dove in and brought him up (Marx helped lay him out by the side of the pool) and began mouth-to-mouth resuscitation. Campus Security was called; soon the College physician and two men from the Amherst Fire Department Rescue Team arrived. They all took turns trying to revive Penny for upwards of 35 minutes before the Medical Examiner pronounced him dead.

Ward was out of town at the time, meeting with alumni groups when he heard. Upon his return to Amherst he set about learning as much as he could about what had happened the day before. A Black Steering Committee and the Afro-Am Society wrote him, insisting that he inquire into the circumstances of the case, which says more about the tenseness of racial relations at the time than it does about Ward. (Could he have done anything else?) Thursday evening a memorial service was held in Johnson Chapel.

At dinner at the Dentons afterwards, Ward met Penny's father. It was a night made the more difficult when an assistant (black) dean confronted Ward and told him that something he had said to Mr. Penny had "deeply insulted" the man, but there was no use explaining because Ward wouldn't understand. (The dean, appointed by Plimpton, would be gone by the end of the year.) Ward later wrote Penny asking for clarification, saying how much it pained him to think that he had offended him. The answer was that Ward's telling him that though someone was clearly at fault, nothing would be accomplished by talking to the many people who had already given their accounts of what had happened, and that the lifeguard in particular had already gone through enough, the latter, it has to be said, indeed deeply insensitive to the feelings of the man who had just lost his son. And though it was understandable that Ward was again trying somehow to bring everyone involved together, his suggestion that they and possibly others meet over a meal the next day was, as Mr. Penny said, "most inappropriate." On that day, Friday, before Penny left to go back home to New Orleans, he called Ward to say that he was going to sue the College—which he did at the end of November.

He and Penny corresponded in the days and weeks that followed. Penny wanted to know exactly what had happened, saying that the circumstances were mysterious, suspicious, and that they "strongly indicate[d] negligent action"; he hoped there would be a change in policy—"to save some other kid's life." He wrote the senators from Massachusetts, Edward Brooke (an African-American) and Ted Kennedy, to apprise them of what had happened in their state. Ward was distressed, especially by Penny's suspicion, but he dealt with the legal and personal consequences of Penny's suit against the College as openly and fairly as he could. Was it possible that charitable institutions were immune? Or that their liability could not exceed $25,000? Ward assured everyone that were either to be the case, the College would not hide behind any legal technicality. A settlement was reached a year and a half later, for how much Ward did not know, nor did he want to know. As he said in a letter to Shinn, "I do not know how adjustors or lawyers arrive at a dollar figure for a life, but would be hard pressed to say that either $60,000 [the amount the company had proposed] or $135,000 [the amount Penny sued for], was fair." The case was closed.

What struck Ward most throughout was the character of the man who was Penny's father. (Not irrelevantly, he was "a letter carrier.") Ward would not forget his example. In July 1975, he wrote to Penny, "I hope if tragedy ever touches my life that I may have the dignity and courage you have shown me." More than a year after that, he described Penny to Shinn as "a fine and strong man, one for whom I have not just respect but awe. I know I could not have borne myself with the dignity and strength he has during this entire affair."

A year later, on October 14, 1974, the Black Culture Center was dedicated to the memory of Gerald Penny. (It occupied the first floor of the Octagon, not the whole building, the difference causing an unfortunate confrontation between Ward and the Afro-Am Society.) There was no place on the program for Ward. Two days after the ceremony he wrote the "Brothers of the Afro-American Society." He assured them, "I feel no slight, only puzzlement," and enclosed a copy of what he had intended to say. Less than a page long, it ended, "While we are together, let us hope we can teach one another how to care for one another. Perhaps we may even hope we can teach ourselves how to love one another." His cover letter ended on the same note: "I still cherish the hope we can learn to care for one another and to help one another." True to form, he continued to envisage a society in which individuals would be treated "equally and fairly." True to form, he overestimated how much he could do to bring it into being.

Had he and Barbara not been out walking their dog on Sunday, November 3, 1974, another tragedy might have occurred. As it turned out, it was only an "incident," but it was one that had enormous significance for Ward. The day before, the Board had voted in favor of coeducation. The evening after, at an assembly meeting, Ward addressed an audience of only fifty students—for after all, what more was there to say about coeducation? He began by referring to the decision but, as he said, he wanted to "seize the moment" to talk about something else, something that had happened over the weekend that probably only a handful of students knew about, but that was to him, he said, as important as the coeducation decision. Hockey players from Charlestown, the center of Boston's Irish mob activity, had come to Amherst to scrimmage with the varsity team on Saturday and Sunday. A member of the Amherst team was from Charlestown. His father, active in Charlestown's youth program and coach of the team that was made up of 17 and 18-year-olds, had proposed the scrimmages. They were more than good enough to provide adequate pre-season competition. On Saturday, the day before the first scrimmage, nine of them accosted a black student verbally (with "Nigger this, and Nigger that," and "What do you think about busing?" the student later said) and then physically. (The student made light of the scuffle. "I have a few scars," he said.) Opposition to court-ordered desegregation of the Boston public schools ran high, especially in working-class neighborhoods in Boston. At Amherst, the black students were still trying to cope with the recent experience of one of their number, a freshman who had been picked up by four white youths while hitchhiking to UMass, taken to some out-of-the-way spot, beaten, and left stranded. There were rumors of other such incidents.

On Sunday, about 35 black students went to the rink and demanded an apology for what had happened the day before. One Charlestown player said he was sorry; hardly satisfied, the students then went to the Octagon to discuss the situation. They concluded that the time had come to take the matter into their own hands, and, accordingly, armed themselves with pipes and metal clubs and chains, and headed back to the rink. It was then that they met the Wards. Why was the scrimmage allowed to go on? they asked him. He agreed and followed them down to the rink. Inside, two crowds formed, one on each side of the plexiglass that surrounded the rink. The black students started to shout at the players on the ice. According to Steve Hardy, the "seasonal assistant" to the Amherst coach, the students had already given Ward "holy hell." Hardy and the head coach had begun talking to the players, saying, in Hardy's words, that "they would get to the bottom of it," when "in walked Ward." "We called all the players off the ice," Hardy goes on. "Bill Ward calmly but sternly told the Charlestown crew that Amherst College did not tolerate racial taunts and they needed to get their gear and leave campus immediately. They did so without incident." He told the Amherst team that he would be back the next day to talk to them before practice. Again Hardy:

> And so he did. He used it as a teachable moment. What I remember most are the long drags on his cigarette (Lucky Strike, maybe) as he talked about his upbringing and about values. It was a first-rate talk from a classy guy. I don't think I ever saw Bill in person after that practice, but his image and his leadership have always stayed with me.

It was a rare situation, one in which he could confidently be the man who had grown up in South Boston, the teacher and the moralist, and the president of Amherst College, all in one.

At the assembly meeting the next day he said that the events left him "fearful and sad." What most upset him, he told his small audience, was that "our Black students believe they must act by themselves, for themselves, and do not think they may turn to the College for support." "You will understand me," he said, addressing no one in particular, "when I say there is room for white hands in the circle of brotherhood." Convincing black students that this was so would be difficult, but he knew that it would be the more difficult because, as he said, he couldn't be at all sure that white students shared his vision—not the ones he had encountered on Sunday, anyway. "I wonder how many of our own hockey players understood why we asked the hockey club to clear the ice," he said.

The "problem of the color line" at Amherst would remain a problem throughout Ward's presidency; it would remain a problem throughout the century, as W.E.B. DuBois had famously predicted would be the case, for the country as a whole. During Ward's presidency it got worse. One specific problem, one issue, one incident followed another, the tension created by each building up to one terrible event. Most of them occurred during Ward's last two years, the worst just before he left.

When Smith withdrew its support for a summer tutorial program for ninth and tenth graders from Springfield, Ward had Amherst take it over, to see how it worked. Though it hobbled along throughout his presidency, the answer from both perspectives was *badly*. Over the years, the pressure on the administration to find and hire qualified black and (soon) other minority faculty increased. Positions for them were to be found not only in Black Studies but "in all disciplines," and the Afro-Am Society wanted to take part in the selection processes.

Beginning in the fall of 1977, another demand, or set of demands, made by students and faculty in what was called the South Africa Support Committee, was that the College make: one, "a commitment to the principle of corporate withdrawal from South Africa"; two, that in keeping with that commitment, it support, or where necessary, introduce "share-holder resolutions calling for the withdrawal from corporations in which it [held] stock"; and three, that it divest if after two years these resolutions failed. The issue was on the agenda of the Board for two years, there were many meetings large and small with Board members on campus and in New York, culminating with a three-hour meeting of the Support Committee and the Investment Committee of the Board in the fall of 1978, after which the Board reaffirmed its policy of monitoring the behavior of firms in which it held stock that did business in South Africa to see that they abided by the so-called Sullivan Principles that required equal treatment of all employees regardless of race.

"One of the most disturbing aspects" of the debate, Ward told the faculty, was "to be regarded as if one were immoral." "It was not a different morality," he said, but rather "a different judgment." It was not like the debate over coeducation, in which one could profess to support coeducation in principle but oppose it at Amherst. No one was suspected of supporting apartheid while opposing it in principle. Though Ward would seem to have been justified in letting the decision process take its course, when he defended the trustees' position in a faculty meeting, he was accused of even worse. "Before you begin to bury yourself in even more rhetoric," one man said, "one could have made the same arguments for supporting corporate involvement in Nazi Germany." But it wasn't an issue behind which the community could be mobilized. South Africa was another country.

All the while, race relations among the students did not improve. In April 1978, the *Student* printed a two-page article with a two-part title: "Racial Misperceptions/Disharmonious Community." It was the result of four weeks' interviewing by students. Seven were listed. In their summary, the editors seemed to speak only for the average, typical—white—Amherst student:

> As a community we grope along. The liberalism of our education, this institution's penchant for insulating us in the modes of self-scrutiny, run smack into the subliminal barriers to inter-racial relations which is all too often an unconscious product—or prejudice—of our personality before we get to this place.

Two days later, about twenty black students occupied the office of the paper for three or four hours, protesting the inclusion of the name of the chairman of the Afro-Am Society in the list of the students who had worked on the article. (In fact, he had worked on it for a matter of days, objected to what he called the methodological and political focus, and quit.) The students demanded that the editors apologize and print their apology on the front page of the next issue along with an article *they* would write. In that issue, in their editorial, the editors described the takeover, acknowledged that they thought the chairman's presence would lend credibility to their project, and printed a correction in which they explained that the student had not worked with them for long.

In February 1979, black students and other students of color would also occupy the office of the *Student*, this time demanding a page of their own as a regular feature of the paper. A particularly enraging—a terrible—example of the limitations of the paper's and the College's racial attitudes was the inclusion in the "Homunculi" awards of "The winner of the Gerald Penny Swim Contest," accompanied by "Better luck next year," which went to an unsuccessful peer counseling program. The debate that ensued was ugly, so ugly as to cause Ward to call an all-campus meeting. At this one he spoke at unusual length with more than his usual earnestness and fervor. He spoke about "the tension between the ideals of the institution and the social reality of the institution" and about the gulf between the two. He said he believed that there was "on all sides a yearning for brotherhood and decency among us," but he had to add, "It is not the reality of the College. I am sad to say it is not." Then looking ahead to when he would be leaving Amherst, he looked back: "The one dimension of my responsibility to the College which will send me away sad, frustrated, and incompetent is to have to say that I and you have failed to realize human sympathy and simple decency when it most counts and is hardest to achieve." Clearly tired, he reached for that moment in Emerson's essay "Experience," that moment at the very end when Emerson says, in the face of ridicule and defeat, "But, up again, old heart!" That was well over a century ago; he could not go on to quote what followed—"There is victory yet for all justice." Rather, he intoned, "If America is to be a great nation, we must have the will to do it," from Martin Luther King's Nobel Peace Prize acceptance speech, and applied it to the College: "If Amherst is to be a good place, you must have the will to do it."

At one point in his talk he had defined the ideal of the College by asking this question: "How do we honor—and I mean honor, not just put up with—how do we honor the diversity among ourselves while asserting the value of our shared and common life together?" It was the question that he had been asking since he left Harvard, if not before. During the run-up to the controversy that centered on the *Student*, he met with the editors in his office. In his frustration, one of them said that there were times when he felt like just giving up. Ward jumped on his comment, "suddenly passionate," and said, "in the firmest of tones....You *never* give up."

The final and most pressing racial issue that Ward faced was the College's orientation program, its introduction of incoming students to the life of the College and the town. Orientation is seemingly a minor occasion, one that students are not likely to think much about once classes start, one they think less and less about thereafter. But the question orientation raised in the late '70s was precisely, "How do we honor the diversity among ourselves...while asserting the value of our shared and common life together?" and it was a heavily loaded one, the more loaded because the students entering in the fall would encounter Amherst College's first answer to it the minute they arrived on campus. It had been, in effect: Amherst College honors your diversity first; Black Freshman Orientation will be a time for you to affirm your identity and solidarity and thereby enable you to understand and participate more effectively in the common life of the College that will begin three days later when the rest of the freshman class arrives. In the five years of its existence, by no means all of the incoming black students had taken part in the program, and as Ward would point out, not all parents were eager to have their children identified as blacks rather than as just students at the outset either. But so far as those who identified themselves as "The Black Community of Amherst College" were concerned, Black Orientation was successful.

In early April 1979, though, the administration worked on a proposal that would replace Black Freshman Orientation with an "ethnic day" (or a day and a half) that would be added to regular orientation, during which students of any minority group could identify themselves and formulate their own programs. Assuming that this was what had been decided upon by the administration, without its having consulted with the Afro-Am Society or any of its representatives, black students protested against the plan and then against the proposal when it turned out to be only that. Rather than bring the administration and the students closer together, a week of debate and meetings only raised the level of tension between them.

And then just after midnight on Monday the 16th a six-foot cross was burned on the lawn outside the all-black Charles Drew House. In a letter that he immediately sent out "To Fellow Men and Woman at Amherst College" Ward announced what had just happened—"at the close of Easter Weekend and Passover"—and followed his announcement with four sentences that more closely resembled those of "the evangelical preacher of earlier days" than any he ever wrote or uttered:

> May God forgive whoever did so cowardly and contemptible and hateful an act.
>
> May those of us who are merely human understand, in our hearts and

minds, the meaning of this shameful act.

May each of us extend the hand of brotherhood to our black brothers and sisters and banish from among us the meaning of that fiery cross.

May anyone who can help us discover who did so ugly a deed, please do.

He signed it, "In sorrow."

The black students living in Drew House came across the street to Valentine Hall (once again armed with clubs and the like) where several black women lived and escorted them back across the street to what would have been relative safety. In the morning, about 100 students occupied the Dean of Students' office in Converse Hall for four hours, and then, because they expected a decision on Black Orientation and because they were sure what it would be, they staged another sit-in later in the day. The cross-burning...Orientation...Orientation...the cross-burning. Reaction to one fueled reaction to the other. In the preceding days and in the days to follow, according to the chairman of the Afro-Am Society, there were cross-burnings at Hampshire and at the University as well. At an emergency meeting Monday afternoon, the faculty unanimously deplored the action and called off Tuesday's classes. The decision on Orientation was postponed until that afternoon. In the evening, more than 1,000 students, faculty, and members of the administration attended an all-college meeting in the gym. All the black students sat together in one block.

Before the meeting Ward made his decision known: an "ethnic day" would replace Black Freshman Orientation. But Ward said he had called the meeting to address what was far more important: the cross-burning, the "obscene" cross-burning he called it, the cross-burning which was the more "obscene" because, as he announced at the outset, he had proof that the fire had been started by two black undergraduates. There was much heated talk—and one climactic moment. Towards the end of the meeting, a white student addressed Ward slowly and formally. Either the administrators planned to abolish Black Orientation all along, he said, and were "lying through their teeth" when they said they had not made a decision, or the plan was "vicious, racial retribution" for "actions of past days." Ward's temper flared up, fueled by the fact that he and the leaders of the Afro-Am Society had arrived at the orientation decision earlier in the day. "I knew some idiot in this audience would bring up that subject. I have put up long enough with the lack of civility by some students," he shot back, and vehemently denying both accusations, exclaimed, "I want from you, sir, an apology." When none was offered, Ward walked out, leaving the crowd in silence. Gifford took over and assured the audience that there had been no decision until that afternoon and that it had been arrived at at the urging of the black community. During the speeches that followed, the crowd began to disperse. Thirty or forty students returned to Converse where they continued their occupation of the Dean's office.

At the end of the week "The Black College Community" reissued its set of demands, the first of which was that the decision on Black Orientation be reversed, moreover that it take place before other students arrived on campus, that black students have full control over it, and finally, that the program be sanctioned by the administration and a letter stating their endorsement had to be sent to incoming black students and their families. The black students had a clear sense of the man with whom they were dealing. As Frederick Douglass said in his autobiography, it was the liberal masters that the slaves knew to rebel against, not the heartless tyrants. In his final interview, Ward appreciated not only the students' appreciation of him but also their sense of timing. He told of a black student who had come to him when it was all over and said, "We've always seen you as the one person we could be sure would understand and be sympathetic," and added laughingly, "We wanted to get everything nailed down before you left."

Ward said he would respond to the demands in the middle of the next week and went to Washington for a trustees' meeting and then returned to Amherst before the meeting was over. The numbers of those occupying Converse had doubled over the weekend. On Sunday night the black activists had caucused and emerged and told those who were asleep in the lobby that they were going to chain and lock the doors of the building and that they wanted the support only of those who were willing to stay behind.

Ashley Adams, a white activist, called what followed that week "a great example of good administration killing bad radicalism....[Ward] let the building occupiers drift into irrelevancy." He was, throughout, furious over the cross-burning. Rich Read, the editor of the *Student*, who had been meeting with Ward at his house, said he was "seething mad" as he walked with him over to Converse. But once Ward got there, he spent time talking to supporters who gathered outside and of course allowed them to bring food to those inside. When campus policemen spotted an open window and started to crawl in, intending to clear the building, Ward stopped them. The students who had occupied Converse identified themselves—for which Ward respected them. In his final interview, he recalled Westover: "My own experience," he said, "made me more aware that students who chose that action were acting on principle, that is, consciously violating one set of values because of a greater commitment to other goods, or other ends."

In the days that followed he spelled out what he thought were the pros and cons of Black Orientation. He said, for example, that a separate orientation implied an admission that there was racism at Amherst but that Amherst's way of dealing with it was just to forewarn incoming students, not recognizing it as a College problem and taking steps to eliminate it. There would be no more Black Orientation. And speaking to the black community's other demands, he said the college would continue its efforts to hire black faculty and administrators and (what became common practice in all hirings) students would be consulted but not take part in final decisions, the trustees' policy regarding South Africa would stand, and the tutoring program in Springfield would remain a budget item.

The occupiers came out and judicial proceedings began. They were charged with "serious violations of the College's statement on Freedom of Expression and Dissent, and its statement on Respect for Persons" and were suspended for the time they spent in Converse (the only serious consequence being the recording of their suspension on their official transcripts). Black students at first refused to accept the fact, but two of them confessed to burning the cross—strongly influenced, it was alleged by some, by an assistant professor in the Black Studies Department. In a letter to the students who'd confessed, Ward called their act "a malicious provocation of and assault on the emotions of all the members of Amherst College, an action which constitutes a cynical manipulation of others for your own political ends, whatever they may be." When judicial proceedings in their case were announced, he brushed aside the chairman of the Judicial Board, saying he wanted the students expelled on the spot, but it was pointed out to him that the Judicial Code did not permit him to suspend students. Hearings took place. The students were defended by a faculty member, in this case Jim Mariness, as the Judicial Code would have it. About 30 black students supported the argument that the cross-burning was, in Mariness' words, "an act of desperation, not insurrection, brought on by accumulated experiences of racial disparagement experienced all across the campus by black students at the hands of faculty, students, and staff." Mariness himself concluded, "If you had heard all of the students' testimony, you would have thought that an act of desperate protest was justified. It was a revelation to me." Of course not everyone agreed—certainly not Ward. Most thought nothing could justify the manipulation. The two students were suspended (getting no credit for the term) and given the option of returning in the fall. Ward had to be content with putting his own stamp on the Judicial Board's decision. In his letter to the two students he added that they would be trespassing if they weren't gone in twenty-four hours and, "Still further, I solemnly warn you that any verbal or physical intimidation of other members of the College community will lead to prompt legal action against you."

Two weeks later, in an op-ed piece titled "The Unrest of Black Students" that he submitted to the *New York Times* and the *Boston Globe*, he said of the preceding days in May:

> Underneath the sensational 'public' events, what was going on was probably the best eleven days in the life of the College in recent years, days in which whites and blacks, pushed together by the emotional traumas which followed one upon the other, spoke openly about their uneasy existence together. The real challenge before the College was not how to handle the immediate crisis, but to begin to imagine ways to sustain the openness which was realized, without the awful pressure which made it possible.

Neither printed it, but we, at least, can appreciate the fact he could imagine that the ideal of "the spirit of the place" that he spoke of at the outset of his presidency had been realized; or at the very least that he managed to impose that meaning on events, lest his bitterness and anger prevail at the end.

Rand Richards Cooper, an Amherst student during the Ward years, has written perceptively about Ward's seemingly endless attempts to inspire and lead young men and women to realize his ideal: "There was often a note of something plaintive in his remarks about 'this place'—as if he was repeatedly invoking some dream place that could never be reached or achieved, quite, and yet had to be perpetually invoked. The beauty of the idea came over time to seem rather like a yoke. He couldn't ever pull the load to the top of the hill—but he couldn't unhook it either." There is something admirable and moving about Ward's ability to tell himself that at the very end of his presidency, under the most trying circumstances, he had seen his vision of an Amherst in which people spoke openly about their existence and their learning together fulfilled this one last time.

COMPENSATION/RESIGNATION

IN JUNE 1975, in the Commencement issue of the *Student*, there appeared an insightful article on the state of the College at what was the midpoint of Ward's presidency. Looking back, it said, "Since the second half of the decade of the Sixties, Amherst has set for itself a role, one which defined the College in some sort of tension with the rest of society." "That spirit," it went on, "which President Ward more than anyone else embodies, gave Amherst the sense that it was different, that it would consider problems in a more enlightened way, that relationships here could be on a higher plane." We have seen Ward define and embody that "spirit" many times.

But things had changed, the article went on, changed for one reason and one reason only: the economy. "We now know better. We now know that conditions of the economy—I would say structural more than temporal—fundamentally determine that we are not exempt." Now, "besides a few special relationships and a higher potential for intimacy, Amherst is not so different"—not so different from the rest of society, no longer on a higher plane. And such was indeed the case. Due to the war the federal deficit rose, as did unemployment. Every economic indicator was in decline. "Stagflation," the combination of inflation in the economy and the stagnation of business, had set in. Accordingly, students' thinking about their careers, and the faculty's concern about their salaries, would become increasingly important in the second half of Ward's presidency, the latter ultimately putting an end to it.

As a result of downturns in the market, the endowment had begun to shrink—by $10 million in 1973; by $14 million, from $87 to $73 million, in 1974. The Alumni Fund had recovered from Westover and had begun to set records by 1975, but inflation more than offset the gains (inflation, as was often pointed out, that was 2 percent higher in the academy than in the economy as a whole), with the result that the College had to contend with annual budget deficits. In 1973 the trustees began to make plans for a fund drive but the next year they called it off. Tuition was raised by relatively small amounts during these years (though in 1975 it was still $1,000 less than what it was at Yale, Harvard, and Princeton), but the increases could reduce deficits by only so much. And finally, soon after the end of the '60s the number of applicants, the number of Baby Boomers of college age, declined. The market in which Amherst traded was no longer dependably a seller's market.

The faculty was a constituency that had caused Ward relatively little trouble in the first half of his presidency. It was, on balance, sympathetic with him over Westover, entirely behind his way of handling racial conflicts, and confident making its own case for coeducation. The debate over the curriculum was more a debate within the faculty than with Ward. But when economic issues were at stake he had to go head-to-head with the faculty. Their salaries—and their egos—were at stake. At least as early as the spring of 1974, as he had warned, it was going to be difficult to see to it that professors' salaries kept up with inflation. For their part, they were worried about not being able to maintain the lifestyle to which they were accustomed, if not worried about making ends meet. What would strike one witness, a *Student* reporter, about the faculty meetings was what extraordinary gifts of oratory, "what passionate principle [was] applied to the cause of self-interest."

In April 1977 the war began, ironically, when Ward tried to describe the economic situation as clearly as possible to the faculty. Believing, as was typical of him, that after he did so, different points of view would be rationally expressed, tolerated, and somehow reconciled, on the 20th he sent the faculty a copy of a three-page statement on "Faculty Compensation" that he had given the Board as it prepared for its spring meeting earlier that month. Ward told his campus audience that at that spring meeting, just past, he had asked the Board to change the language of the 1971 resolution on "Faculty Compensation" in order to dispel any ambiguity about administrative policy and practice. He said that his statement was "self-explanatory" but that he would be happy to respond to any questions at the upcoming faculty meeting. The change of language was slight, but rather than clear up any misunderstanding, it and his "self-explanatory" gloss on it raised questions and led to heated debates, the temperature of which would not go down until after Ward left Amherst two years later.

To be specific, as we must, the resolution that the trustees had passed in April 1971 read:

> The Trustees' general objective is to maintain faculty compensation at a level no lower than that of other institutions of highest quality, so that Amherst will remain capable of attracting, retaining, and suitably compensating eminently qualified faculty members.

Though it did not come up at the meeting of the trustees, it is worth noting that this resolution had replaced the Board's "statement" in 1958 that it was

> the general objective of the Trustees of Amherst College to raise faculty salaries to a level such that they will be as high as those of any other college in the country and such that Amherst can compete with the universities for faculty members.

The days were heady under President Cole and would continue to be on Plimpton's watch. But being good readers of economic indicators, in April 1971 the trustees replaced "any other college in the country" and "compete with universities" with "other institutions of higher learning." The difference was enormous, the change radical. Three months later Ward became president.

By 1977 no one could ignore what the indicators pointed to. Concerns about inflation, budget deficits, and salary levels had been deepening. Ward felt it was important to share his statement on Faculty Compensation with the faculty. At their meeting, he began gingerly. Citing "the somewhat looser rhythm of one's life," a life, moreover, involved with young people, and "the high degree of autonomy and self-determination over what one will do," he pointed out that, "there are enormous non-material satisfactions in the life of a professor." (Years later, when he was playing tennis with the man who was then president, one professor added another "satisfaction." Pointing to the view of the Holyoke Range to the south, he said it was worth at least $2,000—and lived to regret having done so when the president took to adducing what he had said in discussions about salaries.) Behind Ward's remarks about the satisfactions of professors' lives lay the relatively modest condition of his own finances when he embarked on his career and his questions about who should be paid more, professors or secondary and elementary school teachers, both of which we have noted. But on this occasion he went on to acknowledge that after their years of training and of their slow rise through the ranks, professors did not feel all that highly rewarded, and he ended by withdrawing to the safe conclusion that "one should not insist too greatly on the other delights of the calling, however real they may be." It is likely that many faculty members could hear the undertones of Ward's sentences, but what he brought out into the open by sending them his memorandum to the Board, and what would be the cause of the confrontations to come, was his clarification of the 1971 resolution. After quoting it, he said:

> Some faculty read that resolution to mean that Amherst will maintain salaries competitive with the best of the Ivy League universities. Others read it as measuring compensation against other four year undergraduate institutions of the highest quality. The latter interpretation has, in fact and practice, been administrative policy.

Ward's administration had been measuring Amherst salaries against those of professors at "other high-quality undergraduate colleges," Williams, say, and not Harvard, all along, and the faculty had lost purchasing power, lost it *because* they were being compared to faculty members at Williams and not at Harvard.

His explanation of the standard of measurement was that Amherst wanted to hire the best candidates possible at the lowest rank because Amherst was, in a phrase that some found demeaning, "a home-grown institution," and that its faculty couldn't command the kinds of salaries Harvard professors could. Harvard could hire fine young teachers from its graduate schools, or from other institutions, because it was known as "an excellent training-ground for researchers." Very few of them would get tenure. At that level, Ward said, Harvard sought "the best in the world of whatever it is seeking." But almost all tenured Amherst professors had started at Amherst, so Amherst sought to entice very good graduate students, possible future senior members of the faculty, by offering them salaries that could compete with or exceed those of junior faculty members at Harvard. Ward wanted to make all that clear.

The headline of the *Student* account of faculty meeting was "Tempers Flare at Faculty Meeting." Given the tenor of faculty meeting—"the incredible screaming and stand-up attacks," that one faculty member recalls—the paper's reporters and editors would return to such metaphors again and again that spring and throughout the following year. And not only were they in keeping with the fury of many people but also with the venue, the very fact of the Red Room in Converse itself, so called because of the brilliant red carpet that covered every inch of the floor. The room seemed like a site of bloody conflict, not only because of the carpet but because of the relatively small size of the room (with a capacity of only 140) and the five rows of black seats that ascended one above the other, leaving Ward and Gifford and a recording secretary down below at ground level, as if in a pit, or on the dirt of a bull ring. La Plaza de Toros, Hugh Hawkins called it.

One faculty member at that meeting said the old resolution wasn't ambiguous at all. It made no distinction between colleges and universities; it was the goal, the ideal, that mattered. Given what Ward had said, another concluded that Amherst was "a dead-end" and speculated that just as students were tempted by Harvard, Yale, and Princeton, so too might faculty be lured away by those schools. (Not long after, he himself left not for Yale, Harvard, or Princeton but for the University of Connecticut.) A third, an Economics professor, said, "It's not up to me or you, the market will choose. The longer you stay, the poorer in terms of purchasing power you get." One man added that Ward's timing couldn't have been worse: though the ILS curriculum would be voted in that spring, a version of it was on the agenda. (It was defeated that night. The faculty was in no mood to commit itself to the additional work that it implied.) Given the nature of the proceedings, defending the status quo was a little like saying the view of the Holyoke Range was worth $2,000, yet at least one man did. Ward's former colleague in American Studies, Gordie Levin said, "We make more money than 80 to 85 percent of the people in the country, and that's not a terrible situation to be in." To a small minority, the faculty, as Professor Latham once put it, was just rattling its golden chains.

The situation got worse. In the fall, the IRS announced that the difference between what the faculty paid in rent in subsidized housing (a treasured benefit) and the fair-market value of rental property in town was taxable income. More generally, the morale of the faculty declined as it read more and more into what Ward had said about its compensation. At a faculty meeting in February of the following year Professor Kearns, a young member of the Committee of Six, cited chapter and verse. He listed eight administrative "actions or omissions" which he said indicated how little respect Ward and his administration had for "the job that we, as teachers, are doing here." First and foremost was the memorandum that Ward had sent to the trustees the previous year which declared, in effect, that "the faculty is not entitled to Harvard's salaries."

The others followed: a proposal to have departments and programs visited and reviewed by committees made up of alumni and professionals; another to review candidates for promotion more closely and to review all tenured faculty members periodically; no assurance that the administration would make up for losses suffered by the IRS' ruling; restrictions on faculty travel to and attendance at professional meetings; and the administration's limiting the number of faculty before anyone knew that it would be teaching a demanding new ILS program. All could without much difficulty be interpreted as evidence of a lack of respect for what the faculty did. Kearns concluded by saying it wasn't just a matter of money. His main point, he said, was to ask: "Why doesn't the administration believe that what we are doing here is as important as I think it is?"

Gifford distanced himself—and Ward—from Kearns' attack by indulging in a little irony: "I hope you never achieve an administration that is equal to your anxieties, for if you do it will mean the College has reached a very sad state," but that was not Ward's way. He had been criticized, he was offended, he was wounded; he responded directly to Kearns' charges. He began by saying that what the faculty was doing was extremely important and that the only question the administration had in mind when it made policy was how the faculty could do better what it already did well, and then he added a note that couldn't have appeased anyone: Thinking there was any other purpose behind the establishment of visiting committees and reviews, he said, might suggest a lack of security. He regretted using the phrase "home grown," but he had to repeat that Harvard's way of elevating professors to the highest rank *was* "radically different," after which he went on to address the issue of compensation. The headlines of the *Stu-*

dent report that followed were: "Harvard Statement Draws Fire/Flames Fly at Faculty Debate." As the discussion went back and forth, Ward became more and more impatient until, in the words of Professor Dizard, "with a set jaw," he said that "comparison with Harvard's senior faculty and Amherst's was self-serving and worse. I don't recall his exact words but he basically said that the senior faculty at Harvard was in a league that the senior faculty at Amherst was simply not in, so the comparison was bogus. Who, he implied, did we think we were?" The up-shot? "A pall descended and the meeting quickly adjourned." The next day he wrote a letter to Allen Guttmann, another former colleague in American Studies, who was on sabbatical in Germany, in which he said, "I worry about the self-pity of the faculty....The refrain (played rather loudly last night at faculty meeting)...goes: we are great and dedicated teachers, straining ourselves to the limit, working so hard, but are underpaid, undervalued, underappreciated, especially by an unfeeling and authoritarian president."

The question of his estimation of the faculty's worth came up again two months later. In April, at the meeting of the Board, Ward reported that the reaccreditation team from the New England Association of School and Colleges was also concerned about faculty morale. In its exit interview with Ward, the chairman of the team told him that their report would be difficult to write because though the college was generally in excellent shape, there seemed to be "a 'metaphysical' problem of identity for the faculty." Ward conceded that there was and explained it by saying that many members felt their commitment to teaching was not so highly esteemed as scholarly productivity at research universities.

At the next faculty meeting, in his account of the Board meeting he spoke about the reaccreditation team's concern, said that he shared it, and that he wanted to address the discontent, adding that he wasn't sure about its source. At that point DeMott spoke up. What was hard for him to understand, he declared, was "how there can be any mystery about the unhappiness," and he proceeded to explain to Ward, and anyone else who needed an explanation, that, "There was a time when the kind of teaching that we aspire to was vexing, it cost you a lot, it cost you your career." The one you chose when you started out in the profession was more valued than was the commitment to research and writing of those at other institutions. But things had changed: "I think that at some point it was decided by the administration and the trustees that the commitment to arduous teaching was no longer something we ought to respect." Ward's response was a version of what he had said at the faculty meeting two months before: "Surely what we do here is not only *as* important; for education it's probably *more* important." It did nothing to weaken the opposition to him that had built up over the compensation issue, and had built up generally.

He was surprised by the faculty's reactions, but he had said what he had said: if you were as good as Harvard.... There it was. Teaching might be more important than research. He had said as much many times. But the dichotomy was too simple. Amherst proudly claimed that faculty members did both; Harvard's faculty members taught. When you got to the bottom line, Amherst faculty members were not going to be paid as much as Harvard faculty members. Were they as good? When you compared the two on the basis of more than simply teaching as against research.... well, Harvard's pre-eminence was and has always been assumed, perhaps too easily, but arguably its faculty *was* better than Amherst's. Certainly Ward thought Amherst's had little cause to complain.

In his oral history interview a little more than a year later, he recalled Greene's saying to him after the meeting in February, "Bill, you've just made the worst mistake you could make....You're asking the faculty to recognize reality. They never will do that." But in that interview, with nothing left to lose, Ward expressed no regrets. Quite the contrary. He came out and said more: "Despite the loss of real income, I really can't buy the language of exploitation or repression of people on tenure making in the thirty-thousands, with the working conditions we have at Amherst. It just seems to me a kind of rhetoric which is so far out of touch with reality that I tend to get impatient with it."

At their meeting in April it became clear to the trustees that they had to do something about faculty compensation. One recommended that they solicit faculty views and concerns before they issued any report; another warned that there was no way to begin talking about "comparative productivity figures" without making the faculty defensive and asked if there were a way to get the faculty itself to come up with the relevant information. Ward replied that there was a way and that it would be done. A seemingly small procedural matter: let's have the faculty provide us with the information we, the members of the Board, need in order to proceed to do something about their compensation. You can't resist the most hackneyed of expressions in describing what followed: it was the straw that broke Ward's back.

Early in the fall Ward sent a memo to the Committee on Priorities and Resources asking it to provide him and his administration with the information they would need in order to have a recommendation about compensation ready for the Board's meeting in January 1979. At the faculty meeting in October it was again DeMott who protested. "If ever I saw a classic case of faculty co-opting, this is it," he said—"this" being having the issue presented by three faculty members (a chemist, an historian, and, as chairman, a classicist) who had met with "management," namely the president, the dean, the director of development, the treasurer, and the comptroller. (There were three students on the committee, but it is hard to imagine their getting a word in edgewise.) DeMott said he was "sorry to sound upset, but this stinks." And there was another matter. DeMott and others had heard about a trustee position paper that recommended that tenured members of the faculty be evaluated before being promoted to the rank of full professor—this at a time when the faculty itself was just beginning to discuss new language that might go into the *Faculty Handbook* concerning how *it* should proceed in the matter of promotion. Asked about the trustees' position, Ward replied that it had to do with the possible need for such an appraisal in light of legislation relating to the extension of the retirement age, called DeMott's reaction "fevered," and then, at a pitch that was itself "fevered," said he was "fed up" with remarks indicating suspicion, and that he was not "going to sit here and take that kind of implication about [his] morals or motives." DeMott's response was that his remarks were not meant as a personal attack, but he considered what he had heard a "basis for suspicion." The meeting wound down with the addition of two economists to the membership of the CPR, and assurances that the faculty would see whatever document the CPR produced before it was forwarded to any other body.

The straw was the document. It provided the information about comparative salary figures, where it went and how it got there, that the Board had asked for. More to the point, though, it was a 67-page document on salaries that had been prepared by the treasurer and was submitted to the Board before the faculty was given a chance to see it and barely before the faculty members of the CPR had had time to read it. Upon learning that this was the case, a large faculty contingent met informally and agreed on the wording of a letter to the Board, drafted by Professor Fink and polished by DeMott (two of the three faculty members of the Long Range Planning Committee, we may recall) that said that they trusted that the Board would treat "this premature collection of data, recommendations, and conclusions...with the disrespect broken promises deserve." After the meeting, Fink went to Ward's house to show it to him rather than send it directly to the Board—to prepare him, lest he be set up as a target of its opposition. (Wanting precisely that, DeMott berated him for doing so.) While Fink was there, Barbara asked, "Why does the faculty dislike Kurt Hertzfeld so much?" Ward's response was that it wasn't the treasurer they were after. By then he had learned to recognize when he was being insulted.

Another result of the informal meeting was an emergency meeting of the faculty, called for (as was required) by eight of its members, on November 7. It began with the presentation of a motion by Greene, on behalf of the Committee of Six, that stated that the faculty accepted Ward's "regrets" that the administration had forwarded a "preliminary format" of the CPR's findings to the Board without adequate time for review by the faculty members of that committee and without prior knowledge of the faculty. In the discussion that followed, Ward said that he had objected to the use of the word "apologize" in the original wording of the motion, that he had drawn a line when he saw the phrase "broken pledge" in the letter to the trustees. "A mistake was made," he said. "I regret it, and I regret all that flowed from it." Furthermore, it was not a report but the projected design of the document that would be submitted in January; Hertzfeld added that it was not a matter of substance, but rather a preliminary gathering of data. Once again, DeMott led the charge: the issue wasn't whether the word should be "apologizes" or "regrets." No, he said, it was a "very well reasoned and powerful document" that argued that because faculty members were "not exposed to change" they were "happy with [their] compensation"— in sum, "a very powerful rehearsal for continuing the compensation policies that we have had for the last six or seven years." Professor Birnbaum (who was as sharp a thorn in Ward's side as DeMott throughout these debates) glossed DeMott's point by reading passages from the report that, he said, devalued the work of the faculty and characterized the atmosphere in which it worked as that of "a country club locker room," and then went on to say that in gathering data the CPR should note that "the low-risk quality" of faculty life did not apply to younger members of the faculty and that it might also provide "recent unemployment figures among members of the Board of Trustees and their annual rates of increase in compensation." And while they were at it, he added, they might also indicate the compensatory housing arrangements and rates of salary increases given to the College's administrators over the preceding ten years "in which we have been enjoined, ourselves, to live more spiritually." Gifford's response was, as ever, judicious. He urged everyone to concentrate on the issue of faculty compensation, and to "go forward not as factions but with the best interests of the institution at heart." He agreed that there was a need for "an adversary process," but he thought that the best document that could be forwarded to the trustees would result from an adversary procedure followed in a way that was not adversarial in tone. The motion to accept Ward's "regrets" passed without dissent.

After the meeting Ward spoke positively about the prospects of the administration's working together with the faculty on the issue. The week before he had said, "there is something else going on—but I don't know the question to ask. I think it is a larger, more amorphous issue." Now he felt better. The meeting had dispelled his fear that there was more at issue than faculty salaries. But obviously there *was*: a week later, he sent a letter to the community as a whole in which he announced that he was resigning as president.

It was a short letter. In it he gave two reasons for his resignation. The first was that the Board had begun to draw up plans to raise $43 million, which would require more of a commitment than he was prepared to make; the second was that the time had come for him to seek "a new professional opportunity." In *his* interview for the Oral History Project, George Shinn, a man who did not mince words, said Ward "had no patience....He left me in the lurch." And indeed he had acted impulsively once again. He had said to Barbara the night before he resigned, "I don't think I can go on enjoying this job." She had responded by asking him if he had heard what he had just said, after which, without a word, he had gone upstairs and written Shinn. Impulsive, but we can easily understand how Ward felt after what he had been through that fall and how it followed that he would rather do something—anything—other than raise money for Amherst College for the next three or four years. And Shinn knew there was another reason why Ward had resigned. The faculty had a game, he said: "Let's get the president." And so they did. But in this case, it was more to the point that they had gotten *to* the president.

WARD OFTEN said that he did not mind being criticized, that he found it liberating, that he rather enjoyed it, in fact. Early on, at some level, he didn't believe that he *was* being criticized. He was not inclined to think ill of people; he was not inclined to recognize some people thought ill of him. More than anything, for example, DeMott's behavior just perplexed him. But if they *were* criticizing him, he thought he could deflect or erase their criticism by his manner and by the way he oversaw the process by which he and they resolved issues together. Midway through his presidency he told a *Student* interviewer that he wasn't worried about his popularity. "I found enormous liberation when I realized there was nothing I could do without being beaten on"(which suggests that at another level he thought he was rather consistently being "beaten on"), but that it was relief to know there was nothing he could do about it. Two years later, a *Student* review of his performance had it that, "he says he doesn't feel constrained by any sort of necessity to please everyone; rather, he feels a curious freedom in the knowledge that no matter what he does, 'Someone will be unhappy.'" But towards the end, he lost that sense of "curious freedom."

At the outset he thought that because he came from the faculty, the faculty was behind him. In his oral history interview he said he wouldn't have accepted, and wouldn't go on to accept, the presidency of any other institution: "I don't understand these people who want to be presidents of colleges or universities," he said. "I accepted the presidency of Amherst College because I was on the faculty; I knew the place and cared about it." But coming from the faculty was a major part of the problem: he knew the "place" and – *but*—the "place" knew him. As Jill Conway said, he didn't have enough "space." Ward saw the problem but his response was to try to narrow what space there was. He saw that "when you are in office there's a danger people will not treat you as a human being; they see you as simply an office....You're caught in the center of that tension between role and self always." He wanted to be seen as a human being first and foremost. That was his way. It was his ideal for himself and for his students. For a time, in his time, it looked as if it might be the way of the world. Plimpton before him and those who would come after saw that to be a successful administrator you had to be a little less obviously human. But Ward thought that "the most wounding thing in the job [was] when you hear the kind of gossip or speculation by people imputing to you a motivation which you know just never existed." Ward might have avoided "the danger," relieved "the tension," if he had told himself that what he was going through was what the person who held his office *would* go through. But Ward took things personally. He was hurt when a faculty member questioned his motives, or when one said "in print...that [he] had lost the confidence of the faculty," and he added, "not that they said it, but that nobody else would say that they didn't share that position." When that happened, or rather, as he said, "when it started to make me feel hurt, I decided I was losing my capacity to put up with that probably inevitable kind of behavior and decided that if that's the case, probably it was time to move along." He felt hurt, so it was time to quit. Hurt, "very hurt and annoyed," one professor said after he was gone. "You could see it in his manner at meetings...he was huffy, offended, cold." Another added, "His one major fault was that he desperately wanted to be liked. When you are in the position he was in, there are people who don't like you. That tore him up." He knew the job required what he called "aesthetic distance," but he couldn't maintain it. He couldn't stand apart—couldn't play a part.

Eventually he had to admit that there were those who were trying to hurt him. In December he described his response to them in a letter to Greene: "There came a day when I found, in my heart, I wished no longer to work with and serve this Faculty," a faculty that thought "that a President who does not cheerfully and wholeheartedly serve the Faculty can not continue to be President." He went on to tell Greene that it was his "own failure not to have seen that the self-esteem and the pride of the Faculty needed to be constantly re-assured," but he couldn't provide the necessary re-assurance. He thought "it would demean the Faculty," and perhaps himself, if he did. He couldn't "cheerfully and wholeheartedly" serve a Faculty that put so high a premium on compensation or whose egos were in such need of being stroked and—it followed—who thought that he was increasingly inclined to serve the Board of Trustees rather than to serve them.

By the end, his doubts about the merits of the faculty's case would be strengthened by what he thought was its relatively light teaching load. (During the Plimpton years it had just up and reduced its load to two courses a term on its own.) It hadn't been mentioned in any of the fall meetings, Ward noted, "But Amherst," he said, "really is one of the most privileged places in terms of teaching load, leave policy, sabbatical leaves, and so forth....I would say quite bluntly that the faculty could take on more teaching." And as for the faculty's view of those who were not academicians, he said he thought "most academics and intellectuals have terrible stereotypes about how the world functions and what people are. It is easy to talk about the 'corporate' type or something like that"— or "trustee type," he might as well have said.

"Things flew apart at the end," Levin said. In the six months that remained to him he had to preside over the increasingly heated discussions of compensation. Birnbaum summed them up in one word—"shambles"— and regretted his "role in Bill's exit from the Presidency, since after a while, [he] was kicking a man who was down."

Ward took more of the blame that he needed to. "Coming out of the faculty, as a teacher and scholar and intellectual historian," he said, "I may have brought some ability to the office, but looking backward, it is easy now to see that the financial dimensions of management have left a good bit to be desired," but those "dimensions" were not just, not even primarily under his "management." His statement was in the conclusion of a "Memo for the Record" that he wrote after a late February faculty meeting out of his sense of the "need to brief the Board of Trustees carefully...and give [it] a sharp sense of the depth of faculty concern about salary," and distributed to the faculty lest they think that he was once again bypassing them.

Ward wanted the Board to know that the decline of the faculty's purchasing power was still at issue. One member of the CPR had asked rhetorically at a faculty meeting, "Should I not think of giving ten percent less time" to the College. "Do I not owe it to my family to apportion my time elsewhere in gainful employment?" And there was the faculty's belief that in effect they were subsidizing families that were far wealthier than they were, doing so because Amherst's tuition remained lower than tuition at comparable institutions. What was more, they thought that since 1971, when Ward took office, the administration and trustees had been "self-conscious about the effects of tuition and investment policy and have intentionally meant to exploit the faculty." Few if any on the faculty had gone so far as to say "intentionally," but just in case, Ward ended that section of the memo by saying, "Those are hard words, but that is the way the faculty is thinking."

In fact, tuition would rise and the trustees eventually agreed to what the CPR had called for in its report two months before: the restoration of the levels of "real" salary and compensation for all ranks to the level that existed in 1968, "especially among the full professors." (They also said that they "intended that compensation at Amherst College be competitive with that of the superior colleges and universities in the United States," differences of opinion as to which they were—colleges *or* universities—being a thing of the past.) Several years later, comparing presidential notes with Paul Bragdon, Ward talked about the issue of faculty compensation. He talked about it "wistfully, with perhaps a touch of bitterness," Bragdon remembers, "the message being that things might have been different for him had the Trustees acted affirmatively earlier on the outstanding issues of concern to the faculty."

Ward was a former faculty member whom the faculty turned on, in part because they thought he had come to side with the trustees. But the way the trustees set up the search for his successor would indicate that they had never really welcomed him to their side. Originally they had it that they would be in full control this time around: they would conduct the search themselves, while only consulting with faculty and student representatives. They quickly changed their minds when they registered the campus' reaction (unanimous opposition and another emergency faculty meeting); faculty and student representatives became members of the search committee as they had been when Ward became president. The trustees gave up some control over the search procedure, but then they announced that Amherst alumni would be given "strongest preference." If their trying to reverse the process by which he had been chosen did not offend Ward, their desire that his successor be an alumnus must have. If *it* hadn't, it offended one member of the Board, Willard Wirtz, in his name.

"There is clearly implicit linking of the handling of the presidential succession and the development program," Wirtz wrote Shinn in December. Five of the six members of the search committee had been together at Amherst in the '50s; two younger members of the Board, one a college president (i.e., Bragdon) had not been included. But what was more, it was "a heartless reflection on Bill Ward and on such people as Prosser Gifford." "In short, and perhaps too bluntly," Wirtz said, "I get the strong impression of Lord Jeffery riding that sometimes not-so-white steed of his roughshod over the prostrate form of some pretty loyal and fine people solely to gratify some other less principled adherents. In my view this makes a mockery of the Board, diminishes the College's stature and is a bad way to choose a president." Then he too resigned—from the Board. It went on to choose Julian Gibbs, an alumnus who had been in the running eight years before, as Ward's successor. Gifford would stay on through the following fall term and made no comment as he left except to say that twelve years was enough for him and the College.

Over the years, Ward had lost the support of the Board, the faculty, and, going back to Westover and the admission of women, the alumni. It was the students, as a constituency and individually, who admired him most. Upon assuming the presidency he said he hoped to maintain the close relations that he had had with them as their teacher, and though that proved impossible, and though their admiration declined over the years, he never lost their support completely. It was appropriate that at his last Commencement he ended his charge to the seniors with a tribute to them. "All too rarely do even the good teachers stop to think how they learn from you," he said, "how they profit in their individual lives in helping you to learn." It had been his good fortune to be in touch with the change that young people embodied. Commencement speeches usually dwelt on what students will take away from college. "We never tell you about, or thank you for, what you bring *into* the College." But that is what Ward did.

One might conclude that he should have remained in the classroom and in his study, do what he did best, be a teacher and a writer, but having been on the rise at least since his days as a graduate student at Minnesota, he wasn't about to stop. He was on the make, making himself. He wanted to be important. But he was not just crassly ambitious. What he was doing, others could do and, moreover, do together, their worth as individu-

The portrait of Ward by Richard Yarde that hangs in Johnson Chapel

als contingent upon their respect for their fellows and their efforts on behalf of the common good. That was his ideal, his version of the American dream. He had imagined it could be the reality of Amherst College.

But it didn't turn out to be. He began his Charge—there at "the College on the hill"—by citing John Winthrop's vision of "the city on the hill," his "Model of Christian Charity," which was what Ward called the "political charge" that Winthrop delivered to the Puritans before they landed on the shores of Massachusetts. The city was to be "a model, a pattern for all the world of the good society." But, quoting St. Matthew, Winthrop had warned, "if our hearts shall turn away so that...we shall be seduced and worship other Gods, our pleasures and our profits, and serve them...we shall surely perish." He was "giving voice to the American dream of an ideal society," Ward said, but by his account he knew already, even before his ship had landed, that "the lure of an open continent, rich land and opportunity...would seduce individuals to betray the ideal of a common good." Admittedly it is on a very, very small scale, but one might say that between 1964 when Ward arrived and 1979 as he was preparing to leave, something like that had occurred at Amherst.

But that wasn't the kind of thing the president of a college said at Commencement. Instead, Ward celebrated an Amherst that had not changed much since its founding, celebrated it in "the old language" that had it that "through one's calling one served the social good," and he asked the seniors not to forget that their lives had no meaning apart from all the others with whom they would live their lives. He did not mention how the idealism of the students who were at Amherst during the '60s and the early '70s had devolved into students' concerns about their careers, but he did confess that Amherst had not lived up to his expectations, adding that if it was anyone's fault it was his own. He did not see how the educational ideal that he had defined innumerable times—to develop individual minds and imaginations and at the same time to teach what it meant to be "a decent and humane person"—could be reached after all. "I do not know how to do the latter," he confessed.

All told, what did he think, how did he feel about Amherst? "I loved being at Amherst College; I love the fact that I am gone," he later said.

FINALLY, THERE was the practical question: what was he going to do now? One thing was certain: he would leave the academy entirely. He was asked to consider being a candidate for other presidencies but he declined. Nor was he tempted by any other academic position. The field in which he had distinguished himself now lay fallow, at least by his standards. After scanning the program of the upcoming American Studies Association Annual Meeting, complete with the titles of eighty-five meetings, he saw that, "There are no sessions on politics. There are no sessions on economic structure. There are, in short, no sessions addressed directly to the problems of power in the United States." Worse, by far, than Amherst. But even if the field was fertile, he no longer wanted to work in it in any capacity.

When he resigned he had told the *Student*, "There's a manic hilarious side of this and that is that I don't have the faintest idea of what I will do or what I'd like to do." The first part might have been true, manic he may have been, but the second was not. He had something he had to do, that he had agreed to do, and that was an entirely fitting thing for him to do. In the spring of 1978, Michael Dukakis, the governor of Massachusetts, had called Ward and asked him to serve as chairman of the Commission Concerning State and County Buildings in the state of Massachusetts, a less sanitized version of which was the commission that was created to investigate corruption in the awarding of public building contracts, and he had accepted. He would not be paid and while he was still at Amherst he would spend only a day a week working in Boston. He knew where he was going and what he was going to do once his presidency was over.

Academic life was a life apart, but he had retained a sense of how the world beyond functioned and "what people are," and he had a chance to engage it and them again. Moreover, that world was, and those people were, literally "political." The life out there was inestimably larger, perhaps tougher, but it was the life in which he had developed, implicitly as a youngster and then explicitly as an authority on Jackson, the ideals that he thought Americans as individuals and citizens should and could live by. The challenge was much greater but it was more immediate, more direct. The stakes were higher, but if he could succeed.... There was no telling what it might lead to.

He did go to the American Studies Association meetings in the fall of 1979 after all. That year they were being held in Minnesota, where he had begun his ascent in the academic world. Barry O'Connell saw him there and reported back to the secretary of the American Studies Department. "To my relief he looks again in good health and without signs of visible nervous distress...though bitterness remains in some abundance," he wrote. But, he added, "I am sure the time in Boston will do wonders." And indeed it did.

FOUR

Pro Bono Publico

"The Commission, the commissioners themselves and the staff they have recruited, is wholly dedicated to one single thing. We will do our work in a way which wins—one would like to say, restores—the confidence of citizens in this state that someone actually does care for the public good. That is what lies behind the pat phrase, pro bono publico. *That means we serve without pay. It means far more than that. It means we serve the public good. That is an antique notion in the conduct of professional and public life in these United States. It is. One feels almost a fool to say it, to say one is wholly committed to it, willing to give time and energy, all one has to it. We are citizens. We are bound together in a public body."*

(Ward before the Joint Judiciary Committee, March 6, 1979)

"It has been the single most intense and interesting experience of my life. If the Commissioners did not get paid; if we served as we Latin School boys say, pro bono publico, *I can say for myself it has, in another sense, been a wholly rewarding experience."*

(Ward in a lecture titled "The Common Weal and the
Public Trust: Politics and Public Morality," October 1980)

THIS TIME IT really was. Ward's experience as chairman of the Commission Concerning State and County Buildings in Massachusetts really was "the single most intense and interesting experience" of his life—"a wholly rewarding experience." In the words of Nick Littlefield, Jr., the man with whom he worked most closely on the Commission, "Against all odds, his work lived up to his idealism." It was the one time.

It would prove to be an extraordinary, arguably a unique, Commission.

In its two years, eight months, and eighteen days of existence it would not just bring a prodigious amount of corruption to light, but it would also establish pro-active procedures for overseeing the awarding of future contracts and subsequent construction that would guard against, if not entirely eliminate, future corruption. Ward would be remembered more than thirty years later by Barney Frank, who was a State Representative at the time, as having done "an excellent job of navigating through the tough political climate and [taking] advantage of the opportunity that scandal presents to make some real improvements." "Robby" Robinson, the *Globe*'s City Hall and State House bureau chief for two decades, said of Ward, "There is no one quite like him in the modern history of Massachusetts politics, no outsider who ever walked onto such a treacherous political stage and yet had much positive impact." And it wasn't just the work and what it accomplished that was so rewarding. It was also the way the work went and the life he lived while doing it. Everything about him and around him fell into place.

In October 1979, after the Commission had been in existence for a year and a half, just before the Commission's hearings, the long-awaited "public phase," was about to begin, the *Globe* introduced Littlefield and Ward to its readers. Littlefield was, like Ward, a Harvard graduate and, like Ward, a charismatic man, but otherwise they were very different. Littlefield was descended from an old New England family; after college he had gone on to London to study opera at the Royal Academy of Music. He appeared on Broadway in *Kismet* and went on tour in *My Fair Lady*. And then he left the stage for the University of Pennsylvania Law School. Upon graduation he worked for four years in the U.S. Attorney's Office in New York City, specializing in fraud and narcotics cases, after which he lectured at the Harvard Law School on prosecuting corruption cases. He was the perfect choice for the Commission's Chief Counsel, or "Executive Director," as the position was also called, or more informally, "the boss of the investigations."

Although Ward's educational background was ostensibly similar— Harvard, graduate school, teaching—what the *Globe* emphasized was his Boston Irishness. "John Ward, a feisty Irish scholar with Boston roots" was the headline of the half of the article devoted to him. In Boston these qualities would be a tremendous asset. (Thanks to *Roots*, the TV series based on Alex Haley's novel that traced his ancestry back through slavery to Africa, talk of "roots" was common at the time. Ward himself said of his Commission experience, "This is my own version of Roots—to come back and to see how the state conducts its business.") "He wasn't going to be blinking in the sunlight," Dukakis said. "He was, shall we say, acclimated to Boston culture. It's intensely political and part of that is its Irishness." There was no need to go into details. It was enough that he had grown up in Irish sections of town.

It was in this article that Ward was quoted as saying that he was lucky his name was Ward, that had it been Carrigan or Casey, his forbears' names, he wouldn't have been chosen to be Amherst College's president. As head of the Commission too it was probably better that his name was Ward. There was enough Irishness in his past to be usable—but not too much. Having become familiar with the ways of the men on the Amherst Board of Trustees, he knew how to work with powerful men from other parts of town as well, especially with the crusading director of both the news and the editorial pages of the *Globe*, Tom Winship, a strong and obviously influential supporter of Ward's work, with whom he often ate at their private social club, the Tavern Club. "He was able to talk easily with the political powers on Beacon Hill. He could be Irish...without pulling his identity out of his pocket and waving it around like a flag," said one commissioner, Frances Burke (who was chair of the Department of Public Management at Suffolk University, a block away from the State House). Robinson said that though at first he thought Ward was naive, he soon realized that he had the requisite political skills, he was "politically savvy," he knew how to nurture relationships. By way of explanation he added that you wouldn't have immediately said that he was Irish. He said Ward looked and walked and talked like a Yankee. Ward was back in Boston, this time at home anywhere in town.

But most important, as the historian with the long view going back to the time when Andrew Jackson was president, as the idealist intent upon making present-day government work and upon inspiring people to be responsible citizens—in a word, to do all he could to make the promise of American democracy a reality—Ward was in his element. The academic world had been one in which the politics were so vicious, as the old adage had it, because the stakes were so low. In all the years he had spent in it he had retained a sense of how the *real* political world worked; now he had a chance to engage it. Though inestimably greater, the challenge was immediate and in a way simpler. As he wrote Allen Guttmann, he found "the politics of the State House child's play in comparison with the psychopathology of politics in small institutions."

The contrast made his work on the Commission all the more satisfying. Nobody was jealous of him. There is nobody we know of who wanted his job, nobody, anyway, who would not have given the absence of compensation a second thought. And there was no competitiveness. He was the chairman; all those who worked under him had their appointed roles. There is no evidence of anything but respect and admiration for the way he oversaw the Commission's work—oversaw, represented, was "the face" of it, Littlefield said. To Littlefield himself, Ward "was far more than a boss for me. He was a teacher, friend, and role-model whose character and historical perspective enriched my work and whose high standards inspired my best effort." The Commission's deputy counsel, Tom Dwyer, said that Ward's independence and "great moral compass" made the Commission work. He led meetings the way he led seminars and tried to run faculty meetings at Amherst, allowing everyone his say, asking questions, reconciling divergent views. It was obvious to everyone who had any connection with the Commission, or simply had any knowledge of it whatsoever, that he was, in words that cropped up more than once, "clean as a whistle." In Boston he had nothing but success. Comparing his days as president of Amherst as we must (if for no other reason than that when he began his work on the Commission, he had one more year to go as president), we can more readily see how and why he became increasingly impatient in his dealings with the faculty over compensation, and with students who suspected him of not being forthright in his efforts to bring them together as equals.

And another significant contrast: in Boston he was in a world of men. Nothing remotely like coeducation was at issue. (On a practical level, when a provision about fair representation of women in hiring practices on construction sites came up, it was pointed out that there just weren't enough likely candidates around to fill whatever quota of them was proposed, so the idea got nowhere.) In the day-to-day workings of the Commission, in offices or in hearings, there were women in subsidiary and supportive positions, but with the exception of Frances Burke, the only woman whose name comes up in accounts and recollections of the Commission, none in a position of authority.

It was like being at Boston Latin again, or in the Marines. It was especially important that he feel at home with the speaker of the House, Thomas McGee, and that in turn he make McGee feel at home with him. Ward courted him, did so by coming on not as the former president of a prestigious college but as just another Boston Irishman and former Marine like McGee himself. One prominent legislator thought that Ward might have been motivated by too strong a desire to be liked, that he might not have had to try so hard (after all, ultimately his allies on Beacon Hill did have the requisite number of votes), but there is no doubt but that he was politically successful, most notably when the bill establishing the office of Inspector General was being debated. McGee was vehemently opposed. He saw it as what he called "a new branch of government in the control of one person." Were the bill to create the I.G. to pass, McGee said he would move to Russia. Ward went into McGee's office, the two of them talked about their war experiences, they even smoked cigars. Not only did they come to an agreement (a six-member panel would temper the I.G.'s subpoena power), but the two men emerged from McGee's office to announce to the press how they had settled the issue, in effect to hold a press conference, which was something McGee had almost never done before.

Then, after he had left Amherst and moved to Boston, there was the tenor of the life Ward led. "He simply loved walking across the Common, looking at the statues," Barbara said, and loved "going back to Dorchester [and] talking with ex-Marines." And there was the different kind of life that *they* led as a couple. In apartments first on Commonwealth Avenue and then on Beacon Hill, and often at Ward's and everyone else's favorite restaurant, Locke-Ober's, the Wards led, by all accounts, a much more easeful and happy life than they had led in Amherst. Finally, it is worth noting that nobody has mentioned his being subject to "dark, Irish moods" during the two and a half years he spent in Boston.

TO DESCEND into the world in which Ward worked, it was in April 1978, in his third year as governor of Massachusetts (and Ward's penultimate year as Amherst president) that Michael Dukakis signed into law a bill "providing for an investigation and study by a special commission relative to corruption involved in certain state and county building contracts"—i.e., the Special Commission Concerning State and County Buildings. Most prominent among those contracts, in effect the reason why the commission was called for, was the one awarded to the consulting management firm of McKee-Berger-Mansueto, the supervisor of construction at the new University of Massachusetts campus on Columbia Point in Dorchester. The reward of the effort that it takes to follow the story of the corruption involved is at the very least an appreciation of what the Commission was up against. (The volume in the *Final Report*, one of twelve, on "The Investigation of MBM and Related Entities" is 321 pages long.) Ward would have said that it is the kind of story all of us, as citizens, ought not just to know but to care and do something about.

In the fall of 1976 and the spring of 1977, Joseph Di Carlo and Ronald MacKenzie, two Massachusetts State Senators, were indicted and put on trial for extorting money from MBM to fix a legislative investigation into the job they were doing. (In March they were sentenced to a year in prison and fined $5,000 apiece.) During the trial, allegations were made about possible wrongdoings by state employees who were not involved in the so-called "conspiracy" case, about the Bureau of Building Construction (BBC) and its Design Selection Board (DSB) in particular, and about kickbacks to firms and individuals involved in other state construction contracts. It turned out that the coordinator of the DSB had done consulting work in Chicago for MBM in 1972 while he was a member of the DSB and that he was one of five members of the BBC who had spent a week cruising in the Caribbean in a yacht owned by one William Masiello, who was head of a Worcester, Massachusetts, architectural firm that had been awarded many public contracts. He, in turn, had been named in the "conspiracy trial" as having advised MBM to make a $10,000 political contribution to a "Mr. X," who turned out to be Albert "Toots" Manzi, a fundraiser for Dukakis' predecessors, Edward Volpe and Francis Sargent. To explain "conspiracy" is to move one step further into the shady world of Boston politics. Di Carlo was Senate majority leader, likely to be its future president, a position that Billy Bulger coveted and eventually occupied as a result of the exposure of Di Carlo by an FBI agent. The agent was not just any FBI agent, but one who had grown up with Billy's brother "Whitey," who passed on information to that agent about the Italian mafia while getting a free pass to eliminate as many Mafiosi as he deemed necessary for his own, as well as his brother's, advancement to the top, to the top of the Senate in his brother's case, in his case to the top of the criminal underworld.

It seemed that a lot of corruption was involved in the state's awarding MBM that contract, and that a lot of money changed hands in the process, much of it for inferior construction—or for no construction at all. In January 1978, the state auditor released drafts of reports on the construction of the UMass Boston campus that showed what the investigation that Di Carlo and MacKenzie fixed had omitted. For example, after four years, more than $3 million would be needed to repair defects, and the BBC had paid MBM $457,272.48 for "services never received by the Commonwealth," and there were $914,000 in change orders that the director of the BBC had authorized over the objections of most of his staff. As would be made clear in the course of the Commission's existence, public buildings in the Commonwealth had been poorly planned, badly designed, negligently supervised, shoddily constructed and paid for at astronomical rates. Whatever crimes were committed were not victimless. In its summary of the *Final Report*, the *Globe* pointed out the consequences to every taxpayer:

> Since 1968, the state has spent $7.73 billion on state construction projects with severe defects.
> Each Massachusetts taxpayer has spent an average of $3126 for severely defective construction since 1968 and will have to pay an average of $857 to repair the defects.

Referring to the fact that at least five overlapping investigations into the MBM contract were underway, State Attorney General Francis X. Bellotti, said in late January, "It's insane the way it is now," and called for a special commission. Two state representatives, Andy Card (a Republican who later became George W. Bush's White House chief of staff) and Philip Johnston (a Democrat who would become regional administrator of Health and Human Services for New England during the Clinton administration and chairman of the Massachusetts Democratic Party) echoed his call and proposed that it have the power to subpoena documents and individuals, to request grants of immunity and to refer evidence to appropriate prosecutorial agencies, and that provisions of grand jury secrecy extend to private hearings. Later, before the Joint Judiciary Committee, Card added that the ultimate goal of the Commission should be to recommend legislation that would address the issues that the commission had defined. Endorsing their proposal, in an editorial, the *Globe* said that "unlike a crime commission, the panel's investigation should be limited to the case at hand," but that its mandate should be "broad enough to get out all the facts, to allow examination of the state's procedures for drawing contracts, provisions for oversight and record keeping in connection with campaign funds." Common Cause wrote legislators urging them to set up an independent "Blue Ribbon Commission"; a popular talk show host became an influential advocate. (He later testified before the same committee that 8,432 people had written him in support of the creation of the Commission.) A bill was filed on February 6, 1978, and admitted in the Senate two weeks later, during which time Dukakis cancelled 17 state contracts, worth more than $11 million, with Masiello's firm. On April 12 the Commission bill was signed into law by Dukakis.

The Commission would consist of seven members—a retired Supreme Court or Superior Court justice, a lay person who had never served as a member of the general court, a dean of a law school or president of an institution of higher learning in the Commonwealth (who would chair the Commission), the president of the Massachusetts Bar Association or another member named by him, a registered architect and a registered engineer—all appointed by a theoretically disinterested party, the secretary or the auditor of the Commonwealth, or by the governor himself, and one person, the state attorney general or a member of his department, who worked in government. (There was a limit to how much autonomy the legislature was willing to grant the Commission.) The commissioners would themselves hire their chief counsel. All of them would serve without pay—pro bono. Their investigation and study of corruption and "maladministration" would include but not necessarily be limited to the MBM contract; yet, it was argued, because of the expense that would be involved, and because of the impending application of the statute of limitations, they could not examine any contract awarded before January 1, 1968. The Commission had subpoena power. If any witness refused to testify "on the basis of his privilege against self-incrimination, the commission [could] apply to a justice of the supreme judicial court for an order granting immunity to said witness." The Commission would submit interim reports in July 1978 and April 1979 and a final report of its findings and recommendations, "together with drafts of legislation necessary to carry its recommendations into effect," by December 31 of that year.

That spring the members of the Commission were duly chosen; on May 12 Dukakis announced that Ward would be their chairman. Dukakis did so on the recommendation of John Olver, the former UMass chemistry professor, now the Representative from the district that included Amherst. (His wife, Rose, as we know, was converted to feminism by her experience on the Select Committee on Coeducation at Amherst, had been appointed the Chair of the Committee on the Status of Women by Dukakis.) Dukakis told Ward that the work on the commission wouldn't amount to all that much—just a day a week. In July the commissioners announced that Nick Littlefield was their choice for the position of Chief Counsel.

FOUR MONTHS after the Commission bill was passed, in July 1978, McGee and Billy Bulger announced in a letter to the legislature that "the commission was officially constituted." Soon after, Ward wrote down some of his reflections on the nature of the Commission and the work that he imagined lay ahead. They are the first indications of the spirit in which the Commission's work would be undertaken under his leadership and that would prevail throughout its existence. It would be, like the document itself, elevated in principle and in tone.

After a short summary of the Commission's broad mandate ("to inquire into the past in order to make recommendations for the future") Ward described three characteristics of the Commission that would define its sense of itself and the image that it would present to the public and the legislature. First was a restatement of the Commission's mandate that emphasized "correction in the future and not just punishment in the present." The Commission was not embarking on a witch hunt. It would not be like the Crime Commission of the late '60s that had thrilled the public with its findings—WASP investigators exposing a host of shady Irishmen. If it uncovered "corruption or flagrant maladministration" it would report it to the proper office, and it would go further: it would propose legislation intended to bring about reform. Second, tapping into his most deeply felt and firmly held political convictions, Ward said, "we will conduct ourselves and the work of the Commission in a manner which inspires confidence in the integrity of our work. We should, in effect, offer a model of what citizens of the commonwealth may expect of their servants." As he said repeatedly in his presentations of his democratic ideal, the conduct of the Commission's business should meet the highest standards of procedure: "The power granted us is a temptation if not guarded against. We should not lightly use it because we can easily destroy reputations and careers. If, humanly, we err, we should be strong enough to say so publicly and at once, so no innocent person is harmed by us. We need, in sum, to be tactful and judicious." Eventually "volunteers/work study students, student interns and voluntary paralegals" from 21 educational institutions across the state, and two, Columbia and Yale, outside it, would join in the work of the Commission. He did have to restrain some of the more fired-up crusaders among them. According to the *Globe*, he also cautioned Commission members "to curb their aggression when questioning some witnesses," adding that he preferred to call them "guests." And third, Ward wrote, "we must agree to act as 'a Commission,' a corporate body." Of course it would be impossible to say nothing to the media, but individuals should be careful not to speak for the Commission itself. "When the Commission speaks, it should be through its chairman." (No letters from the faculty going directly to the trustees.) He, as chairman, would be cautious himself. If at all possible, he would "discover the consensus of the Committee before making any announcements or pronouncements." And though he did not say so in these reflections, he did on other occasions: there would be no leaks. As Littlefield said, "He was fiercely opposed to any leak coming from within the Commission—and it never did."

All very well, but how exactly was the Commission to proceed? Though not everyone would have used the analogy, everyone knew that anyone, any Commission, looking into "corruption involved in certain state and county building contracts" in Massachusetts *and* trying to do something about what they discovered was like Hercules working away in the Aegean stables. But again Littlefield: "Ward was no conventional muckraker. He was as interested in the quality of the raking, as in the quantity of the muck." And more. He was interested in the result as well—in clean government in the future. But how was the Commission going to succeed in its labor? How was it to confront what the "The Commission's Narrative" called "the tremendously complex and confused system," a system so complex and confused, they soon discovered, that it could hardly be called a system at all? As Ward said in the first volume of the *Final Report*, "Ultimately, the Commission had to reconstruct the universe it was charged to investigate."

The investigative procedure they chose was to study private firms' business operations and particular building projects and individuals involved in the construction process by summoning and examining their books and records. The going was difficult. They began without knowing any crime had been committed; they could analyze records for months and emerge with nothing to report. But the method had proven successful in other cases, one in New Jersey, for example, another in Maryland, the one that resulted in Spiro Agnew's being charged with bribery and extortion and his subsequent resignation as Nixon's vice president. The process of preparing charts and chronologies that compared inflow of money, outflow of money, expense vouchers and invoices, meetings with participants and events in the contracting process, double-checking invoices to see whether or not services had actually been performed, calling witnesses and obtaining more documents to corroborate statements they had made, which would lead to summoning more witnesses who might provide more information was dizzying, but this model had proven successful and it was therefore the one that the Commissioners had begun to emulate. At strategic points they would publicize their findings, which is to say, they would use public hearings as a way of inspiring the legislature and the citizenry to call for reform.

In the beginning, as the "Narrative" calmly puts it, the commissioners "underrated the magnitude of the findings" and of the need "for wholesale reform of the system and the scope of corruption in it." By the end, they had to have the help of literally hundreds of people, all listed by Ward in the "Acknowledgments" in the first volume of the *Final Report*, everyone from "the firm but friendly Capitol Police who maintained strict decorum at public hearings" (and whom one can easily imagine Ward greeting on the way in or out as if these officers might be from Dorchester too) to Littlefield, whose appointment was "not only the most important decision, it was the best decision the Commission made." In between are lists of lawyers on investigations, lawyers on legislation, CPAs, former IRS and FBI investigators, paralegals and editors, administrators, secretaries and receptionists within the Commission, auditors, resource groups (specialists on public construction procurement systems, campaigns, public management, construction industries), "systems hearings witnesses," 134 "Others," beginning with the United States Attorney and ending with the volunteers, the work-study students, interns, and paralegals who represented the future to Ward. There are more than 200 of them, more than half the number that had graduated from Amherst College each spring while he was there. He had always hoped that among the Amherst graduates there would be a goodly number who would go on to care and work for the betterment of American society. They might, they might not. He could be more hopeful about the "young people" who had worked with the Commission. They had demonstrated their willingness to do just that. "If the next generation has the enthusiasm, the interest in public service, and the capacity for hard work these young people showed," he concluded, "then there is hope for the future." (His hopes were well-founded: in 1985 they made up half of the federal prosecutors investigating corruption in the state.)

The story of the Commission is the stuff of fable or romance, or of crusaders, Thoreau might have called them, going forth to reconquer "this Holy Land [call it democratic America] from the hands of the Infidels," knights slaying dragons, virtue triumphing over vice, complete with "virtue rewarded" to a degree that nobody would have predicted, but the details are mundane, one political ploy, one questionable financial deal after another, the whole leading to the conclusion that Ward drew in the *Final Report*: "Corruption is a way of life in the Commonwealth of Massachusetts." Nothing fabulous, nothing romantic. And though we will give some details, some of which might be considered sensational, some even comic, what is finally most impressive about the story is the sheer amount of hard and efficient work that went into the making of it under Ward's leadership—it and its relatively happy ending.

THE OBSTACLES the Commission faced were seemingly insurmountable—but not to Ward. The most daunting was the most pervasive and the most difficult to pin down: cynicism. At a hearing before the Joint Judiciary

Ward testifying on Beacon Hill

Committee in March on amendments to the original mandate, proposed by the Commission and Card and Johnston, it was the first thing Ward spoke about. He did so in his introductory remarks about the importance of the Commission. Everyone seemed to agree on its importance. He himself couldn't have been more emphatic about it: "I will flatly say to you that the work of the Special Commission Concerning State and County Buildings engages, in its small way, the single most important issue which confronts this state and this country; the capacity of the ordinary citizen to believe the social order is decent and fair." So why did he feel it was necessary to belabor the point? He answered by way of an anecdote. A television reporter had asked him if he was surprised by anything he had discovered so far, and he had said no: "I imagined that almost any citizen of the Commonwealth of Massachusetts would expect to discover exactly what the Commission has discovered, a widespread pattern of favoritism, ambiguous dealings, outright illegality in the generations of cash, and probably corruption." But he was shocked. "Perhaps you, as legislators, are beyond shocking. I am not," he said. What shocked him was the need for a commission, shocked him "that it requires a special resolve of the Legislature to inquire whether people who do business with the state, or people who are responsible for the conduct of the business of the state, need to have a special body to insure whether they are responsible to their professional ethics or their public trust." The legislators knew what the situation was. So too did people "out there," people who "already know more than the investigative staff can discover, people smug in the confidence we can never discover their betrayal of the public trust." And beyond them was the general public; in it, he went on to say, there was, "to put it brutally, cynicism." They too knew. (Months later Ward would cite a Clark University survey: only eight percent of the people of Massachusetts believed that their government was not corrupt.) They knew, and they didn't think there was a thing that could be done about it. He told the committee that members of the Commission had spoken to "Chambers of Commerce, Rotary Clubs, the Massachusetts Bar, other professional associations, and students at colleges and universities in the state"; their audiences were "wholly skeptical that we in our work will make any difference at all in the conduct of public life in this state." That was what shocked him.

Many, probably most, people in those audiences would have called him naive, but his response would be that theirs was a lowly, cynical perspective. He did not view the situation the way they did. He was an idealist. He thought something could be done to reform the system. We know he was not an innocent, but he did have a lot to learn—and he wanted to learn. According to Bob Turner, who reported on the Commission's activities for the *Globe*, "He was "interested in seeing how things worked," and he was "very determined, smart." Andy Card's responses to Ward track these stages: cynical at first, given the number of investigations he'd seen come to nothing; then skeptical as he watched Ward at work, but finally a believer and an advocate because he saw that Ward was a "real idealist, truly independent, and not arrogant." Ward was not setting himself above or apart from anyone else. His ideals were not merely personal, not ones he could live up to alone; they were ones everyone had to live up to if there was to be a true democracy. Ward went on to speak to those ideals before the Judiciary Committee. As he said to its members, he and everyone else involved in the work of the Commission were embodying them right then and there. They were "citizens," working pro bono for the Common-wealth, for the common weal. Add "political savvy" to Ward's qualifica-tions and you can say that if anyone could lead a commission in such a way as to give citizens reason to believe that those they elected were respon-sible to them, he was that man. He was beginning to make big strides on the high road.

(From time to time we must remind ourselves that though he had re-signed the previous November, and would soon be without a job, Ward was still Amherst's president, and that that spring he had more to contend with than he had had since he had been arrested at Westover eight years before. He was embroiled in debate with his faculty over compensation; students opposed to the College's investments in South Africa and his plans for orientation occupied Converse Hall; the cross-burning brought the College to a halt. Occasionally we ought to be even more specific, to note, for example, that after the meeting with the Joint Judiciary Com-mittee he had to go back to preside over a faculty meeting that night that would include discussion of the idea of professors devoting ten percent less of their time to the work of the College because their purchasing pow-er had declined by that much.)

Cynicism may have been the major obstacle, but there were many oth-ers. There were the ways of large bureaucracies—budgetary constraints, made the more acute when, say, paychecks to members of the commis-sion's staff were as much as four months late, problems with office space, not just size but relocations, four forced moves in the first ten months, for example. Perhaps they just went with the territory, or perhaps they were ex-amples of what Ward called "covert resistance." If the latter, one assumes Dukakis would have had something done about them, but he had been de-feated in the Democratic primary in 1978. After that, the obstructions were more clearly not innocent, nor were they very well hidden. The man who succeeded Dukakis as governor in January 1979, Edward King, was not, and had reason not to be, happy about the existence of the Commission. He tried to slow down or halt its progress at many stages along its way.

In the first stage, in the first full year of the Commission's existence, 1979, the obvious means of slowing down its progress was trying to see to it that there wouldn't be enough money. A month went by. No money, nothing came from King's office other than word that he didn't think there was any emergency. When Ward and Littlefield met with him in February 1979 (at Ward's request) King said he wasn't familiar with the Commission, he hadn't had time to read about it. Ward explained the Commission's mandate. He said the Commission wasn't interested "in creating scandal"; he didn't want to be put, or put King, in an adversarial position. When King said he wondered why the Attorney General couldn't do the investigating, Ward explained further: the Commission had been created because the public didn't trust political agencies to investigate corruption impartially. There happened to be funds left over from a previous allotment, but wisely, just in case, in late January the Commission had applied for a federal grant from the Law Enforcement Assistance Administration. Its award of $209,500 helped tide them over.

The amendments to the original mandate were intended to clear away other obstacles that King wanted to remain in place. The first and most important one pushed back the date of contracts that the Commission could investigate indefinitely by adding the words: "and concerning design, survey, boring, soil exploration and feasibility contracts and other investigative study contracts awarded before January 1, 1968, which relate to construction contracts for state and county buildings awarded on or after January 1, 1968." Years often elapsed between the initial authorization of a building, the designing of it, and the eventual award of a contract to build it, nine years in one case, as many as five in others. It would be impossible to discover the source of problems, to find out who was at fault, who was benefitting, without being able to examine contracts awarded before January 1, 1968. The second amendment was intended to make it clear that the "state" that awarded contracts meant "the Commonwealth of Massachusetts and public instrumentalities established under general or specific laws," thereby ensuring that any building paid for by taxpayers' dollars was a state or county building. Another had it that the Commission's life would be extended six months, to June 30, 1980. Investigations were already under way, so much was turning up, there had been so many delays. "We are still embroiled in the bureaucratic process of securing the necessary funds to continue and complete our work," Ward pointed out, and, moreover, there was the final report that they had to submit. Nobody wanted the work to go on forever, but everyone wanted to get it done and done right—which would eventually lead the commissioners to ask for and be granted a further six-month extension to December 31, 1980.

In late May the House approved the amendments to the original re-solve, but the Senate did not immediately take up the bill. Weeks later, when it did, there were changes. The language about "public instrumen-talities" had been deleted. The House counsel had taken out the language without informing the speaker; he told Ward and Littlefield that what he had done was the kind of thing that could be done any time; it was a not a substantial change; he would reinstate it. And out of nowhere there ap-peared a new amendment. A year into their work, the commissioners were to be joined by an eighth member. He was to be a retired judge (the hypo-thetical judge that had been in the legislation that created the Commission but never found), and he was to be appointed by the governor. Not worth a headline. Just the kind of thing you come upon on the roads leading up to the State House. Maybe not worth raking, but you had to wonder. Who was it that wanted to have someone new on the Commission, perhaps some-one who would talk about what investigations were going on? Card said, not unreasonably, that "the proposal was made in King's interest." What-ever the case, you had to agree with Card's characterization of the whole incident: it was "very bizarre." Another move by King was more serious: in a letter to "The Honorable Senate and House of Representatives" he moved that the amendment that enabled the Commission to investigate contracts awarded before January 1, 1968, be stricken. A lot had happened before that date that he didn't want to come to light.

In 1964 King had become the executive director of the Massachusetts Port Authority; he'd remained in that position until 1974 when Dukakis was elected governor. There was no love lost between the two men; one of the first things Dukakis did upon assuming office was fire him. In his ten years at Massport, one of those "public instrumentalities" that the Commission almost lost the authority to investigate, King awarded many contracts, including the lion's share of those for work at Logan Airport, to Desmond and Lord, a firm whose president was Richard Thissen, "a close friend and traveling companion of King" and a contributor to his success-

ful campaign against Dukakis in 1978. Supposedly a design firm, supposedly on the up-and-up, what with a name like Desmond and Lord, it em-
ployed not architects but men who were essentially what Littlefield called
"fixers," men who saw to it that contracts went to those whose political
contributions were the highest. To enlarge the picture, according to the
Final Report, the fees received by Thissen's firm "and its joint venture part-
ners for these services, represented 98 percent of all the architectural fees
paid by Massport between July 1, 1968, to June 1, 1978." And it followed: in
the summer of 1979, the work that Desmond and Lord supposedly oversaw at Cape Cod Community College, Southeastern Massachusetts University, and Salem State College was under investigation. Eventually Bellotti's office filed a $3 million suit against them for their faulty design work.
Coming full circle to campaign fundraising, Thissen had been Governor
Peabody's "leading financial supporter" and (again it followed) Desmond
and Lord had received more contracts during Peabody's administration
than any other firm.

King tried to amend the amendment, to get the legislature to return to
the original language of the bill they were to vote on, and thus to prevent
the Commission from investigating contracts awarded before January 1,
1968, but it took the House less than 30 seconds to reject his amendment
by voice vote. No senator even moved it. After that, the Commission was
finally (relatively) free to get on with its work. And having moved to Boston at the beginning of July, Ward was free to give that work his undivided
attention.

THE COMMISSION'S investigative strategy was two-fold: it focused
on "the award of contracts to design firms, consultants and suppliers" and
on "the performance of contractors and sub-contractors." It had become
the Commission's working hypothesis that "corruption involving public
officials was most likely to occur at the point where discretion was exer-
cised by a public official, and where substantial sums of money and profits
were to be made by private firms who were the beneficiaries of the public
official's discretionary decision." The award of a contract was the public
official's first "discretionary decision." The second, "the area of greater
discretion," was in his supervision of a contractor's performance. The con-

tractors submitted bids. A contractor who could be sure that his performance would not be well scrutinized could get away with using inferior
materials and with cutting corners. He knew that he could go ahead and
bid low and thus win a contract; he knew he could still make a profit by sav-
ing on his performance. How, on what basis, did the public official come to
his decisions when he awarded contracts? Why did he look the other way
while supervising a contractor's work? How could a contractor knowingly
perform badly and be confident that he would suffer no consequences? In
his summary of the Commission's work in the *Final Report* Ward's answer
is simple: "The name of the game is cash....When bribes are paid or money is extorted, and the two are opposite sides of a single coin and hard to
distinguish, there has to be cash." And cash it was—what the "Narrative"
calls "the tell-tale sign." (Legitimate businesses and businessmen wrote
checks.) After reviewing several hundred contracts and contractors, the
Commission focused on six where they thought corruption was most likely to have occurred.

On March 19, 1980, Ward addressed the Joint Committee on State Administration about the construction reform bill that the Commission was
working on. Again he made the point that the Commission understood its
mandate to be to put in place "a comprehensive system of administration
which defines responsibility and locates clearly so the Commonwealth
may with assurance say to the public that it does its business well," but
that as things stood, there *was* no system. In his remarks you can hear how
much he had learned, you can hear the authority in his voice.

Examples of corruption had been coming to light for months as a result
not only of the Commission's investigations but of the attorney general's
as well. There were the three projects of Thissen's firm, Desmond and
Lord. There was—the most sensational example—the library at UMass
Amherst, supposedly the tallest library in the world, that had been closed
in August after it was discovered that "design deficiencies in the ironwork
posed a 'catastrophic' threat to life and property." At a later hearing, Walter McCarthy, a commissioner who was professor of civil engineering at
Southeastern Massachusetts University, deplored the fact that "an insid-
ious thing like that creates the failure of a beautiful structure like that."
(The *Globe* put it put it more graphically: "Bricks came hurtling down, en-
dangering passers-by.") A few stories like these had made the papers after

the Commission's hearings in the fall; many, many more would appear during the public hearings that would soon begin. Ward cited a handful of other examples and explained why each was symptomatic of a general problem. There were five courthouses in Worcester County within a 25-mile radius, each costing a million dollars. Which was to say, "there is no single responsibility for overall planning." At the Concord State Prison a designer had been paid three times for designs for a building that had never been built. Which was to say, "when an individual project is approved, there is no prior analysis of the needs it must meet to determine whether it should be built at all"—and to say more, "since 1968, the state has paid more than 20 millions of dollars for design plans for buildings which have never been built." At UMass (again in Amherst) a power plant had been built at a cost of $11 million, a plant that had never worked. Which was to say, "When projects are built, there is no supervision to see they are built well," to which he added, "in a timely fashion at reasonable cost," because he also spoke of the millions wasted on delays ("On average, construction takes 170 percent of the time estimated in the original contract," he pointed out) and overruns. Then addressing the Joint Committee directly, he said that "since the administration of the state is your essential business," it should discover how many contracts had been awarded by state agencies over the last ten years. In a year and a half the Commission itself had not been able to find out how many contracts it had been charged to investigate, nor even how many buildings the state owned or leased. "We are not asking you to reform a system," he told the Joint Committee. "We are asking you to create a system."

In its summary of the Commission's life, the *Globe* cited 17 examples, examples that should have more than satisfied those who wanted some shocking details. Among them were the UMass library and the Tilson Farm Power Plant. There were the nine buildings comprising Cape Cod Community College, supported by jacks and scaffolding and so porous that mushrooms grew on carpets; Bridgewater State College, where the baseball diamond was underwater unless there was a drought (and when there was, it was an uphill run to first); the Haverhill Parking Garage that began to collapse before it was finished; the seven-story elderly housing project in Melrose in which the cost of the defects equaled the original design and construction cost; another building for the elderly in Randolph, where the water leakage was "profuse" and the ventilation system didn't work; and the Worcester County Jail, where—it seemed only right—officials had given up using surveillance cameras in some areas after spending $23,000 in repairs of a security system that cost $60,000 and where one automatic cell-locking system simply didn't work.

The hearings that would put all of the corruption on public display began on March 28th and ran for fourteen weeks. The setting was Room 436 on the second floor of the State House, a relatively small room, wider than deep. The commissioners sat at one raised and slightly bowed desk; behind them were rows of legal tomes. Before them, in 43 days of public testimony, ninety-six witnesses appeared, their testimony eventually covering more than 4,000 transcribed pages. The *Globe* described the atmosphere of that first day as "much like an opening night at the theater." TV cameras were lined up six in a row, cameramen and photographers jockeyed for position amidst a maze of wires and tripods. Before the hearing started, Deputy Chief Counsel Dwyer briefed as many as fifty reporters about the documents that would be involved. A veteran reporter said he hadn't seen anything like it in fifteen years, not since the Crime Commission presented its allegations against state officials. The excitement didn't abate during the Commission's run. Nor did the media coverage. Three of the twelve rows of seats were reserved for reporters. Some days that was not enough. Some days there would be as many as six reporters from the *Globe* alone checking in for story leads. Littlefield would remind the commissioners that they needed to expose a bribe a day by noon—otherwise the Commission wouldn't be in the evening editions.

And there was Ward, running the whole show, and then a few hours later appearing in the papers and on the news. He was undeniably important, what he always wanted to be. That had to have pleased him. But we must go on to say that what was theatrical about the hearings was as nothing compared to what they meant to him and to those who followed them. When it was all over, Littlefield put it best:

He did restore confidence. The people saw on the television news, night after night, at the public hearings, an easygoing man with a long, sparkling, craggy face, looking out over his half glasses, whose single motivation was the public good. He was in charge, at the center. The people knew he fought for them. They looked up to him because he was incorruptible; no one could touch him.

As he said, "his work was living up to his idealism"—finally.

The hearings gave ample evidence of the "pattern of campaign contributions" that governed how building contracts were awarded. The testimony of Frank Masiello and his brother William, given under a grant of immunity, was especially clear. It was all about "political contributions," or "campaign fund-raising," or, under the pressure of questioning by the Commission, Frank Masiello had to admit, "bribery." He told about being "the middle man" between Daniel, Mann, Johnson & Mendenhall, the Los Angeles firm that received the design contract for "the multi-million dollar Holyoke Community College" and "Toots" Manzi, a fundraiser for Governor Volpe. Manzi had originally told Frank that without a contribution of around $70 thousand to $80 thousand DMJM wouldn't get the Holyoke contract. He later agreed to $22,000. No checks. Cash. After a DMJM official came through (one installment being $6,000 worth of five-dollar bills, stuffed in a briefcase, which he delivered to Manzi's grocery store in Worcester), his firm was awarded the contract by the Administration and Finance Commissioner. Masiello's firm was listed as "the project consultant." In order to keep the contracts coming, Masiello himself had given monies to Governor Peabody's campaign as well. Masiello described the workings of the latter in some detail: a three-room suite in the Statler Hilton, consisting of a waiting room, a room in which you met the governor and told him you were interested in making a contribution, and a third, in which your pledge was recorded. If you couldn't come up with the funds right away, you were told a loan could be arranged. Subsequently, the Commissioner of Administration and Finance would put a check or a dot next to the firm he wanted to get the contract—and that was that.

Among the other players, among the many witnesses who appeared before the Commission, were government officials who had a hard time seeing that anything was wrong. Governor Peabody himself, for example, told the commissioners that he saw no problem with his or any other administration's awarding contracts to "people who support your campaign, who believe in your candidacy, and who put you in office." He admitted that "many of the buildings resulting from the contracts he had awarded did not live up to expectations," but, he said, "compromises had to be made to raise political funds." He cited the case of the UMass library, and then went on. "I'd always hoped [it] might be called the Peabody Library," he said, "but after I visited it, I decided I didn't want it to be called the Peabody Library anymore." (Safe now, it is called the W.E.B. DuBois Library, named after one of the truly great sons of Massachusetts.) The man in charge of handing out architectural contracts during Peabody's administration explained that the better firms didn't apply for contracts because they knew that campaign contributions were expected in return. But all you needed was average competence. Then in awarding contracts "we favored the person who was one of the governor's supporters," the man said. "I make no apologies for that."

The Commission staff grew, they covered more and more ground in their investigations—literally (at one point they traveled to Puerto Rico, Great Britain and Switzerland in their investigations)—but they never lost sight of where they were headed. Their goal was to propose reforms and to see that they became laws. They would not make the mistake that the Crime Commission had made a decade before. They would not wait until the very end, until their final report, to make recommendations that would never be adopted because they were not around to explain and defend them. The deadline for filing legislation to be acted on during the legislature's 1980 session was December 5, 1979.

In the fall, as the commissioners worked on proposals, they consulted with government officials, representatives from the industry, and public interest groups, with a group of managers who worked with the Port Authority, the Department of Correction, and the Department of Community Affairs, and a group established with the help of the Massachusetts Construction Council. Realizing that there was a connection between public officials' "discretionary decisions" and their need for campaign funds, they authorized a study of Massachusetts' campaign financing laws. The man Ward named to direct it was Rich Read, still an Amherst undergraduate at the time, and still the editor of the *Student,* who worked with the Commission over the summer and then commuted weekly to Boston in the fall. The commissioners also held public hearings, nine of them, with fifty-three witnesses.

On December 5 among the almost 8,500 pieces of legislation that

were filed were three from the Commission: H.5619, "An act providing
for the establishment of Inspector General; ("an apolitical investigative
body to prevent and detect fraud, waste, and abuse of public funds," as
the *Globe*'s "Overview" has it); H5620, "An act to improve the system of
public construction in the Commonwealth," a law that "tightens architect
and contractor selection procedures"—the two together running to about
200 pages); and H5567, "An act prohibiting civil and criminal fraudulent
acts affecting the Commonwealth" or what it called "commercial bribery"
(which increases "substantially the ability of law enforcement agencies to
prosecute individuals and firms found to have defrauded the Commonwealth or its cities and towns"). A fourth, a "late-filed" campaign reform
bill, was added and admitted in June. This last would fail for a simple reason: as Barney Frank said, those who had succeeded in getting elected, by
whatever means, were not likely to vote for a change in the way their campaigns would be financed in the future. What progress the Commission's
remaining three pieces of legislation made was very slow.

There was the sheer number of bills, and the amendments and the
amendments to the amendments, before the legislature. There were the
House and Senate committees that had to consider bills and iron out their
differences before they reached the House and Senate floors. The Commission had to spend time defending itself in lawsuits challenging its legitimacy for one reason or another, filed by men who, with good reason, did
not want to appear before it. There was, in other words, democratic business as usual. There had been what Ward had called "covert resistance"
when the Commission was trying to get started, and for reasons we have
noted, King and his staff maintained their distance for most of the time
thereafter. But King's resistance could be active and overt as well. He had
begun "quietly" to implement "some of the Commission's administrative
recommendations in an attempt to prove Commission legislation unnecessary," and there were rumors (that proved to be facts) that efforts were
being made to refer the Commission's legislation to a Contracts Commission. The Commission alerted its supporters and also informed the State
Administration Committee that inasmuch as the Contracts Commission
would be dominated by industry representatives and the Bureau of Building Construction the move would have been like putting a chicken in the
fox coop, and the effort failed.

All the while, prorogation, the final session of the legislature, was rapidly approaching, and no action had been taken on the Commission's bills. It began to look as if the leadership might win, might successfully run out the clock, but backers of the Commission and Commission members met in late May and agreed to support a recommendation by Barney Frank that a letter be sent to House members urging them to vote on the Commission's proposals before prorogation or to vote against prorogation until their proposals had been defeated or acted upon by the governor. In early June the House passed a resolution to that effect by a large margin.

The final legislative session was traditionally chaotic and draining but this time around, according to the "Narrative," "The mood in the State House ran from nervous exhaustion to a condition of outright lunacy." The session went—nonstop—from 4 p.m. on July 3 until 10 a.m. on the 5th. Forty-one hours straight. One representative said, "We're throwing papers out the window, saying 'Help, we're held hostage.' This is unbelievable. We're all so tired we don't even know what the heck is happening." A mechanical bird was launched at one point, hovered over the chamber, and crashed in the midst of what a commissioner called the "organized confusion" below. "Anyone who loves sausages or democracy shouldn't see them being made," an AP news analyst said. "All that was missing from the wild scene," a Lowell newspaper reported, "was the gushing lava." Somehow 200 bills were passed and sent to the governor, among them the Commission's three. "It's a tremendous victory," Johnston told reporters. "It's extraordinary when you think that only a few weeks ago it looked like all was lost." Just four days before, McGee had told the commissioners "there was no way the contract reform bill would reach the floor of the House this year," and yet by three in the morning, the House had passed it and sent it on to the Senate.

But it wasn't as if a new day dawned. The story of the Ward Commission's "victory" wasn't over, even after it was over, even after those three bills were signed into law by King. Reminiscent of what had transpired the year before, when the bill to amend the legislation that brought the Commission into existence was mysteriously altered at the last minute, the Inspector General bill underwent two changes that were so radical that "reminiscent" is not really the word, nor is anything so dramatic as "the last minute" applicable. The changes were not discovered until after King had signed it into law, so nothing could be done about them, and the changes were more damaging than the deletion of "public instrumentalities" or the addition of an eighth commissioner. One involved, again, the Inspector General's subpoena power. It was blatantly self-serving. As altered, that power did not extend to the records of any legislative committee—in effect, any records of the legislature. The other, the deletion of "the power of the Inspector General to refer cases to any prosecutorial body, including the U.S. Attorney" with, literally, a stroke of the pen, was absurd. In Ward's acidic summary, "As the bill now stands, the Inspector General is in the preposterous position of not being able to refer a case to a federal prosecutor when he knows a federal law has been violated. It happens to be a crime not to refer evidence of a federal crime to federal authorities. The great and General Court of the Commonwealth of Massachusetts has created a high office in state government which forbids the incumbent to do that. Both changes were made surreptitiously. By whom no one knows."

The three bills the Commission had filed were signed into law by mid-July. The work of the all-important Inspector General was delayed for months by the turf war waged by King and Bellotti and the state auditor over the selection of the man who would hold the office, and because Bellotti did not think that his office was "a crucible for fact that a trial would have provided," he prosecuted far fewer cases than the Commission expected. Ward concluded that it had taken the Commission more than two years to look into the awarding of construction contracts, and it would take more than ten years to "create a climate of opinion where there is public trust because political leaders manifest the will to serve the public good."

In the five or six months remaining in the life of the Commission, it completed its ongoing investigations and referred evidence to law enforcement agencies, reviewed the legislation that had been enacted to see where it could be strengthened and what new legislation it might file in December, and prepared its final report. Ward's essay summarizing the Commission's experience appeared in the first of its twelve volumes. It is one of the finest pieces of writing he ever produced.

True to the standards of a professional historian, he writes at the outset that though he and his fellow commissioners knew that few would read the report, and that those who did would read only those sections in which they had a "special interest" ("We are not naive," he says), they knew that "lofty general observations" would not have much weight "without the ballast of a detailed, empirical account of the particulars." Thus 12 volumes. In his essay he said that the particulars were "set, however, in a general design":

First, what have we learned?
Second, what have we proposed to do on the basis of what we have learned?
Third, what do the first two say about politics and about the future?

In our effort to tell the story of the Ward Commission, we have drawn on the first two sections frequently. The third is evidence of the further evolution of Ward's democratic ideals, and it can help us understand what lay ahead for Ward himself.

From the beginning, the commissioners and their staff knew that though the public would be more interested in scandalous acts and dramatic examples, their task was to propose legislation. Some might imagine the world of politics was one "of good guys and bad guys," but Ward considered it "a complex process of ordinary people, by and large, trying to do their work under circumstances which inevitably affect how they do their work." The goal, the ideal, as it had been Ward's for decades now, was "to make government effective and honest." To reach it,

One must work at both dimensions: get good people to become active in politics and make public life an estimable and honorable calling; and, at the same time, design the institutional arrangements of government to attract good people and, more, to make it possible that they can do their work well.

As things stood, "the institutional arrangements of government" were certainly not attractive. The cynicism that had shocked him early on persisted. More and more people had become aware of the Commission's work; the large majority of them thought that it had done a good job and that the time and money spent by the Commonwealth was well spent. But among those very people, almost 60 percent still thought "things would go on as they always have and there would be no improvement whatsoever in the future."

Ironically, Ward went on, special commissions were not the best means of improving government. Their very existence was proof that governments could not be trusted to correct "the ills of public life." Not only were they commissioners who worked outside of government, they were *privileged* commissioners who worked outside of government, "insulated, by virtue of their own social and economic class, from the very social and economic pressures which it is the business of politics to mediate." The experience of the commissioners and their staff had been "intense, educational and rewarding in ways that money, the usual coin of the political realm, could never measure." But given their very nature they could not create confidence in government. That would depend on the press and television (though he never had anything very good to say about television), on citizens being informed and inspired to demand good government, and above all, on those who were elected and appointed to govern well. "All the commissions and all the legislation in the world cannot create that indispensable and necessary condition," the condition that he imagined existed in Jackson's day, "the will and the desire of people in government to serve the people." The Commission's experience of the resistance, the opposition, the subversions of those in power made him wonder.

And now? December 31, 1980? "The Commission ends with words of seasoned skepticism." The Commission's words, yes, but, most assuredly Ward's words as well:

> One needs to be precise: skepticism, not cynicism. Skepticism means that, whatever one's doubts, one must act as if one can make a difference. One never knows where the limits are until one presses against them to discover whether they are, indeed, limits or simply self-created excuses not to act, not to try.

His experience heading up the Commission had grounded him. His oft-repeated final words—"Keep the faith"—now had traction. The faith was specifically faith in democracy—by now, in his case certainly "seasoned."

When you think back over the political situation that Ward confronted, the political atmosphere in Massachusetts at the time, especially the "system" that wasn't a system, that the Commission sought to reform, and, and when you consider that by the accounts, thirty years later, of such authorities as Andy Card, Barney Frank, Nick Littlefield, and John Olver (like Frank, later a member of the United States House of Representatives), politics in Massachusetts are more honest than they have ever been. More specifically, when you hear Philip Johnston, now a trustee of the University of Massachusetts, say of the millions and millions of dollars of ongoing new construction on the Amherst campus that there has been "no whiff of scandal," you have to marvel at what Ward and the Commission he headed accomplished.

And we should recognize another important indication of Ward's legacy: the John William Ward Public Service Fellowships, established in 1986 by then U.S. District Judge Mark Wolf, that enable students at Ward's old school, Boston Latin, to work with public officials in the summer as interns. Since the program's inception, well over 300 Boston Latin students have worked with a wide range of public officials who have sponsored them—department heads in governors' and mayors' offices, state representatives, attorneys general, the inspector general, the police commissioner. The fellowships introduce young men and women to the rewards and importance of public service; they enable them to experience what it could be like to act, as Ward said one must act, "as if one can make a difference."

THE COMMISSION'S work was done. As the end approached, Ward's hopes still seemed to be high. He repeated almost verbatim what he had said on the eve of his departure from Amherst: "It's very exciting to quit a job and not know what you are going to do. It's a great feeling." But this time he was whistling much later in the day. Soon he, unlike his fellows commissioners, would have no paying job to return to. Back in April, while protesting against the delays on Beacon Hill, the *Globe* pointed out that Ward wanted to wrap things up. He had "no substantial income and has been working selflessly on a full-time basis for the past 18 months. But he has to come up with a suitable executive or administrative post—and soon—if he is to avoid going broke."

The College had given him compensation for the fiscal year 1979-80 (what amounted to the equivalent of an assistant professor's salary), and he did have *some* work. In September, George Carmany, an Amherst alumnus who knew of Ward's reputation in American Studies, acting upon the recommendation of "Spike" Beitzel, a prominent member of the Board of Trustees who was well aware of Ward's financial predicament, recruited Ward to come down to New York two days a week to work for him at American Express, where he was head of the Office of Strategic Planning.

It would overlap with his work with the Commission the way *it* had with his final months at Amherst; he would commute to New York and stay at the Harvard Club while he was there. Obviously it wouldn't lead to what he knew he really wanted to do, which was (what else could it be?) to work on social issues, on political issues in Boston. But, he said, "I'm not quite sure what that would be."

He sent out more than a score of letters asking for recommendations. Would that he had gone into politics when he was young. He never did stop thinking about it, going so far at one point (in one of what he called his Walter Mitty moods) to imagine starting a third party. He even had a name for it: The Commonwealth Party. For a time he pinned his hopes on being named the head of the Greater Boston Chamber of Commerce, or of HEFA, the Massachusetts Health and Educational Facilities Authority, an agency that helped nonprofit organizations get the financing they needed, but as fall approached, he was still doing what he called "vibrating the network" of connections without any success.

In November, in a speech to the Massachusetts Municipal Association, he said, "To try to create the conditions for a decent public life seems to me the highest calling there can be so that the old word, our 'commonwealth,' has meaning." By then, though, he could foresee that he would never respond to that calling in the way he wanted to respond. Nobody in Boston had hired him; nobody *would* hire him. It didn't help that the American Society of Public Administration recognized him for his work on the Commission as "the outstanding private citizen in the Commonwealth of Massachusetts." Nobody was sure what to make of him, or of what he would do to them. In the public sphere, politicians had been wary of him from the start. He later said that because of his having chaired the Commission, "the private sector" viewed him as "political and controversial" as well. He had confirmed that cronyism and corruption was everywhere. People were embarrassed by what he had revealed, Andy Card said. As a consequence, they were unwilling to break "the habit of cynicism." Robinson summed up Ward's effect on everyone in one word: he was "radioactive." In effect, Turner said, he was "driven out of town." In December Ward told a *Globe* reporter, "It did make me feel the town was a little small," and he recalled his saying to Barbara, "so much for good citizenship."

It was the beginning of the end.

FIVE

At the End

"Your son sounds like one of those rare people who is capable of knowing that he does not have the final Truth but, in all humility, was able to work and act with decency and humaneness and not fall into the selfishness of despair."
(Ward to the parents of a young academic who had died, July 1972)

"Yet despair, if it can remain genuine despair, is not the worst of emotions; it testifies, at least, to the earlier presence of desire."
(Ward in "Anarchy and Authority in American Literature," n.d.)

A T AMERICAN EXPRESS, Ward was once again an educator, a seminar leader, this time sitting around a table with twenty or twenty-five bright young men and women with MBAs, discussing the relations between cultural and business trends in America. What he was doing, he told the *Amherst Bulletin*, was intended to amplify "their awareness of the kind of social environment in which they're involved....[T]hey want me to make an educated guess on what the needs of American society will be in the 1980s." He would be there for eighteen months, maybe two years. "A lily pad for him," George Carmany later called it.

Early on, Ward circulated a position paper in which he introduced himself. Its title, "Some Reflections on Technology. American Express and Social Values," opened up a range of possibilities. "As an historian," he said, he would "bring to the Office the perspective of a student of American society and American values on the social environment in which the Company does its business; hopefully, to identify trends which may influence the Company's future development." Attention would be paid to advances in technology. He pointed out, for example, that the company would soon be putting its travel business on computers, that customers would no longer go through travel agents, and that American Express owned 50 percent of Warner Cable Communications. What was one to make of all that? He said he recognized that his interest in their work together had to bear some relation to their interest in making a profit, but he would insist on the larger political and social issues that he had focused on throughout his working life: the importance of the individual and the ideals that he expressed this time as no less than "justice, health, and peace." It was "the general area, the larger environment of implicit values and attitudes, which interests me the most," he said—adding, a little lamely, "and which I hope may also interest you."

Upon his return to Boston and the Commission's offices, he exclaimed, "Would you believe someone would pay you to do what you love most? They're paying me to sit and listen to me talk—it's wonderful!" He enjoyed it and they enjoyed him. The vice-president for corporate planning described him as "at his best at forcing us to think," and yet as Carmany said, when it came to "harvest time," the time when you compared the cost of the labor with the yield, you had to conclude that the experiment's success was limited.

In October, at the Kennedy Library, in a series of lectures commemorating Boston's 350th anniversary, Ward gave one titled "The Common Weal and the Public Trust: Politics and Public Morality." It was one of the more impressive speeches of his life. In glossing the ideal of serving the public good, he made it applicable to realms beyond what was literally political, and in the process made the challenge of realizing those ideals seem more difficult than ever before.

He devoted a major portion of his speech to "Ethnic Politics and Rational Politics," the difference between them providing him with another reason to question just how effective commissions were. The members of his Commission, he said, represented "the new middle class," the class that came into being in the census of 1870 and was presently "the single largest occupational group in the nation." The class had its virtues. It treated people as individuals; they were free to pursue their own goals in life; if they succeeded they did so because of their merits. A person was, in sum, "the bearer of his or her own meaning." But, he went on, there are kinds of associations that can be strong and justifiable, relations within the family being the most obvious. The Commission's investigations had taken no account of them: "The system of values which it took for granted, embodied, if you will, had little or no relation to the structure of values of many of those it investigated." *Their* "system of politics" was "personal and familial"; it was grounded in neighborhoods and shared ethnic associations. (There were signs of it that you couldn't ignore in those neighborhoods—real signs in front of dwellings that had Ward's picture on them, bracketed by the words: "Wanted! For a Witch Hunt Against the People of Massachusetts.") Witnesses didn't see the problem with awarding contracts to friends; that was the way they did business. But they and the ethnic politicians among them had little power and few of the privileges that went with power. His conclusion was sound and sobering: "The universalistic and individualistic values of the middle class have not been universal and individual after all; rather they have been used to sanction the interests and advantages of certain groups of society."

Both systems had their downsides. In that of "the new middle class," relations with others tended to be impersonal; one's sense of one's own worth was defined only by one's work, with the result that the individual became lonely, "involved only in transient and fleeting relations with others." Among those who had been excluded, there was, as we have seen, "outright extortion," "direct bribery," "favoritism," "a tolerance for poor workmanship and shoddy service." What underlay both, what most disturbed Ward, was "a loss of a sense of the meaning of *public* virtue and the reduction of judgment on public servants to individuals and personal criteria."

What was a good politician to do? It followed easily enough from his formulation of what was at issue: he was to embody what was the best in both worlds. "The politician, when he is good, translates social policy into personal terms," mediates "between principles and programs and the concrete individuals who make up the public." Elaborating on the responsibility of the public leader, he said, "The good politician must educate the public. That is, he must create the public by defining those issues which he believes are the important questions, questions to which citizens must attend....the good politician must be an educator." That could have been John F. Kennedy. "Surely," Ward said, "it was his intense engagement with and passionate voice about what the American people should be about for which we remember him." Just how seriously, for just how long, Ward entertained the possibility we cannot say, but in describing the good politician's responsibility we have to imagine that he also had in mind the goals of the educator, the teacher, and by his definition, the college president he had been:

> having educated the public, after defining issues of importance, [he] then becomes the preservation of the democratic process, namely, the participation of those outside the doors of government in discussion and reflection on what should be done. It requires no less than the capacity to learn from others, the ability to "hear" and to empathize with points of view alien to one's own.

In sum, once again he was arguing that the process by which decisions are made is more important than the decisions themselves.

He began the final section of his speech ("Politics and Public Morality") by confessing that because he had been an academic ("lived by my mouth," as he put it) for so long, he had gotten "irritated with talk and more talk," and he contrasted that life to that of the politician who could not just "lay out all the complexities of a subject" and think he had fulfilled his responsibility. A politician had to make decisions, he had to act. Then sounding like a man running for office, he laid out "an agenda for Boston and the particular actions it requires." In doing so, though, he raised the bar so high we can't imagine any politician clearing it. What remained was just the man speaking, one who, like the ideal politician, had "the moral courage to speak for social justice," but in his case not an opportunity to work to bring it into being.

He singled out and cited one passage from the entire lecture series commemorating Boston's 350th anniversary:

> the people of South Boston have more in common with the people of Roxbury than they do with the cosmopolitan elite which looks down on Irish and black alike from their secure and usually suburban setting, except, of course, their common needs as a social and economic class are obliterated by their racial hatred, the rock on which all reform movements have finally foundered in American history.

And then he provided four examples of powerfully organized institutions, orderings of social life in Boston, that denied the potential of individual

citizens: the public schools and hi-Tech industries that extolled the virtues
of vocational education but sorted and classified children "as products to
meet the changing demands of the market"; "members of the fashionable
social and eating clubs" whose "criteria of social standing and importance
do not extend, say, to the accomplished professionals and intellectuals who
created and continue to struggle to sustain Freedom House in Roxbury";
the banks that did not "exhaust the criteria by which to define responsible corporate citizenship"; and, finally, "the one Holy Roman and Catholic
Church that had seemed to forget "its historical messages, the meaning of
a sanctified life, a life of good works, an ethical life." He ended—almost
defiantly—by pointing to one of Machiavelli's heroes (in his *History of Flor-
ence*) who "deemed the greatness of their native city higher than the salvation of their souls." (Small wonder that he hadn't found a job in Boston.)

Seven months later, in June 1981, on the verge of leaving Boston altogether, he spoke at Commencement at Suffolk University. This speech too
seems to ring loud and clear for being delivered in a vacuum. He began by
once again citing John Winthrop's lay sermon, "Model of Christian Charity," the sermon about "a city upon a hill." Ward noted that Kennedy had
alluded to Winthrop's "city upon a hill" in presenting his vision of "the new
frontier in American politics." As we know, he had alluded to this vision
himself in his charge to the last graduating class he addressed at Amherst.
In what was becoming itself more of a "lay sermon" than a Commencement address, he asked, what was "the application" of Winthrop's words?
"What does the ancient text have to do with us today?"—us, today, Suffolk
University, founded for the many immigrants "who had fled European
shores in search of the American dream." Suffolk embodied "the dream
which brought John Winthrop to Boston, the ideal that as a community, as
members of the same body, we have an obligation to others and not just
to our own pleasures and profits." Now 88 percent of the university's law
degrees and 84 percent of all degrees went to students who lived outside
of Boston, students who were not hoping to realize the American dream.
Why? Because they were already living it.

But he was not talking about just Suffolk. The University's history represented a national trend, a "major social problem." Bringing more statis-
tics to bear, he went on to talk about "white flight," more precisely, "middle-class flight," from America's cities, now "the homes of the brown and

the black, the poor and the undereducated, the elderly and welfare recipients." In describing the Boston area he just barely kept his indignation under control:

> a fourth of the population in one some form of welfare, in a city where the public school system is a mockery of the traditional role of public education as the vehicle for equality and opportunity, with transportation and basic services in steady decline, and old neighborhoods bisected by the turnpikes and highways which carry the successful from shining towers downtown back to the distant suburbs in the evening.

What he said applied to all the ten cities that he cited: "What, then, of our 'city upon a hill,' the millenial dream of a good and just and fair community of equal citizens? We can shrug, of course, and say it was just a dream. The reality is a city of the poor and undereducated."

But he ended his speech, a commencement speech, after all, the way he had ended many speeches like it before. "We can confront reality and can change it," he told the graduates. He said that the degrees and titles they were about to receive (Doctors, Masters, Bachelors) carried with them, in words that he had intoned many times as president of Amherst, certain "rights and responsibilities," but that more important to him was the title Citizen:

> in a democratic society, the greatest title of them all is "citizen." And the essential responsibility of the citizen, whatever one's calling, wherever life takes one, is to have the moral imagination to see, and the will to act on the age old dream that, yes, we are a community, members of the same body, bound together in a common enterprise, the creation of a decent and humane society.

And in these final words he gave as lofty expression as he ever gave to the ideals that he had imagined realizing for years as a writer, a teacher, a president, and as head of the Commission. But this time *his* fear was stronger than his hope, and his tone the more passionate, not just because of the undeniable truth of what he had observed, but also because he was all but certain that he was not going to be in a position to do something about corruption and injustice in American society.

From time to time he thought of writing a book, or at least a few articles, about his Commission experience, specifically about the convergence of politics and economics in Massachusetts. Nothing came of the idea. In the fall he taught a seminar on "Corruption and Politics" at the Institute for Politics at the Kennedy School at Harvard, and he served pro bono on a panel that helped the Boston School Committee with their system of awarding the city's $40 million school-bus contract. Neither came close to requiring the kind of commitment he wanted and was prepared to make.

IN MAY 1981, Ward wrote Commager that he and Barbara "would dearly love to stay in Boston," and that there were "two interesting, well-paying jobs in the private sector" that he had his eye on, "only to discover the work of the commission [was] now a disadvantage." "The consequence," he said, was that they would probably end up in New York, "although my flesh says I don't want to go." Not that he had, or wanted, a future at American Express, but he didn't have any choice.

In June, though, when he learned that the American Council of Learned Societies would soon be looking for a new president, his spirits lifted. In his next letter to Commager he asked for his former colleague's support, adding that he knew "a good bit" about the Council: he had been the American Studies Association's delegate to what were called the Conferences of Secretaries, the gatherings of the principal executive officers of what had become the forty-three learned societies that the Council represented; he had been on a committee of college and university presidents that had sought ways to generate financial support for the Council; and going back to his "salad days," an ACLS fellowship had helped him get started in the profession. A few months later, he told Barbara that he had learned that Robert Goheen, the president of Princeton when Ward began his teaching career there, was also being considered for the position. "Well, there goes that job," she replied. "You don't have a chance against Goheen." But he had more than a chance. Much to his (presumably doubled) delight, in early October he had the job. He would start at the beginning of the new year and work two or three days a week and take over completely on July 1—which he did with gusto.

Filled, it seemed, with more high hopes, after a week as president he was as enthusiastic as he had been when he first went to work for American Express. What he said to Barbara was a version of what he had told the commissioners after his first few trips to New York: "Can you imagine someone paying you to read, to talk about ideas and the academic profession," adding this time, "and you don't have any *students* or *alumni*?" In *its* enthusiasm over Ward's appointment, the *Chronicle of Higher Education* couldn't resist a little hype. To Boston and Irish, the qualifications that Dukakis and others said would make him an ideal chairman of the Commission, it added an unlikely third: Tough Guy. "A Boston 'Street Fighter' Defends the Humanities," their headline read. More accurately, the article quoted his description of the Council as "the principal privately administered national representative of the humanities in the United States" and went on to explain the Council's mission. It sought to advance humanistic studies in *all* fields of learning. It awarded fellowships and grants to scholars, set up conferences and symposia, organized committees of researchers to identify and develop new area studies programs, and sponsored the publication of reference books and research guides; it also furthered international exchanges among scholars and promoted close relations between associations at the Conferences of Secretaries that it held twice a year.

In April 1982 the Wards left Boston and moved into a large apartment on Prospect Park West in Brooklyn. In spite of what his flesh had said the year before, he was as excited about the move as he was about the job. On New Year's Day 1983, in a letter to the secretary and his former colleagues in American Studies at Amherst, he told of how the apartment "looked down on Olmsted's splendid park, with the Brooklyn Public Library and the Brooklyn Museum four blocks away, the Botanical Gardens across the Park and the other exposure giving upon the Verrazzano Bridge and the Narrows." He missed Amherst, missed Boston and the politics of Massachusetts (adding, "that is probably just ego on my part") but, he said, "the mood pales beside the excitement of New York. My adrenalin and pulse rate rise 38 percent when I hit the street. I even enjoy riding the subways." It was true, though, that "97 percent of the riders are brown, black and poor." As he had told the graduates at Suffolk University, that was the reality of America's cities.

One of the first things he did as president was oversee the Council's move to a former factory space on 45th Street between Second and Third

Avenues. With the sizable amount of money that was saved on rent he hired an architect and did what his successor called "a splendid make-over," mahogany bookcases and all. His office "was simply a wonder to behold." He updated the spirit of the place as well—by the way he treated women, for example. He made it possible for his "executive assistant and director of member relations" to arrange her schedule to accommodate the fact that she was a working mother who lived outside the city; he put a woman on the Investment Committee; he organized two retreats a year for the secretaries.

The work of advancing "humanistic studies in *all* fields of learning" was work for which his years in the academy as an educator and an administrator had prepared him. He oversaw it efficiently. He himself reached out to the member societies in a way that none of his predecessors had, meeting with leaders of 35 of them, creating two seats on the ACLS Board for representatives from them. His democratic impulse led him to support what his executive assistant called "Joe Scholar" by increasing the number of members from the societies' lower ranks and the size of their fellowship stipends. He delivered innumerable speeches and talks and reports both here and abroad, and appeared before Congressional committees. The occasions and the subjects of his presentations rippled out from the most immediately practical (talks on "The Market and the Future of Humanistic Scholarship" and "Jobs or Citizenship: The Community College and the Humanities," and testimony before the subcommittee of the House Education and Labor Committee) to what mattered to him most, to education in and for a democracy (speeches on "The Relationship of Scholarship in the Humanities to Society," "Learning, the Humanities and a Democratic Society," and "The Humanities in a Democratic Culture"), and, finally, from education in America to learning in and about other countries ("The Sense of History and the Assumptions of American Foreign Policy," and opening remarks at the plenary session of the ACLS-Soviet Academy of Sciences Commission on the Humanities and Social Sciences, and a report to the Committee on Scholarly Communication with the People's Republic of China), these last when he led American Council of Learned Societies delegations on trips to those countries.

All were informed, all were inspired by the ideals that had lain behind everything he had done for three decades, most obviously and explicitly those having to do with what he considered to be the aim of education in America. "The humanities," he would point out, is a noun, referring to the organized study of certain traditional fields of learning; "humanistic" was an adjective that referred to a certain perspective on learning. It was a liberal arts and not a vocational, a general and not a specialized or departmental education that he was calling for. Furthermore, it had to entail an increase in the power of every individual in society, not to be materially or socially successful, but to be able to live the fullest possible life. As if recalling the headmaster of Boston Latin, he said, "Learning is involved in living a life, not how to make a living." He set his sights high and they ranged far and wide. Humanistic learning bore "an essential relation to society, especially in an ostensibly democratic culture." The ideal individual that he had presented to his classes and written about many years before not only respected the individuality of his fellow citizens but acted and voted in support of the good that could be theirs in common. Now, in the context of the mission of the ACLS, he argued that the private delight that one took in learning ultimately took one "to a vision of what ideally a human being may become and, so, for the need of a social and political order which will carry one there." Having testified persuasively before governmental committees on Beacon Hill, he spoke confidently and eloquently in Washington, before the subcommittee on Education and Arts and Humanities of the Senate's Committee on Labor and Human Resources, for example. On that occasion he said that "A society which does not nourish such things as history, language, and philosophy is a decerebrated society, not capable of what it might yet become, a society not yet fully human," and then went on to say that "beneath [was] a more fundamental relation," which was

> what it means to be human, to make sense of life and experience, to understand what it means to be a self in society in which one lives, what ethics are required, and what standards of justice are legitimate. The restless drive and deep desire to have satisfying answers to such questions defines the human condition. That is what humanistic learning is about.

It couldn't be "the province" of just a few, of just "a learned class." "It must entail the increase in the power of every individual in society." And updating one more belief, one that he had expressed again and again as president of Amherst (and hardly ever mentioned as Chairman of the Ward Commission), he would often say that that individual and the social order had to be "humane." He said that a scholar who is committed to humanistic learning is committed to the creation of a humane social order. The full life enjoyed by the right kind of scholar "must entail" the full life enjoyed by every member of society; "inevitably" Ward's humanistic learner was committed to bringing a just society into being. One thing *had* to lead to another. So it had seemed a decade earlier, when he became president of Amherst. Now all one could be sure of was that it worked out in his rhetoric.

His ideals were all there: the life of learning, conducted by individuals in such a way as to inspire them to create a humane social order, a true democracy, and maybe, just maybe, somewhere beyond, maybe sometime in the future, a peaceful world order. But otherwise there was so much that wasn't there. He was almost always preaching to the choir, or worse, to silent parishioners. Lacking were voices challenging him, students asking him "Oh yeah?" and "So what?," colleagues in debate with him, readers reviewing his book and his articles. He was less of an educator than he had been at Amherst, or even on Beacon Hill. He was just an administrator and a spokesman for the institution he headed.

Moreover, his relations to the people he worked with were nothing like his rapport with his fellow commissioners and the scores and scores of other people who contributed to the Commission's success. His background, even where he lived, was different. The men on his seventeen-member staff were, by one man's account, all "WASPY men," all "highfalutin humanists." Most of them lived on the Upper East Side and walked to work—and wondered why a man would want to live in Brooklyn and ride the subway. They were like his "corporate acquaintances." They "pale when I tell them [what] I actually do," he said in his New Year's Day letter to his former colleagues. "They, of course, have not been underground for eleven years." In a word, at ACLS he didn't fit in.

By the end of his first year he saw that this would be his last job. His letter ended on that somber note. He managed to list some good things about it. It was "fine, interesting, various, good staff to work with"; he had "a sense of engagement as well as a sense of freedom." The only "unsettling" thing was

> to realize that here I am sixty years old, that I will work eight to ten years, and this will be my last job! All of a sudden the horizon line comes up close:

a curious psychological mood. I have always enjoyed whatever I did, but part of that was that I would move onto something else, something new, and now that is not true.

And though he loved the city, Brooklyn anyway, Barbara was not happy with the move from the start when "everything which could go wrong, did go wrong," he reported in his letter. She sprained her ankle badly, "which put her in bed with half-opened boxes all about for the first ten days and," he went on, "those who know how compulsive she is in settling in will have some sense of how easy that was." Their car was broken into and then, far worse, she was "held up at gun point of a warm, lovely Friday noontime." He tried to put the best face on the situation by saying, "But all that happened in April, the cruelest month, and has now receded to cocktail anecdotes to prove we are acculturated to New York."

In time, for her sake one has to assume, they bought a house, a '50s ranch-style house with a pool in the back, in Westport, Connecticut, and he commuted to work in New York with riders a few of whom might have been brown or black, but none of whom would have been poor. He became one of those whose lives he had deplored in his Suffolk Commencement address, who rode the train that carried "the successful from shining towers downtown back to the distant suburbs in the evening," except that he didn't consider himself among "the successful," not at all. He now felt his life was "useless." And all the while, his marriage was unraveling.

A letter he wrote in the spring of 1976 in response to the news of his former student, Robert Fein, that he had just married begins to give us a sense of the dynamics of his own marriage. "If I don't sound too self-congratulatory, may your marriage be a good one, as good as Barbara's and mine," he began, and then went on to say it wasn't that their life together was "ideal or perfect, not by a long shot." He said he had trouble with the word *love*; he had had "fierce discussions with Barbara about that emotional fact." He didn't know what the word for their relation was, but he said that from his perspective "what happens is, for me the realization finally that it is not that I love that woman who is separate from me, over there, so to speak, but that who I am, my self, is she." And he went on: "The separateness is still there, but at the same time she is a constituent part of my being, and there is no way that I could ever say my life could be without her, because that is a contradiction in terms."

Ward had trouble not just with the word *love* but with "the emotional fact of love." Yet somehow his wife was a part of him and he a part of her. It wasn't enough to say that he and Barbara were two different, autonomous, people who loved each other, be thankful, even a little "self-congratulatory," and move on—as Emerson would say, that they were the "very two" that were necessary for them to be "very one." No, they were as one. He was she, she he. At least he was part of her, which is to say, less abstractly, that he needed her, that his dependence on her went very deep.

It is hard to imagine Barbara's holding her own—or even trying to hold her own—in a "fierce discussion" about the meaning of love. She was one to come quickly to the point, and her point could be sharp. We know that from Ward's own reports. He'll tell someone she avoids hearing him lecture if she can, or that when someone asked him a question she might interrupt with her own question: did he want a fifty-minute or just a short response? Maybe just "poking fun," maybe just slight jabs. Her reaction to the "Talk of the Town" piece in the *New Yorker* unquestionably went deeper. He described it in a letter to Dwight Morrow, Jr. He hadn't told her or anyone else that it was coming out. When she saw the opening description of him as "an animated, handsome, dark-haired, keen-eyed, unpretentious man of forty-five," she looked at him and said, "without a flicker of irony, 'I never would have thought of using the word 'handsome' about you." "So you can see," he added, "the kind of support I get at home."

What strains there were in the marriage were accentuated by his being president. Barbara was the last of the old-style presidents' wives, a full-time resident, seemingly a full-time hostess. In looking back at the several days of a colloquium on Creativity, she estimated, in Ward's words, that she had "served dinner to 175 people." She did her unpaid job, she was long-suffering, but as she told a young professor, she thought the presidency was a job for a bachelor. When another asked her how they managed as a couple, she said that they were "good actors." Drinking helped. When it didn't, they protected each other, she by putting an end to a meeting at their house when it was obvious that he had had too much, he by telling a student bartender to cut her off when he thought she had reached her limit. But though he wasn't about to hear good things about his looks, she did give him good counsel. If he was frustrated by the alumni, she reminded him, "There are some rather interesting people; you must remember you taught them," if by the faculty, she pointed out that were he still a professor he might well be among those who made life difficult for the president. She edited his claims about his humble beginings, she had him face up to his need to be important and to others' desire to undercut him. She kept him honest.

But it wasn't enough. He needed her—and he needed more. He would have his ideal. So there were other women. What must have been the climactic affair took place in the fall of 1984 on the China trip, a month-long combination "summer camp and graduate seminar," the Princeton historian Nell Painter called it, on which a delegation of about ten Americanists lectured and consulted with scholars at universities and research institutes in six cities. As had been the case before, Ward made no attempt to hide his relations with the woman. After the trip, Barbara asked him to move out. In the words of the divorce petition filed in Bridgeport Superior Court on June 27, 1985, the marriage had "irrevocably broken down." As he once said, she was "a constituent part" of his being, and "there is no way I could ever say my life could be without her." But for her, the show was over.

In July he traveled to Hungary to sign an academic exchange treaty; it was there that he delivered his last public address. It was titled "Individualism: An American Ideal." Back in New York he was, in effect, homeless. For a short time he stayed at the St. George's Hotel in Brooklyn, once the largest hotel in New York, with more than 2,600 rooms, but by the time Ward stayed there it was in a condition that prompted him to refer to it as "a welfare hotel." Then he stayed at the Harvard Club.

Ever since coming to New York his spirits had to have declined, his moods darkened. Peter Forbes, who was often in New York ("Boston expatriates," they considered themselves) met him regularly, on Thursdays, for martinis at the Century Club. On one occasion, Ward talked about his experiences during World War II, and then, his mood darkening, about the very fact of the war and about the human condition generally. On another, he told Forbes that he found the Harvard Club "convenient but uninspiring" and questioned him about buying an apartment. As an architect, "I had some experience with that process," Forbes later said. Ward's "subsequent suicide seemed odd. Buying an apartment speaks of a future, no?"

In the middle of July Ward called Marx in Boston—called him in distress. Marx came down to New York and the two of them took a long walk in Prospect Park. Ward's mood had changed, he talked about recommitting himself to ideas and to scholarship, he said he had ten good years left in him, he didn't mention why he had called. Marx didn't ask him—something he has always regretted—and returned to Boston. Two men of a generation that was not inclined to open up or probe. Or maybe two men just behaving like men, the one not wanting to expose himself, the other not wanting to follow up on what he might have thought the other was not saying.

Easier than talking to him, or any man—one might even say it was "natural"—was opening up to a woman. Ward talked to at least three about taking his own life. He had called Ellen Ryerson several years before and so alarmed her that being many miles away herself, she called a mutual friend who went immediately to the hotel where he was staying, only to learn that he had checked out. He talked to Janice Denton just before the end. By then he was, in her words, "a lost soul," going on about the entitled faculty of Amherst College and about the wreckage of his life. But she was in Amherst. She knew no one she could call. There was nothing she could do. He had lunch with the third, Richard Schlatter's daughter, in mid July. Ward had known Schlatter since his Princeton days. Now they saw each other often: Schlatter had recently been helping out two or three days a week as an "executive associate" at ACLS. Ward's mood and talk so alarmed her that she told her father to contact Ward and arrange to see him immediately.

At the memorial service Schlatter told of a dinner he and Ward had had eight months before, of their "talking as only the closest of friends can do and then only rarely," and of his receiving a letter from Ward the next day, a letter that ended with these words: "I realize now how deeply I care for you and in saying that I realize all the more my own problem. I do not believe that anyone cares for me, even when they say they do." Schlatter recalled his own reaction: "He was, of course, wholly and tragically mistaken and even when he wrote it to me I did not understand that he meant it." But now, eight months later, he did take his daughter's warning seriously.

Schlatter and another man, Arthur Trottenberg, a classmate of Ward's at Harvard, who worked at the Ford Foundation, invited Ward to lunch at the Century Club on August 3rd—and the pattern repeated itself. At the luncheon, to both men Ward appeared to be in good spirits. Trottenberg was also aware of the fact, as he later put it, that Ward "never thought he was a success, never felt he was loved," but it didn't make any sense to him any more than it had to Schlatter. "This was not a man suffering on the surface from profound unhappiness," he said. "There was nothing to indicate the depth of despair."

After lunch Ward went back to his office at ACLS. He was the "naturally ebullient Irishman" and much more. He was also the empathetic idealist who believed that men, especially young men, could express their individuality by working to bring a just and humane society into being. (The next day he was scheduled to go down to Washington to defend the humanities before another Congressional committee.) That afternoon he had an appointment to talk with Daniel Warner, Amherst Class of 1968. Almost twenty years had passed since Warner had taken an American literature course with Ward, but he admired him for the stands he had taken as president of Amherst and remembered him as a man who would be willing to talk to him, perhaps help him. After graduation Warner taught in Harlem and the South Bronx and then, in 1972, moved to Europe to teach "in a private school on a mountain top in Switzerland." He was in New York because his daughter was undergoing a second major heart operation. Ward recognized him when he walked in. Ward had in fact gotten hold of his former student's transcript in preparation for their meeting. They sat in his office, Ward rolled up his sleeves, lit up a cigarette and asked what he could do for Warner.

They talked for almost two hours. Ward told Warner that, in Warner's words, he had "a great deal to give to help the world," that he "was being 'irresponsible" doing what he was doing, and that he ought "to come down from the mountain." A "noir" version of Emerson's "self-reliant" man kicked in: "He also told me, and I hear his words as if it were yesterday, 'that you should never take shit from anyone.'" Their meeting ended with Ward's saying that Warner should call him when he decided how he could help. Warner gave him a copy of his resume and left, his spirits lifted. Having thought about their conversation many times over the years, he remembers Ward as being "filled with optimism, especially for me. There was nothing negative, no indication of his personal situation." At the end of the day Ward told his secretary that Warner was "an extraordinary young man who could make a difference" and that he was going to do what he could to help him.

It was Martin Duberman with whom Ward had dinner that evening. Afterwards, Ward went back to the Harvard Club. Duberman would be the fourth man Ward met that day who'd say he had no inkling of the fact that Ward would take his own life that night.

IN A talk on "The Life of Learning" that he gave at the Century Club in March, 1983, Ward had described "the mood of the general society" as "almost sullen, mean-spirited, self-protective, if not downright selfish." He said he caught "no sense of joy and delight, no sense of exuberance and gaiety." There was instead "a mood of pulling back, turning inward, hunkering down," which was to him "the greatest threat to learning."

In May of the last year of his life he gave another speech with the same title: "The Life of Learning." The occasion was commencement at the University of Minnesota, the commencement at which he received an honorary degree. In his speech he looked back to his years as a graduate student. He said they were "a realization of what still seems to me an ideal community of teachers and learners together," of "that ideal republic of the mind and imagination which is constantly a reproach to the actual republic in which we live." In that "ideal republic," he said, "one discovers the answers to the questions, What good is it? What use is it?"

Minnesota had been an ideal community of teachers and students generally, but more specifically and importantly, it was there, as a student of American life and letters, as a graduate student in the American Studies program, that he had begun to evolve his definition of "that ideal"—call it his version of the American Dream—and arrived at his definition of the good life, the useful life as one dedicated to the realization of that ideal. It was the ideal that he presented as a teacher and a writer, that he bore constantly in mind as an administrator and a commissioner, and that he represented personally at a time when Americans, especially young Americans, believed in the possibility of its being realized. But now as he contemplated the state of American society and that of his own life he was not at all hopeful.

As John Winthrop had warned it might, the ideal of the "city on a hill" had receded into the past. And Ward himself had suffered the fate of another American dreamer, the one so memorably described by Nick Carraway:

> He had come a long way to this blue lawn and his dream must have seemed
> so close that he could hardly fail to grasp it. He did not know that it was
> already behind him, somewhere back in that vast obscurity beyond the city,
> where the dark fields of the republic rolled on under the night.

Imagining how the world looked to Ward as it became clearer and clearer
to him that his ideal republic would never come into being is one way of
accounting for why he decided that his life was not worth living.

We may point to more immediately personal causes as well: in the
present, especially his impending divorce. An English professor who had
scandalously left his family for another woman and was going through a
divorce in the middle of Ward's presidency remembers Ward's coming to
him. He said he had three things he wanted to say: your wife will never forgive you (she and Barbara were friends); he couldn't have done what you
have done; and he might be able to help financially but not emotionally. It
was a generous gesture; it was also a revealing one. Ten years later, Barbara had not forgiven him; whether out of loyalty or to spare the children
or out of fear or guilt, or some combination of them all, he had stayed in
a marriage that was not ideal, "not by a long shot"; and he could not help
himself emotionally. In lay terms, he had lost his sense of self, a sense that
had never been deeply grounded to begin with. In the past, there was his
religious upbringing, which he cannot have completely erased or forgotten—his knowledge of the Seventh Commandment especially. And finally,
there were his "dark, Irish moods," or, more specifically, his feeling that he
fell short, his feeling that he didn't really belong in the situation or position
in which he found himself, however much he sought acceptance, and with
it, his fear that he wasn't good enough, that no one really cared for him,
even when they said they did.

In his speech at Minnesota he said that having found the answers to
the questions, "What good is it? What use it?" "one does not forget. One
keeps on striving to realize that ideal again in another place." It was as if
he was summing up his life after he left there many years before. He had
maintained his faith in his democratic ideal, he had striven to realize it
again and again—until he could no longer. So now it was also as if he was
writing his own epitaph.

NOTES

A LARGE MAJORITY of these notes refer to boxes and folders containing Ward's presidential and other papers in the Amherst College Archives. Other notes frequently referred to are abbreviated thus:

Globe: *Boston Globe*

Hampshire Life: *Hampshire Life*, August 30 through September 5, 1985.

Jackson: John William Ward, *Andrew Jackson: Symbol for an Age* (New York, 1955).

"Narrative": "The Commission's Narrative," *Final Report to the General Court of the Special Commission Concerning State and County Buildings*, Volume 9, December 31, 1980.

Oral History: The Friends of the Amherst College Library Oral History Project. Ward was interviewed on June 19, 1979. The dates of other interviews are in the notes.

RWB: John William Ward, *Red, White, And Blue: Men, Books, and Ideas in American Culture* (New York, 1969).

Student: *Amherst Student*.

Preface

ix "look back at us with pride": Letter to Ase Omowale Kuasi, July 1, 1974. Box 11, folder K.
"their own wild dreams": Brotherhood Banquet, National Conference of Christians and Jews, May 14, 1973. Box 1, folder 25, new series.

x a quarter of a million copies: This is the number in Wilson Smith's entry on Ward in the *American National Biography Online*. Smith verified the figure with the Oxford University Press. Phone conversation with the author, March 15, 2011.

xi "play a role in it": RWB, p. 335.
"President Ward's biography": *Amherst Bulletin*, May 31, 1978.

xii "the single most intense and interesting experience": "The Common Weal and the Public Trust: Politics and Public Morality," October 21, 1980. Box 1, folder 69, new series.
"in the world of scholarship and learning": *Chronicle of Higher Education*, July 7, 1982, p. 7.

xiii   "to pay the family bills": "The Life of Learning," March 3, 1983. Box 3, folder 39, new series.

      now "useless": James Hund, phone interview, June 2012.

      Darkness Visible: (New York, 1990), p. 5.

xiv   "the depth of despair": *Globe*, September 15, 1985, p. 25.

      "every twenty attempts": (Cambridge, 2010), p. 13.

      his wife declined: *Globe*, September 15, 1985, p. 25.

ONE: Becoming "Bill" Ward

15   "the presentation of self": Letter to Robert Fein, September 4, 1973. Box 7, folder F.

      "a learned man": *Hampshire Life*, p. 6.

16   "when he walked in": *Globe*, September 15, 1985, p. 25.

      "could be arrogant": *Hampshire Life*, p. 6.

      "in this environment": *Globe*, October 25, 1979, p. 2.

      "where there is money": *Student*, June 3, 1971, p. 5.

18   "not necessary to retain": Letter from Pat Mullins to Calvin Plimpton, December 6, 1985. Copy in author's possession.

      "those one knows well": *The Sixties Diaries: 1960 to 1969*, Volume 2 (New York 2010), p. 500.

      "close to Bill Ward": Phone conversation, October 14, 2010.

      "an alien": Phone conversation, December 5, 2010.

      "a stranger": Interview, October 15, 2009.

      "what he was feeling": *Globe*, September 15, 1985, p. 1.

19   "a world-weary plainclothes cop": *Globe*, October 25, 1979, p. 2.

      "flows over Boston": February 5, 1972.

      "is its Irishness" *Globe*, October 25, 1979, p. 2.

      "knew how to fix things": *Ibid.*, May 13, 1978, p. 3.

20   "equal lack of discrimination: Quoted in Nat Hentoff, *Boston Boy* (New York, 1986), p. 34.

21   "even more from ourselves": Hentoff, pp. 34-7.

      "early in life": Untitled pages in Box 3, folder 39, new series.

23   "The Hero": 60 (May 1941), pp. 6-7.

25   "admitted to Harvard": Untitled pages, Box 3, folder 39, new series.

26   "the establishment at Harvard": James G. Hershberg, *James B. Conant: Harvard to Hiroshima and the Making of the Nuclear Age* (New York, 1993), p. 80.

      "were Harvard men too": *Ibid.*

      addressed the seniors: *Liber Actorum*, 1941, p. 13.

27   "On Shining Shoes": Box 2, folder 30, new series.

28 "present at all Faculty Meetings": After Minutes of Faculty Meeting of June 1, 1976, Box 9.

29 a short tribute to Matthiessen: November 14, 1981. Source unknown. Copy in author's possession.

30 "any particular course": *The Historian's Workshop: Original Essays by Sixteen Historians*, ed. L. P. Curtis, Jr. (New York, 1970) p. 209.
"come intensely alive": *Ibid.*
"far beyond our tutorial relation": Letter to Mrs. Stephen Whicher, July 11, 1973. Box 19, folder W.
"the most elbow-room": *The Historian's Workship*, p. 208.

31 "its moment in time": Report of the Delegation on American Studies to the Committee on Scholarly Communication with the People's Republic of China. Box 2, folder 28, new series.
"ideas and good talk": *The Historian's Workshop*, p. 209.
"brought [him] up professionally": Comment on "Landscape Studies" by John Brinkerhoff Jackson, September 8, 1979. Box 1, folder 66, new series.
"Reflections on American Studies": *American Studies*, XL (Summer, 1999), 39-51.

32 "as fortunate as we are now": *Perfect Witness*, Xlibris, 2009, p. 219.
"the University of Minnesota": *Dictionary of American History*, third edition, (New York, 2003), p. 169.
"was a disaster": "*The Life of Learning*," May 23, 1985. Box 3, folder 46, new series.

33 "The harps are taking over": Phone conversation with Elizabeth Moynahan, October 14, 2010
"your cocktail officiating": Letter of July 5, 1972. Box 12, folder H.
"Not that it matters": Letter to Ase Omowale Kuasi. Box 14, folder K.

TWO: The Writer and the Teacher

35 "writer to 'scholar'": *Student*, May 26, 1979, p. 6.
"teachers and learners together": "The Life of Learning," May 23, 1985. Box 3, folder 46, new series.

36 "what I found in Princeton": *Cures: A Gay Man's Odyssey* (New York, 1991), pp. 1-3.
"uneasily in their chairs": Letter of March 25, 1975. Box 14, folder M.

37 "tight money": Letter from Geoffrey Woolf, October 7, 1973. Box 19, folder W.
"like an equal.": Jonathan Helmreich, E-mail to author, August 24, 2010.
"every page of mine": *Jackson*, pp. vii-viii.

38 "to pernicious results": LVI (July 1951), 906.

"on practical affairs": *Virgin Land* (Cambridge, 1950), p. vii.

"problem through literature": Oral History, p. 2.

"the American past": *The Historian's Workshop*, p. 211.

39   "the overriding national mythology": XXXIX (Summer, 1970), 748.

"a study of popular ideology": *The Historian's Workshop*, p. 208.

"He was the age's": *Jackson*, p. 213.

"some lines of relationship": *The Historian's Workshop*, p. 212.

40   "leader in American history": *Ibid.*

"for personal striving": *Ibid.*, p. 213.

"In the Beginning Was New Orleans": *Jackson*, pp. 3-10.

41   "Coda": *Jackson*, pp. 207-13.

42   "a people's beliefs": XXIV (October 1972), 444.

three criticisms: *The Historian's Workshop*, pp. 217-19.

43   "*imposing* a pattern on history": *RWB*, p. 58.

"the man of iron will": *Jackson*, p. 171.

"so bountifully provides": *Ibid.*, p. 10.

"a humane regard for others": *The Historian's Workshop*, p. 213.

44   "the demands of oneself": *Jackson*, p. 173.

"not against society": *Ibid.*, p. 200.

45   "people can make a difference": *Globe*, September 15, 1985, p. 24.

Encyclopedia Americana: Volume 15 (Danbury, 1997), p. 69.

46   "Of Individualism in Democratic Countries": *Democracy in America*, eds.
J.P. Mayer and Max Lerner (New York, 1966), pp. 477-78.

"Toqueville and the Meaning of Democracy, LTV Washington Seminar,
1982, p.4.

47   "take shape in that way": *Democracy in America*, p. 485.

"equality of conditions spreads": *Ibid.*, p. 488.

"freedom of discussion than in America": *Ibid*, p. 235.

48   "men of great character": *Ibid.* p. 238.

his "non-book": Letter to Henry Nash Smith, January 1, 1965. In the Smith-
Ward correspondence in the Bancroft Library.

"in our nation's history": Quoted in Alan Trachtenberg, review of *RWB*,
Carleton Miscellany, XI (Summer 1970), 106.

"The Meaning of Lindbergh"s Flight": *RWB*, pp.21-37.

"made America": *Ibid,* p. 29.

49   "vision of themselves": *Ibid.*, p. 26-7.

"American genius and industry": *Ibid.* , p, 34.

"his two lives separate": *Ibid.*, p. 25.

"the task of America": *Ibid.*, p. 37.

"The Ideal of Individualism and the Reality of Organization": *Ibid.*, pp.
260-63.

50   "a central role in its creation": *Ibid.*, p. 294.

"Benjamin Franklin: The Making of an American Character": *Ibid.*, pp. 125-40.

"characterized our society": *Ibid.*, p. 126, 137-38.

"all success stories": *Ibid.*, pp. 130-31.

"Who am I?": *Ibid.*, p. 140.

51   talk he gave on John F. Kennedy: *Ibid.*, pp. 140-52.

"Love your self enough": *Ibid.*, p. 151.

"The Politics of Design": *Ibid.*, p. 267-94.

52   "some perspective on ourselves": *Ibid.*, pp. 267-68.

53   Plimpton kept notes: Copy in author's possession.

54   "The Intellectual: Critic or Cleric?": *RWB*, pp. 315-29.

55   "hide it away": *Ibid.*, pp. 315-17.

"bears upon the present": *Ibid.*, p. 317.

56   "The University: The Trouble with Higher Education": *Ibid.*, pp. 330-48.

"higher education is in trouble": *Ibid.*, pp. 330-31.

"pastoral setting like Amherst": *Ibid.*, p. 334.

"play a role in it": *Ibid.*, p. 335.

57   "American education today": *Ibid.*, p. 348.

"the old definitions": XI (Summer 1970), 110.

58   "the year of student participation": *Student*, September 19, 1968, p. 2.

59   "freedom of speech": *Student*, November 8. 1965, p. 6. This includes the *Times* quotation.

"possibly illegal means" *Ibid.*, October 28, 1968, p. 2.

60   "by racist assumptions" *Ibid.*, February 24, 1969, p. 1.

61   appear in the *Student, Ibid,*, October 17, 1966, p. 3.

"Most Relevant Course": *Ibid,*, April 24, 1967, p. 3.

"before Marcus Garvey": *Ibid.*, October 13, 1969, p. 3.

62   "thought out in advance": Gordon Jones, letter to author, January 13, 2011.

63   "occupation of buildings": *New Yorker*, February 5, 1972.

"test of what we do": Letter of November 16, 1976. Box 4, Miscellaneous folder.

"best friend among the students": Rob Hawkins interview, October 24, 2010.

64   and that mattered: Interview, October 31, 2010.

employment opportunities: Interview, January 9, 2011.

in the spring of 1966: Untitled talk, Box 3, folder 53, new series.

65   he signed a letter: *Student*, January 26, 1967, p. 5.

66   their last Assembly: Untitled talk, Box 3, folder 56, new series.

"Can We Go On Like This?: Education and Youth Today": Reprinted in the *Amherst College Bulletin*, LVIII (January 1969), 3-8.

69   "followed by rational action": *Student*, April 28, 1969, pp. 2-3.

70   The editors of the *New Republic*: CLX (May 17, 1969), 1, 5-7.

72   "BLACKS SEIZE BUILDINGS": *Student*, February 18, 1970.
      "black community sets forth": *Ibid.*, February 23, 1970, p.2.
      "true promises of democracy": (Iowa City, 2003), p. 67.
73   Commager's, Marx's, and Kateb's remarks are in *Student*, May 7, 1970,
      pp.7, 9.
74   "one place to another": *Ibid.*, May 12, 1967, p. 3.
      "in many ways a servant": *Amherst Alumni News*, XXIII (Summer 1970),
      7-8.
      "lock-outs, sit-ins, etc. personally": E-mail to author, April 8, 2013.

THREE: The President of Amherst College

76   "Education for What? The Liberal Arts and the Modern World": Box 1,
      folder 42, new series, pp. 3-4.
      "collegial and engaging": E-mail to author, June 2, 2011.
      the "inside" president: E-mail to author, April 3, 2011.
77   withdrew his name: John Esty e-mail to author, November 9, 2011.
      "a most impressive man": Box 19, folder W.
      "Amherst in 1971": Ronald Varney, e-mail to author, June 2, 2011.
78   "over to the other side": *Ibid.*
      "thinking about complexities": October 10, 1985. Non-alumnus Biographi-
      cal Box, Memorial Service folder.
79   "the self-determination of the professor": Letter of January 22, 1968.
      Commager papers, Amherst College Archives, Box 63, folder 41.
      "being a college president": *Student*, June 3, 1971, p. 4.
80   "thickened incredibly": Letter of February 7, 1972. Box 17, folder S.
      "to answer the problem": Box 1, folder 63, new series.
      "it means to be a teacher": *Student*, February 11, 1971, p. 6.
81   "incipient male menopause": Letter of October 14, 1971. Box14, folder M.
      See also *Student*, June 3, 1971, p. 4.
      "I really wanted it": *Student*, February 11, 1971, p. 6.
      "what the President of Amherst College says": *Ibid.*, p. 1.
      "all too easily forgotten": Letter of August 30, 1974. Box16, folder R.
      a letter to a young man: Letter to John Peterson, November, 1979. Copy
      forwarded to author.
82   "named president of Amherst": *Globe*, October 25, 1979, p. 2.
      "whooped with delight": George Kateb interview, November 23, 2009.
      "I'm it!": *The Making of a Black Scholar: From Georgia to the Ivy League* (Iowa
      City, 2003), p. 5.
      "a haunted look": Interview, December 17, 2009.
83   "some limited achievement": Quoted in Derwent May, *Hannah Arendt*

(New York, 1986), p.71.

"with and by [one's]self": *The Life of the Mind* (New York, 1978), p. 5.

"between role and self always": Oral History.

84   "the president of Amherst College": *Student*, May 26, 1979, p.7.

"with public commitments": Phone interview, October 27, 2009.

"adopt the role of president": E-mail to author, May 27, 2010.

85   "Why not me?": Greene interview, Oral History Project, February 2, 2000.

"enough space": Phone interview, October 27, 2009.

confessed to John Esty: E-mail to author, November 9, 2011.

"when you're being insulted": David Wills interview, November 20, 2012.

87   "what the job was like": Oral History.

"The Spirit of This Place": reprinted in *Alumni News*, XXIV (Fall, 1971).
Merrill's and Smith's remarks are also included in this issue.

88   report to the Board in 1973: Box 1, folder 28, new series.

89   "between myself and students": *Student*, February 8, 1971, p. 1.

"a matter of political right": Box 1, folder 28, new series.

90   Ward approved: James Mariness interview, June 1, 2010.

91   "the future of secondary education": Letter to Stephen Kiss, March 14,
1974. Box 14, folder K.

27-year-old freshman: Steve Roberts, e-mail to author, November 16, 2010.

who came from Malaysia: N. Balakrishnan, e-mail to author, November 18,
2010.

92   1973 report to the Board of Trustees: *Op. cit.*7

"preacher of earlier days": "Education for What? The Liberal Arts and
the Modern World": *Op.cit.*

"here in Massachusetts": Box 1, folder 26, new series, p. 2.

93   a Thursday evening talk: October 2, 1975. Box 1, folder 43, new series.

"will clean it up": *Student*, September 22, 1977, p. 1.

"Sleazing": *Ibid.*, November 8, 1973, pp. 4-5.

94   in a College assembly meeting: *Ibid.*, November 12, 1973, p. 3.

those who wrote letters: *Ibid.*, November 15, 1973, pp. 4-5.

WESTOVER

95   "as persons": *Student*, April 24, 1972, p. 2.

96   "those many years ago": Letter to John Keyes, July 18, 1972. Box 14, folder
K.

97   "do Westover": *Student*, April 21, 1972, p. 10.

"if they wish": "Concerns of the Campus," *Alumni News*, XXIV (Spring,
1972. Box 17, Springtime (Westover) folder.

98   "was in progress": *Ibid.*

"The Ethics of Investment": *Student*, May 8, 1972, pp. 1, 3.

99   a "Message" to the College: Ibid., May 1, 1972, p. 8.

100   to call off classes: Ward's notes for Committee of Six meeting, April 29,
      1972. Box 17, Springtime [Westover] folder.
      crammed into the Chapel: The meeting was recorded. A typescript of it is
      in the Hawkins papers. Amherst Archives, Box 5, folder 8.

101   reprinted in the *Times*: May 13, 1972.

103   "some 1,000 students": *Ibid.*, May 12, 1972.
      "crazy world this is": *Student*, May 11, 1972, p. 2.
      "by the commotion": *Hampshire Life*, p. 8.

104   "The Blooming of the President": *Student*, June 1, 1972, pp. 2-4.
      in *Change*: July/August, 1972.
      published in the *Alumni* News: XXV (Fall 1972), 11-12.

105   "not Amherst's finest moment": Letter from Hawkins, July 22, 2010.
      In a letter: August 15, 1972. Box 14, folder M.

106   from the Alumni Office: Memo of July 12, 1973. Box 2, Alumni Council
      folder.
      "be a man": Letter of July 8, 1972. Box 12, folder H.
      "will have an office": Letter from Robert L. Neill, Jr., September 25, 1972.
      Box 15, folder N.
      to predict the results: Box 19, Westover Letters in Support.

107   "as an Amherst alumnus: Letter of April 18, 1972. Box 3, folder 10, new
      series.
      "judgment deemed best": Statement given by telephone, May 12, 1972.
      Box 17. Springtime (Westover) folder.
      Ward's "indiscretion": John Esty, e-mail to author, September 10, 2011.
      "Statement of the Trustees of Amherst College": June 3, 1972. Box 17,
      Springtime (Westover) folder.

108   "bad for business": Interview with Dick Hubert, August 18, 2010.
      "braced for that!": Letter to Malcolm Diamond, July 19, 1972. Box 6, folder
      D.
      "of identification only": Letter of October 7, 1973. Box 3, Amnesty folder.
      "choose to do": Undated letter. Box 17, Springtime (Westover) folder.

109   "from American bombing": *Ibid.*
      a long list: *The Seventeenth Degree* (New York, 1974), p. 57.
      letter to Henry Nash Smith: October 4, 1972. Smith-Ward correspondence,
      Op. Cit.
      an op-ed piece in the *Times*: December 15, 1974, p. 17.

110   "in good hands": Letter of June 26, 1972. Box 14, folder L.
      "what I did": Undated letter to Duncan Ballantine. Box 17, Springtime
      (Westover) folder.
      interview in the *Student*: June 3, 1971, p. 4.

111   notes for a lecture: Box 17, Springtime (Westover) folder.
      "A Word on Civil Disobedience": *Alumni News*, XXV (Summer 1972), 4-6.
112   two statements: Box 17, Springtime (Westover) folder.
113   "Should College Presidents Take Stands": Box 1, folder 23, new series.
      last interview in the *Student*": May 26, 1979, p. 7.
      "disobedience personally necessary": *Ibid.*, June 1, 1972, p. 7
114   "believed in something": December 7, 1957. Box 2, folder 5, new series.
115   "brass knuckle business": Letter to Marc Pritzer, October 14, 1971. Box 15, folder P.
      "a *Student* interview": February 16, 1976, p. 15.
      "policies I abhor": Letter of July 11, 1972. Box 7, folder F.
116   "I'll *go* to Hell": "Anarchy and Authority in American Literature." Box 2, folder 1, p. 15.

COEDUCATION

118   "the founding of the College": Draft of "The President's Recommendation on Coeducation." Box 21, Recommendation folder.
      "an animated and exciting discussion": L. Clark Seelye, *The Early History of Smith College: 1871-1910* (Boston, 1923), pp. 8-9.
120   in its final report: For it and Ward's response, see *Alumni News*, XXIV (Fall, 1971), 42-43, 51-52.
122   "Looking Backward": Box 2, folder 16, new series.
      "I really don't know": *Student*, February 11, 1971, p. 6.
      "to answer that question": *Ibid.*, June 3, 1971, p. 5.
      "doing to my school": Box 6, Miscellaneous 1975-76 folder.
      told Robert Fein: Letter of September 4, 1973. Box 7, folder F.
123   "to put me on the spot": *Student*, February 7, 1972, p. 1.
      "no longer a question": Convocation, September 4, 1975. Box 1, folder 41, new series.
124   "the decision itself": Oral History.
      Ted Cross, said to him: Letter of November 6, 1974, following minutes of Trustee meeting of November 2, 1974.
125   meeting in early November: Minutes of Trustee meeting of November 6, 1971.
127   "to formulate a decision": *Student*, October 5, 1972, p. 1.
      What he recommended: *Amherst College Bulletin*, LXII (October, 1972), 3-7.
129   according to Guest's minutes: Minutes of Trustee meeting of November 19, 1972.
      "continue to be justified?": E-mail to author, November 9, 2009.
130   letters he wrote Merrill: Dated December 7, 1972 and January 9, 1973. Box 21, Coeducation Correspondence of the Board of Trustees folder.

131   At its meeting in December: Minutes of Trustee meeting of December
        15, 1972.
        "seems to me an injustice!": Quoted in an E-mail from John Esty to author,
        November 8, 2011.
132   "sensible space of time": Letter of December 31, 1972. Box 21, Coeducation
        Correspondence of the Board of Trustees folder.
        "would carry the day": E-mail to author, November 9, 2011.
        "made a hash of coeducation": Phone interview, March 3, 2012.
        Student reporter's words: January 29, 1973, p.2.
133   their meeting with the trustees: Ibid., April 9, 1973, p.1.
        "call him a nigger": *Ibid.*, April 16, 1973, p.2.
134   the faculty did the reverse: Minutes of the Faculty Meeting of April 5, 1973.
        "if I free them": Letter of Ellen Emerson, March 2, 1973. Coeducation Cor-
        respondence of the Board of Trustees folder.
135   "God help us with the alumni": Minutes of the Trustee meeting of Novem-
        ber 2, 1974.
        "to do it for you": *Student*, April 9, 1973.
        "the institutions themselves": Box 20, Visiting Committee Final Report
        folder.
136   "institution for men and women": Minutes of Trustee meeting of October
        18, 1974.
        met in Amherst: Minutes of Trustee meeting of October 19, 1974.
137   forwarded a letter: Box 21, Coeducation Correspondence folder.
        "extracted in many ways": *Ibid.*
        "I was simply empty": "Looking Backward," *Olio*, April 30, 1975. Box 2,
        folder 16, new series.

CURRICULUM

138   "that of the curriculum": Box 1, folder 7, p. 1.
139   "the ideal of a free society": Box 1, folder 20, new series.
        report to the Board: Box 3, folder 12, new series..
140   a little history: Claude Fuess, *The Story of a New England College* (Boston,
        1935), p. 313.
        Piety and Intellect: (New York, 1946), p. 116.
141   his Report to the Board: *Op.cit.*, pp. 11-15.
142   "the life of the College": Box 1, folder 44, new series.
        "The Honeymoon is Over": February 12, 1976, p. 5.
143   its report early in 1977: *Education at Amherst Reconsidered: The Liberal
        Studies Program* (Amherst, 1978), p. 40.
        his 1972-73 Report: *Op. cit.*, p. 4.
144   "an effective liberal arts curriculum": April 21, 1977, p. 1.

"to embody a traditional ideal": *Education at Amherst Reconsidered*, p. xii.
"its educated minority": *Ibid.*, p. 35.

145   "the Calvinistic founders of this place": Box 1, folder 55, new series.
       "What's going on?": *Student*, March 8, 1976, p. 3.
       "The Making of the Liberal Arts College Identity": *Daedalus*, CXXVIII
       (Winter 1999), 22-23.
       "Case Statement": Faculty Meeting Minutes, Box 9, folder 1976, p. 2.

RACE

147   On one occasion: Horace Porter, e-mail to author, May 6, 2013.
149   "one of the great men": *New York Times Book Review*, March 10, 1985, p. 37.
       never talked about it: Oral History Project, June 8, 2011.
150   not an "incident" but a tragedy: Box 15, Penny Case folder. All the docu-
       ments relating to the tragedy are in this file.
153   Hockey players: *Student*, November 4, 1974, pp. 1,15.
154   According to Steve Hardy: E-mail to author, July 5, 2012.
156   "as if one were immoral": Minutes of the Faculty Meeting of April 4, 1978.
       "in Nazi Germany": *Student*, April 20, 1978, p. 1.
       "Racial Misrepresentations/Disharmonious Community": April 10, 1978,
       pp. 6-7.
157   "Homunculi" awards: *Ibid.*, December 7, 1978, p. 7.
       an all-campus meeting: "Our Day to Day Life Together," Box 1, folder 64,
       new series.
       "You *never* give up." Rich Read, e-mail to author, January 10, 2011.
158   "To Fellow Men and Women at Amherst College": Box 6, Cross-Burning
       folder.
159   an all-college meeting in the gym: *Student*, April 18, 1979, p. 4.
160   "before you left": Oral History.
       "drift into irrelevancy": E-mail to author, September 11, 2010.
161   "to other goods, or other ends": *Student*, May 26, 1979, p. 7.
       They were charged: *Ibid.*, May 10, 1979, p. 1.
162   in Mariness' words: E-mail to author, January 29, 2012.
       "The Unrest of Black Students": Box 3, folder 36, new series.
       Rand Richards Cooper has written: E-mail to author, November 17, 2010.

COMPENSATION/RESIGNATION

163   Commencement issue: June 5, 1975, p. 3.
164   "the cause of self-interest": Rand Richards Cooper, note to author, July 23,
       2013.
       statement on "Faculty compensation": Minutes of Faculty Meeting of April
       20, 1977.

167   headline of the *Student* account: April 28, 1977.

168   At a Faculty meeting in February: Minutes of Faculty meeting of February 21, 1978.

       headlines of the *Student* report: February 28, 1978, p. 1.

169   "quickly adjourned": E-mail to author, April 25, 2014.

       a letter to Allen Guttmann: February 22, 1978. Copy in author's possession.

       At the next faculty meeting: *Student*, April 20, 1978.

170   his oral history: Oral History.

171   faculty meeting in October: *Student*, October 19, 1978, p. 4.

172   a letter to the Board: Dick Fink, interview, October 27, 2009.

       an emergency meeting of the faculty: Minutes of the Faculty meeting of November 7, 1978.

173   After the meeting: *Student*, November 6, 1978, p. 1 and November 13, 1978, p. 9.

       In *his* interview: July 12, 2009.

       he had said to Barbara: *Student*, May 26, 1979, p. 7.

174   "without being beaten on": *Ibid.*, February 12, 1976, p. 4.

       "'Someone will be unhappy.'": *Ibid.*, February 23, 1978, p. 6.

       As Jill Conway said: Phone interview, October 27, 2009.

175   "time to move along": Oral History.

       one professor said: *Hampshire Life*, p. 8.

       Another said: *Globe*, September 18, 1985, p. 25.

       in a letter to Greene: December 14, 1978. Box 12, folder G.

176   "take on more teaching": Oral History.

       "the 'corporate' type": *Ibid.*

       "at the end": *Hampshire Life*, p. 8.

       "a man who was down": E-mail, May 24, 2010.

       "Memo for the Record": Minutes of Faculty meeting of February 20, 1979.

       "in gainful employment": *Student*, February 22, 1979, p. 5.

177   "issues of concern to the faculty": E-mail, February 19, 2012.

       given "strongest preference": Non-alumnus biographical box, Resignation folder.

178   Wirtz wrote Shinn: *Ibid.*

       his charge to the seniors: Box 1, folder 65, new series.

180   "I loved being at Amherst College": *Hampshire Life*, p. 9.

181   "power in the United States": Box 1, folder 66, new series.

       "what I'd like to do": *Student*, November 15, 1978, p. 1.

182   "Boston will do wonders": Letter to Freidel DeWitz, October 25, 1979.

       Hugh Hawkins papers, DeWitz folder.

FOUR: *Pro bono Publico*

183   Ward before the Joint Judiciary Committee: "Narrative," p. 52.
       "The Common Weal and the Public Trust": Box 1, folder 69, new series.
       "lived up to his idealism": "A Remembrance of Bill Ward," October 10,
       1985. Non-alumnus biographical box, Memorial Service folder.
184   "some real improvements": Letter from Barney Frank to author. February
       15, 2012.
       "had much positive impact": "Robby" Robinson, e-mail to author, Febru-
       ary 11, 2012.
       the *Globe* introduced: October 25, 1979, p. 2.
185   "waving it around like a flag": *Hampshire Life*, p. 9.
       "politically savvy": Phone interview, February 16, 2012.
186   "in small institutions": Letter of February 25, 1980. Copy in author's pos-
       session.
       "inspired my best effort": "A Remembrance of Bill Ward," *Op. Cit.*
187   a desire to be liked: Phone interview with Philip Johnston, January 2012.
       move to Russia: "Narrative," p. 122.
       "talking with ex-Marines": *Globe*, September 15, 1985, p. 24.
188   "in certain state and county building contracts": "Narrative," p. 17.
189   In its summary: *Globe*, January 5, 1981, p. 2.
       "the way it is now": "Narrative," p. 4.
190   in an editorial: *Ibid.*, p. 5.
191   "recommendations into effect": *Ibid.*, pp. 18-19.
       some of his reflections: *Ibid.*, pp. 20-21.
192   to call them "guests": October 25, 1979, p. 2.
       "and it never did.": "A Remembrance of Bill Ward," *Op. cit.*
193   "charged to investigate": p. 31.
       "the scope of corruption in it": "Narrative," p. 35.
       "the best decision the Commission made": Introduction to the Final Re-
       port, Volume 1, p. 10.
194   "hope for the future": *Ibid.*, p. 16.
       "Corruption is a way of life": *Ibid.*, p. 21.
       before the Joint Judiciary Committee": "Narrative," pp. 50-54.
196   According to Bob Turner: Phone interview, February 28, 2012.
       Andy Card's responses: Phone interview, August 21, 2012.
199   A lot had happened: *Globe* reports, February 11, May 3, July 14, 1979.
200   The Commission's investigative strategy: "Narrative," p. 78.
201   In his summary: p. 22.
       addressed the Joint committee: *Ibid.*, p. 92-95.
202   In its summary: *Globe*, January 5, 1981, pp. 3-5.
203   "opening night at the theater": March 26, 1980, p. 13.

204   "no one could touch him": "A Remembrance of Bill Ward," *Op. cit.*
       The testimony of Frank Masiello: "Narrative," pp. 97-100, 104-05, 110-11.
       See also Ward's summary, Volume 1, pp. 24-25.
       were government officials: *Ibid.*, pp. 105-06, 112, 142.
206   as Barney Frank said: Phone interview, February 20, 2012.
207   The final legislative session: "Narrative," pp. 152-65.
208   Ward's acidic summary: Introduction, *Op. Cit.*, p. 45.
       "to serve the public good": *Ibid.*, p. 48.
209   The third: "Introduction," *Op. Cit.*, pp. 40-48.
211   "no whiff of scandal": Phone interview, January, 2012.
       "It's a great feeling": *Globe*, September 9, 1980, p. 40,
       "to avoid going broke": April 7, 1980, p. 13.
212   "what that would be": *Hampshire Life*, p. 9.
       "vibrating the network": *Ibid.*
       "our 'common wealth' has meaning": Box 1, folder 72, new series.
       "political and controversial": *Globe*, December 24, 1981, p. 13.
       "the habit of cynicism": Phone interview, August 21, 2012.
       "radioactive": Phone interview, February 16, 2012.
       "driven out of town": Phone interview, February 28, 2012.
       "good citizenship": December 24, 1981, p. 13.

       FIVE: At the End

213   "the selfishness of despair": Letter of July 18, 1972. Box 4, folder C.
       "the earlier presence of desire": "Anarchy and Authority in American Liter-
       ature," Box 2, folder 1, new series.
       "in the 1980s": *Amherst Bulletin*, October 29, 1980.
       "A lily-pad for him": Interview, October 10, 2009.
       "Some Reflections on Technology": Box 2, folder 32, new series.
214   "listen to me talk – it's wonderful!": *Hampshire Life*, p. 9.
       "forcing us to think": *Ibid.*
       "harvest time": Interview, October 10, 2009.
       "The Common Weal and the Public Trust: Politics and Public Morality":
       Box 1, folder 69, new series.
215   real signs: *Hanpshire Gazette*, June 11, 1980.
217   spoke at Commencement: Box 1, folder 71, new series.
219   "I don't want to go.": Letter of May 16, 1981. Commager papers. Box 63,
       folder 41.
       "You don't have a chance": Quoted in letter to Commager, October 5, 1981.
       Ibid.

220   "any *students* or *alumni*": Quoted in *Chronicle of Higher Education*, July 7, 1982, p. 7.
      "Defends the Humanities": *Ibid.*, pp. 7-8.
      a letter to the secretary: January 1, 1983. Copy in author's possession.
221   "a wonder to behold": Stan Katz e-mail to author, October 7, 2010.
      before the subcommittee: Box 3, folder 44, new series.
223   "highfalutin humanists": Stan Katz phone interview, September 15, 2009.
224   his life was "useless": James Hund phone interview, June, 2012.
      A letter he wrote in the spring: Letter of April 25, 1976. Box 7, folder F.
225   "I get at home": March 10, 1972. Box 14, folder M. (The day before, he told Smith the same story in a letter.)
      "dinner to 175 people": Letter of February 5, 1974. Box 12, folder G.
      job for a bachelor": Stanley Rabinowitz interview, May 24, 2010.
      "good actors": Bill Taubman in conversation, September 9, 2009.
226   "and graduate seminar": *Hampshire Life*, p. 27.
      "a welfare hotel": *Globe*, September 15, 1985, p.25.
      "speaks of a future, no?": E-mail, April 22, 2012.
227   "a lost soul": Janice Denton, in a phone conversation, April 27, 2009.
      "that he meant it": Memorial Service folder.
228   "the depth of despair": *Globe*, September 15, 1985, p. 25.
      to talk with David Warner: Letter from Warner, September 11, 2010.
229   "The Life of Learning": Box 3, folder 39, new series.
      "The Life of Learning": Box 3, folder 46, new series.

PHOTO CREDITS

Page 24:   Yearbook page courtesy of the Boston Latin School
Page 86:   Inauguration photo from Amherst College Archives and Special Collections
Page 179: Portrait by Richard Yarde; printed with permission of the Richard Yarde Trust
Page 195: Photo by Jack O'Connell/*Boston Globe* via Getty Images

INDEX

ACKNOWLEDGMENTS

I AM GRATEFUL to the many people who have been willing—often eager—to help me with this project. I have interviewed and talked or corresponded with well over a hundred. Janice Denton, Gordie Levin, Nick Littlefield, Jr., Bill McFeely, Dale Peterson, Horace Porter, Bill Pritchard, Rich Read, Ellen Ryerson, and David Wills read section of drafts—as did Barry O'Connell at a pivotal juncture. Rand Richards Cooper, Amy Demerest, Ben Lieber, Susan Pikor, and David Sofield read drafts in their entirely. Bill Taubman did too and helped again and again thereafter. Their impressions, criticisms, and suggestions were invaluable. I am especially grateful to my former colleagues Hugh Hawkins, George Kateb, and Leo Marx, who supported me in countless ways from the very beginning.

I cannot imagine more pleasant and helpful staffs than the ones working under Bryn Geffert, Librarian of Amherst College, and Michael Kelly, Head of Archives and Special Collections. Emily Boutilier oversaw the transformation of my manuscript into a book with exceptional insight and efficiency. Maryanne Alos and Su Auerbach were very helpful at important stages along the way. Julie Howland and Bette Kanner were always there when technological challenges were too much for me.

My pages on "Westover" originally appeared in an edited form as "Civil Disobedience: A Question of Institutional Involvement" in *The Massachusetts Review*, Volume 53, Issue 4 (Winter, 2012), 701-16.

Finally, I would like to thank Greg Call, former Dean of the Faculty at Amherst, and Peter Berek and the members of the English Department, who through the departments's Thalheimer Fund, made publication possible.

I have dedicated this book, with love, to my children and to my wife.